Talk to Me, Baby!

Talk to Me, Baby!

How You Can Support Young Children's Language Development

by

Betty S. Bardige, Ed.D.
A.L. Mailman Family Foundation
White Plains, New York

·P·A·U·L·H·
BROOKES
PUBLISHING C.º®

Baltimore • London • Sydney

Paul H. Brookes Publishing Co.
Post Office Box 10624
Baltimore, Maryland 21285-0624
USA

www.brookespublishing.com

"Paul H. Brookes Publishing Co." is a registered trademark of
Paul H. Brookes Publishing Co., Inc.

Typeset by Broad Books, Baltimore, Maryland.
Manufactured in the United States of America by
Versa Press, Inc., East Peoria, Illinois.

The individuals described in this book are composites, pseudonyms, or fictional
accounts based on actual experiences. Individuals' names have been changed and
identifying details have been altered to protect confidentiality.

Library of Congress Cataloging-in-Publication Data

Bardige, Betty Lynn Segal.
    Talk to me, baby! : how parents and teachers can support young children's language
development / by Betty S. Bardige.
        p.   cm.
    Includes bibliographical references and index.
    ISBN-13: 978-1-55766-977-3 (pbk.)
    ISBN-10: 1-55766-977-5 (pbk.)
    1. Children—Language.   2. Early childhood education—Parent participation.
I. Title.

LB1139.L3B365 2009
372.6—dc22   2008054784

British Library Cataloguing in Publication data are available from the British Library.

2012   2011   2010   2009

10   9   8   7   6   5   4   3   1

Contents

About the Author

Betty S. Bardige, Ed.D., speaks and writes widely on the importance of early language development and what parents, teachers, and communities can do to promote it. She is the author of *At a Loss for Words: How America is Failing Our Children and What We Can Do About It* (Temple University Press, 2005), coauthor of *Building Literacy with Love* and *Poems to Learn to Read By* (with Marilyn Segal, ZERO TO THREE Press, 2005), and a contributing writer to the second edition of ZERO TO THREE's classic: *Caring for Infants and Toddlers in Groups: Developmentally Appropriate Practice* (2008). A developmental psychologist, educator, and child advocate, Dr. Bardige holds a doctorate in human development from the Harvard Graduate School of Education.

As Vice President of the A.L. Mailman Family Foundation, Dr. Bardige focuses on improving the systems and policies that affect very young children and their families. She led the Foundation's Florida Initiative to improve infant/toddler care and school readiness in that state. She has worked with various educational and family-serving organizations on program development and evaluation, curriculum, and strategic planning, and serves on boards of local, state, and national organizations, including the Brazelton Touchpoints Foundation, The National Association for Family Child Care, and Facing History and Ourselves. She also advises several community-based efforts to promote young children's language, literacy, and emotional resilience.

At Learningways, Inc., a Cambridge, Massachusetts, firm founded by her husband, Art Bardige, Dr. Bardige developed pioneering educational software for young children. In a series of projects for various educational publishers, she authored or co-authored nearly 50 interactive, animated stories and poems with accompanying activities to teach reading, writing, storytelling, and math to children ages 3–8.

The mother of three adult children, Dr. Bardige lives in Cambridge, Massachusetts. She can be reached through her web site, http://www.awealthofwords.com.

Foreword

Since the beginning of time, mothers, fathers, aunts, uncles, grandparents, elders, teachers, and caregivers have taught children the critical skills and abilities they would need in order to survive and thrive in their world. Adults have always modeled and involved their youngest children in gathering seeds and fruits from the forest; milking domestic animals; cutting through ice in order to catch fish; collecting oysters, crabs, clams, and plant life exposed by the receding sea; and hunting animals for their meat and hides so that children would master essential skills by the time they became adults. *In the 21st century, the ability to read well is as much a survival skill for today's children as hunting, gathering, and farming were for earlier peoples.*

As in the past, families, caregivers, and social systems must transmit the critical skills and abilities and provide ongoing encouragement and education if children are to flourish as adults. Academics and professionals have amassed the necessary knowledge, research, and understanding about how to promote language and literacy development for all children. The challenge is that many adults (family members, caregivers, and early childhood educators) are unaware of the incredible, long-lasting impact of simply talking and engaging with babies in conversations from birth. Many adults do not understand that with these simple interactions, they set their children on a trajectory of literacy success.

As a result, a silent, national crisis expands every day, as large numbers of infants and toddlers do not have opportunities to participate in frequent, warm, engaging verbal interchanges with the key adults in their lives. Each day of missed verbal interactions and new words widens the achievement gap that exists between middle class children and those being reared in poverty. The consequences are staggering personal and national losses as hundreds of thousands of children fail to reach their educational and cognitive potential.

In earlier societies, adults were aware that hunting and gathering were essentials skills all children must learn. They understood that everyone who cared for young children played a critical role in teaching them necessary survival and societal skills. They also knew how to teach children—by modeling the ways their elders taught them.

Preparing all children for literacy success in our modern, literacy-based society requires raising awareness about how literacy develops in young children and the key role that adults play in promoting development from a child's earliest days. It also requires that caregivers and families have the opportunity to learn how to promote language and literacy so that in future generations, young parents will be able to transmit their own early experiences, just as humans have done through the ages.

This volume addresses all three needs. It provides families and early childhood professionals with the "who, what, when, where, how, and why" of early language and literacy development. Dr. Bardige's rich descriptions create word pictures of the magic of early learning, underpinned with clear explanations of the current body of research knowledge and strengthened with detailed, practical strategies that can be applied at home, in child care, in preschool, and in the community. This volume provides all of the information adults need to set young children on the right path! It has practical, accessible information for caregivers and provides a powerful resource for families and those supporting families.

For decades, families and professionals across this nation have taught me that when they learn and understand why and how to promote their children's learning, they do so with aplomb. All it takes is awareness, modeling, and ongoing support for families to develop clever and innovative learning opportunities that fit into their unique way of being. It is my honor to share a few of the myriad of ways that ordinary people—families and early education providers—have created unique language learning techniques and approaches that fit them and their families. Armed with the information from this volume and the examples in the stories, I urge you to take these words of Clarissa Pinkola Estés to heart: "I hope you will go out and let (these) stories happen to you, and that you will work them, water them with your blood and tears and your laughter till they bloom, till you yourself burst into bloom."

Everyday learning opportunities can work for each family's lifestyle:

- Jason and Christina find ways to keep everyone in their large family involved during down times such as riding in the car, waiting in lines, waiting at the doctor's offices, and so forth. One way they do this is to make up their own stories. Each child and parent adds a line to a story that begins with just one sentence. Because the younger boys are not able write yet, Christina writes down their sentences as they create them. Each person adds whatever they want to the story, even if it doesn't make sense. Christina adds, "We all have a great time!"

- Sally and John are very interested in wild turkeys, their migration patterns, their reproduction rates, and other facts. They involve their two preschool-age children in this interest. The children have developed keen observational skills; can count small groups of turkeys; can identify familiar groupings of turkeys and what they eat; and can explain how to distinguish males, females, and imma-ture turkeys. They participate with their parents in tracking groups of turkeys online and are able to share a great deal of information with anyone who asks. Preschool teachers were surprised when they tapped into this part of the children's knowledge!

Parents often overcome personal challenges, attitudes, and expe-riences for the children's sake.

- Karen has four children and a full-time job as a child care provider. She also volunteers at her youngest child's Early Head Start pro-gram. When she learned about the power and importance of talking and sharing books with young children, she began a multiyear effort in which she provided workshops for other parents—often several times each week. Recognizing that many family members may not have had positive experiences with books, Karen showed families how to make books with their infants, toddlers, and preschool-age children "When I went to school I did not like reading," Karen notes. "When I had my first child, I did not read to her because I did not like to read. Now I know it's important to help kids like reading. I want parents to have comfortable books to share with their children. If a family makes a book with their child, they know what it is about, and will be able to have fun with it with their baby."

- While attending a book-making session at his child's Early Head Start (EHS) program, Carlos, whose family was living at a homeless shelter, realized that this was the first and only book his children owned. He "read" the picture book with them each evening and came to realize that his children loved the experience. His toddler asked to read the book over, and over, and over again. As Carlos became aware of how much fun he and his children were having with this homemade book, he enrolled in an adult education pro-gram to learn to read. "I want my children to be able to read, and they need my help, so I have to learn, too." The next time the EHS program held a book-making session, Carlos wrote words in the book that he could now actually read!

Language and literacy is for everyone!

- Michael is 40 years old. He has Down syndrome. When he was very young, a preschool teacher, whose name Michael still remembers, told him he would "never read." To this day he firmly believes her prediction is absolute truth. His family never set limits on Michael and encouraged him to be himself. In addition to his limitations, Michael has many skills and competencies. Indeed, while he was the daytime caregiver for his aging grandmother, Michael saved her life by quickly calling the ambulance after she had a massive stroke. In his early 30s, Michael's family began to notice that he would look at the newspaper each morning and talk about things that were in it all day. When he wanted to subscribe to *TV Guide*, they encouraged him to do so. On a weekly basis, Michael highlights the TV shows he plans to watch each day. Michael believes he cannot read, but his family believes that he teaches each of us that language, literacy, and lifelong learning are for everyone!

- Kirsten, age 4, has been diagnosed with autism spectrum disorder. She loves books and enjoys talking about them with adults, but she has difficulty with social relationships. Her mom organized a "book-talk" club to use Kirsten's strengths to help her overcome her challenges. Each week a small group of parents and children meet at Kirsten's home for an hour on Saturday morning. Before they meet, they all read the same book at home. At the meeting, they read and talk about the book together, do a book-related activity, and/or play together. Kirsten's mother has developed a comfortable way for her to connect with other children successfully. Everyone has a great time and learns from one another!

Bilingualism adds to a child's life and school success!

- José is the oldest of three children of immigrant parents. When he entered preschool, everyone encouraged him to learn English and drop his Spanish so that he could succeed in school. But José, who spent a lot of time with his grandparents, kept learning Spanish, even after he went to school. By third grade José was advanced in English without losing his Spanish. His younger brother and sister also fulfilled the expectations that they learn English but did not keep up with their Spanish. All three now have graduate degrees, but José, who is fluent in both languages, has many more career opportunities than his brother and sister. Most important, he has a close relationship with his aging grandparents. As young parents, José's brother and sister are committed to ensuring that their young children learn both languages so that they can add the benefits of bilingualism to their high levels of skill in English.

- Dani was born in the United States to immigrant parents from different Asian countries. Dani's parents follow the one parent–one language rule when communicating with him, with his mother speaking Bengali and his father speaking Urdu. They communicate with each other in English. Dani has attended an English-speaking child care since he was 2 months old. After spending time with both sets of his grandparents just prior to his third birthday, Dani's expressive use of both Urdu and Bengali grew exponentially. He not only distinguishes words from language to language but he also selects the appropriate types of interchanges and topics of conversation suitable for young children and adults in each language. Kindly, Dani selects words in the language that he knows adults will understand; for example, when spoken to by an English-only speaker who gave him a toy, he responded with an English word rather than using the Urdu spoken by his grandmother.

"It takes a village to raise a child" (Nigerian proverb).

- Maya and her husband have four boys and, while Maya read and talked with her older sons, she was not so conscious of the importance of these kinds of experiences until she participated in a series of trainings when the youngest was a toddler. "I was pretty busy, so I used the older boys to read to the younger ones. The whole family got involved! My grandparents, mother, sons, husband, and anyone who was involved with the boys would read to them. They didn't care about how many times they reread the book. The memories and benefits turned out to be more than I expected. They all still talk about it!"

- When Margaret, who has five young children, learned about the importance of talking with and reading to children, she organized a communitywide effort to collect books from donations and secondhand shops. Margaret and her colleagues at the EHS program put the donated books in places frequented by young children and their families. They selected places where people often have extended periods of waiting, such as Women, Infants, and Children (WIC) and Community Action Program (CAP) offices, and Laundromats. Each book also contained an explanation about the importance of early talking and reading so parents would understand why and how to support their children's growth.

- A group of parents and early childhood providers worked with the local bus company, local merchants, and service groups to start a "Books on the Bus" program in their small city. Books were donated and placed in a safe spot on city buses. Adults traveling with young children could borrow a book, read the story during the trip, and return it as they left the bus.

We all need to know what to do, how to do it, and to receive some ongoing support—all of which are in this volume. And finally, consider one more story, which illustrates the timelessness of talking to your baby:

- Angelica, mother of a 22-month-old, completed training in strategies that promote language and literacy development. Her daughter, who was not using many words when she began using the strategies, responded rapidly and quickly began to use more words and to initiate more verbal interactions. After 3 months, Angelica reported, "This will go on and on! I taught it to my daughter and she will teach it to hers and it will go on and on forever!"

Joanne Knapp-Philo, Ph.D.
Director
National Head Start
Family Literacy Center
Sonoma State University
Camarillo, California

Preface

"Every child needs at least one person who is really crazy about her."
–Urie Bronfenbrenner

Talk to Me, Baby! How You Can Support Young Children's Language Development is for every adult who is "really crazy" about at least one child and for every professional who seeks to harness that passion in the service of a child's development. It explores the fascinating and yet ordinary processes by which nearly all children learn to speak and by which most who are taught learn to read. It draws on the insights of diverse researchers and the inventiveness of a wide range of practitioners to illustrate how parents and caregivers in various settings and circumstances talk to and play with babies and young children in ways that build language, literacy, brain power, and emotional connection. The book grew out of my fascination with young children's talk, my love of playful language, and the passionate desire to see all children get a promising start that infuses my work as an author, developmental psychologist, board member, funder, and advocate.

The research is clear. Children whose families talk a lot and expect children to do so as well are likely to be more verbal and to amass larger vocabularies at younger ages than children growing up in more laconic families. And the talk that makes the most difference is the playful, engaging, relationship-building kind—the serve-and-return interactions that are entertaining, emotionally satisfying, eye-opening, and mind expanding not only for a child but also for the adult who loves her.

As I urge parents, caregivers, and early childhood teachers to increase their intentional use of language-building strategies that are fun for children and adults alike, I'm acutely aware that there are cultural and individual differences in what feels natural, comfortable, appropriate, and fun. Strategies that work well for some adults—or some babies—may be unnatural or uninteresting for others. I thus try to provide a broad range of examples, strategies, and informative research, although my emphasis is on children growing up in the United States and learning English as at least one of their primary languages.

Different cultural and family beliefs and practices about how adults should talk to young children and how and when children should talk back influence the trajectories of children's language learning. So, too, do differences in the quality of the child care environment and in the emphasis placed by teachers and caregivers on book-reading, conversation, child-initiated play, use of more than one language or dialect, intentional teaching, and adult involvement in children's pretend worlds. Such differences give some children an advantage in literacy and formal schooling, and others an advantage in street-corner repartee, oral performance, learning through quiet observation, or bilingual or bi-dialectical fluency. Yet cultures change over time, and what is adaptive in one context may be less so in another.

The illustrative vignettes throughout the book are adaptations of real incidents. I observed many of these directly; others were told to me by parents, grandparents, home visitors, pediatricians, early childhood teachers and caregivers, or program directors and supervisors. Some are composites of several similar or related events. In most cases, I've changed names and other identifying details and represented children's words in standard written English. The children portrayed in these vignettes come from diverse backgrounds, yet they share a special spark—a joy in using words, asking questions, spinning stories, and learning new things. Most of the vignettes catch them at their best or most endearing, in moments that their parents and teachers remember fondly and retell with pride.

Except for its first and last chapters, this book is organized developmentally. The age ranges are wide and overlapping, reflecting the natural variability in the pace of children's language and communication development as infants, toddlers, preschoolers, and kindergarteners. Each of these chapters describes key advances in language and communication development and the research support for a range of strategies that support their full flowering. Each contains tips for talking with children and choosing books they will enjoy. Each also features songs and poems to share, questions children ask (with words or nonverbally), and a set of activities that adults and children can enjoy together. In addition, each addresses common social-emotional advances and challenges and models effective strategies that parents and teachers use as they talk with children about feelings, values, and other important matters.

Whether you are a home visitor, parent educator, teacher, pediatrician, parent or grandparent, or simply someone who loves children, I hope you will find this book enlightening, entertaining, inspirational, and practical. Most of all, I hope you'll do a lot of talking and playing with young children and that you'll help everyone you encounter to see why this is so important.

Acknowledgments

This book has been shaped by many hands. My volunteer editors—Costanza Eggers-Pierola, Ronnie Mae Weiss, Kori Bardige, Wendy Masi, and Marilyn Segal—each brought a unique and valuable perspective. Costanza, author of *Connections and Commitments: Reflecting Latino Values in Early Childhood Programs,* broadened my outlook, helped me to see my cultural biases, and shared the latest research and best resources for second language learners. Ronnie Mae, work/life liaison for Harvard's School of Public Health, tried to set aside her knowledge of early childhood development and education to read as a young parent or as someone new to the field and to rid my text of jargon. My daughter, Kori, a special educator and teacher trainer, reflected teachers' concerns and supplied vignettes that helped to shape the manuscript. My sister Wendy, former dean of the Mailman-Segal Institute for Early Childhood Studies at Nova Southeastern University and director of its preschool, parent/child, and teacher training programs, was my most critical reader. She repeatedly helped me to step back from my writing to reflect on what my various readers would want to know and what they might find confusing, misleading, or tedious. My mother and frequent co-author, Dr. Marilyn Segal, having contributed several of the poems, anecdotes, and play ideas, also reviewed the draft with her ear for rhythm and eye for typos.

I also thank the many colleagues and friends who shared stories of their children, grandchildren, students, and mentees; invited me to observe in their programs or classrooms; pointed me to valuable resources; and shared their own enthusiasm for talking with babies, their questions about young children's thinking, behavior, and language learning, their worries about the stresses today's parents and caregivers face, their concern that too many parents and caregivers are not doing enough talking, and their ideas about how to help. Special thanks go to Sue and Derek O'Grady, Jean Bradley and Chris Hurley, Lei-Anne Ellis, Ellie Szanton, Patti Lieberman, Rachel Masi, T. Berry Brazelton, Jennifer Coplon, Marta Rosa, Sarah Walzer, Barry Fish, Joanne Knapp-Philo, Ellen Wolpert, Jim and Debbie Frieden, Jean Fahey, Marge Petruska, Luba Lynch, Peg Sprague, Ed Greene, Aileen Lynch, Joan Matsalia,

Jeff Johnson, Michelle Morrison, Josh Sparrow, Diantha Millott, Jessica Allan, Terry Ann Lunt, Theressa Lenear, Linda Gillespie, Joan Laurion, Derry Koralek, Rick Weissbourd, Yasmina Vinci, Brenan and Arran Bardige, Lauren Leikin, and Sue Williamson. Finally, I thank my editorial and production team at Paul H. Brookes Publishing Co.—Sarah Shepke, Shauntel Brown, and Leslie Eckard—for their questions, insights, patience, attention to detail, and belief in the power of words.

To my husband, Art, who loves talking with babies,
believes passionately that learning requires active practice
and responsive feedback,
and keeps pushing me to push the messages in this book

The Power of Play Talk

It is Sawyer's second birthday, and he has been excited all day. His mom made him a fire engine cake, his dad read him his new books, and now they are all celebrating at his grandparents' house. Sawyer has opened his presents—trucks, crayons, more books— and is delighted with them all. Now, finally, his uncle hands him the last box—a heavy, oblong container wrapped in shiny red paper.

"Should we open this together, Sawyer?" asks Uncle Josh.

"Open it," Sawyer replies, pushing the heavy box back into his uncle's hands. Josh carefully unwraps the present, revealing a tightly sealed box printed to look like a fire engine. Sawyer stares at the box, shaking with delight.

"Excited," he comments.

"I can see you're excited, Sawyer," Josh replies. "I'll get this box open for you in a minute. I just need a knife to cut the reinforced tape."

Watching intently, Sawyer repeats, "Cut refors tape," as Josh cuts the tape and opens one end of the box.

"Should I cut the rest of the box, Sawyer, or do you want me to slide it out?"

"Slide it out."

"Okay. You pull on the fire truck, and I'll pull the box."

"Fire truck! Fire truck!" chants Sawyer, as the long, red fire engine slowly emerges from the box. Josh cuts the tape holding down the ladder, then realizes that he needs a screwdriver to attach the ladder to the truck.

"Do you want to help me assemble this?" he asks. "This screw is for attaching the ladder, see? Would you like to help me screw it on?"

"Screw it on," Sawyer echoes, as he places his hand on his uncle's and helps turn the screwdriver.

"Look," says Josh, once the ladder has been secured. "You can turn this crank to raise and lower the ladder."

"Sawyer try. Turn crank. Uh-up ladder."

"Look," Josh says. "The doors open. There's even a steering wheel in the cab."

Sawyer picks up the toy firefighter.

"Go in cab," he says, opening the door. "Drive to fire."

"Rev up the engine, fireman," Josh adds, "and turn on your siren."

"Rrr–rrr–oweeo–oweeeo," Sawyer shrieks, as he pushes the fire engine across the floor.

"Hurry! Hurry!" urges his uncle. "This fire is really blazing. You'd better get there fast!"

On first glance, the only thing at all unusual about this conversation is the 2-year-old's command of language. His uncle Josh has no training in early childhood education and little experience with young children; he is just playing with his nephew. But he is curious, and his nephew's rapidly emerging language fascinates him. To engage Sawyer's interest, Josh hands him the present and waits to see what he will do with it. Following Sawyer's lead, Josh asks if Sawyer wants help and supplies it when requested. Josh uses words that are new to Sawyer as part of his normal conversation, then introduces a few more because it's such fun to hear Sawyer repeat them. As Sawyer begins to play with the fire engine, Josh accepts the implicit invitation to join in. Watching Sawyer and his uncle pretend together, it's hard to tell who's leading the game—or who is more excited.

When an adult knows a child well and is in a relaxed, one-to-one setting that fosters intense interaction, it's easy to do what Josh did. The adult can

- Follow a child's lead
- Carry on a back-and-forth conversation, even when the child's part consists of gestures, facial expressions, and one- or two-word utterances
- Attend to a child's feelings and respond to his verbal and nonverbal communications
- Ask questions and offer choices
- Point out and name interesting objects, features, or processes
- Talk about what the child is doing, or about his own thoughts, plans, and actions as he interacts with the child
- Use interesting words
- Join in pretend play
- Build a relationship

What is most unusual about this episode is not that the adult did all of these things or that the child was completely captivated, but rather that, except for the exciting birthday present, it was a typical interchange for Sawyer. All of the adults in his life frequently engaged him in such conversations, and his rapidly growing vocabulary and self-confident use of language made these conversations increasingly interesting and, therefore, increasingly frequent. Sawyer was teaching his family the rewards of "play talk."

MEANINGFUL DIFFERENCES

In 1982, two researchers at the University of Kansas, Betty Hart and Todd Risley, began a study that would transform our understanding of early language learning and its role in priming children for success in school. Hart and Risley had spent the early part of their careers advising and evaluating a preschool program for children from economically disadvantaged homes in addition to working with the university's preschool, where most children came from professional families. Homing in on vocabulary as an indicator of concept knowledge, they tracked the words that children used in their play and conversation, as well as those that they could use correctly on standardized tests. They soon noticed that the vocabulary gap between the children from low-income homes and those from professional families kept widening. The things they were doing in the preschool—providing lots of books; field trips; supported pretend play activities; and focused, vocabulary-building conversations—were helping, but not enough to close the gap.

If this gap was so difficult to close, might it be preventable? Hart and Risley decided to look at what parents did with their children in the years before preschool. Were better educated parents constantly and consciously teaching their children? How could they be teaching them so much by their third birthdays that children who lacked this head start would have difficulty catching up? Perhaps something they were doing in this early period unlocked a door to faster learning so that by age 3, the children would not only know more but also would be able to acquire new knowledge at a faster rate. Perhaps patterns of parent–child interaction were established early and tended to persist, giving some children an ongoing as well as an initial advantage. Perhaps, by carefully chronicling children's early conversations, researchers could identify the patterns that made a difference.

From birth announcements in the local newspaper, Hart and Risley recruited 42 families in various economic circumstances. The study's team of observers began monthly, hour-long visits with the families when the children were 9 months and continued these visits until the children's third birthdays, tape-recording everything the children heard and said and noting the context of these interactions. After years of coding and data analysis, surprising patterns emerged. Hart and Risley reported these findings in two books: *Meaningful Differences in the Everyday Experience of Young American Children* (1995) and *The Social World of Children Learning to Talk* (1999). In a podcast for Senior Dad (http://srdad.com/SrDad/open/open.html), a weekly advice column on the Internet for older fathers, Risley shared a book chapter that he and Hart had written (2006) summarizing the discoveries that had surprised both them and their readers. Here are some of the chapter's key points:

- *On average, infants and toddlers heard a lot of language in their homes:* Family members addressed 340 utterances (1,440 words) to the children in a typical waking hour! Equally important, these utterances per hour included 150 responses to the children, of which 17 were affirmations (praise, encouragement, or indications of approval).

- *Family patterns of engagement and talkativeness were consistent over time:* Parents who were talkative with infants continued to be so with toddlers; those who spoke less or were less likely to use words to acknowledge and encourage their baby's accomplishments when first observed tended to continue these patterns.

- *Differences among families were huge, and compounded over time:* Extrapolating from the recorded sessions to all of each child's waking hours, the researchers concluded that children in the most verbal families would have heard 33 million words by their third birthdays, whereas those in the least talkative families would have heard only 10 million. Some children would have heard 500 thousand affirmations, whereas others would have heard fewer than 60 thousand.

- *Families were alike in the amount of directive language, or "business talk" (initiations, commands, prohibitions), that they used to manage their children;* the striking differences were in the amount of additional talk—conversation, running commentary, storytelling, wordplay, chit-chat, explanation, and thinking aloud.

- *In all families, the "extra talk" (or "play talk") was naturally far richer than the business talk:* Play talk tended to include longer and more complex sentences and narratives, more varied types of sentences, a greater variety of words and a greater number of less common words, and more descriptive language. It was also richer in information, complex ideas, and subtle guidance, and in supports for social-emotional development such as affirmation, engagement, responsiveness, and acknowledgment of feelings.

- *Toddlers' patterns of talk came to match their parents':* In more talkative families, in which adults engaged in more play talk, toddlers did more talking. They, too, learned to talk about things that went beyond the here and now and to use the rich, varied language they heard for a wide variety of purposes that transcended business talk. Hart and Risley estimated that by age 3, the average toddler would have spoken about 8,000 words. The toddlers in the most talkative families spoke about 12,000 words, whereas those in the least talkative families spoke fewer than 4,000.

- *Differences in patterns of family talk are associated with social class, but not perfectly so:* The professional families tended to be the most talkative, though a few of them were among the most laconic. In all six of the families headed by single mothers receiving Aid to Families with Dependent Children support, extra talk was rare, though the researchers did record occasional bouts of sociability and ebullience. Most of the middle-income, working families fell into the average group, but the range was wide and included families at both extremes.

The most striking findings of all were the differences in child outcomes and their strong connection to early language experience. By age 3, the children who had heard 33 million words with 500 thousand affirmations had Stanford-Binet IQ scores that were approximately 25 points higher than those of the children who had heard only 10 million words and fewer than 60 thousand affirmations!

These differences persisted. Children's scores on standard vocabulary, language skill, and basic academic skills tests given in third or fourth grade were strongly correlated with their vocabulary use at age 3 and even more strongly correlated with the language input they had received from their parents in those early years.

In Risley and Hart's words,

> We found that the large differences in the amount of parent talk that infants and toddlers received, particularly the amount of non-business conversation and commentary, was powerfully related to large differences in the size of toddlers' vocabulary growth and to standardized test measures of their intellectual achievement at age 3 ($r = .78$) and later at age 9 ($r = .77$). Parental talkativeness to babies accounted for *all* the correlation that existed between socio-economic status (SES)—and/or race—and the verbal intellectual accomplishments of these American children. (2006, p. 86)

It was the amount of play talk before age 3—not race, social class, or family income—that predicted children's intellectual accomplishments at age 9 and beyond. Indeed, in Hart and Risley's data, the correlations between play talk before age 3 and vocabulary at age 9, as measured by the widely used Peabody Picture Vocabulary Test–Revised (PPVT-R; Dunn, 1981), were nearly as high as those between two close-in-time administrations of the school-age vocabulary test itself. Differences in children's verbal abilities were better explained by the amount of play talk they had heard as toddlers than by race, social class, or any other factor.

The most successful language teachers in Hart and Risley's study were not consciously and continually teaching their children. Much of the time, like Sawyer's uncle Josh, they were "just playing," and often they were "just talking." But the talk that made a difference had particular characteristics that Hart and Risley were able to code and quantify, and their importance for young children's intellectual, emotional, and social development, as well as language and literacy, would continue to be confirmed by research in child development, early intervention, family support, and early childhood education.

Business talk isn't bad for young children or unimportant to their development. Toddlers and preschoolers need clear directions and clear limits. Much of what parents need to teach their children is best taught in a no-nonsense way. But, play talk adds an essential dimension.

Table 1.1 highlights differences between play talk and business talk. Business talk and play talk both have their place in a child's life. Business talk, with its simple vocabulary and sentence structures, can help children interpret more colorful language later. Also, it can signal to children when it is time to be serious and pay attention (e.g., to a teacher during a test). However, it is important that talk between adults and children not be heavily weighted toward business talk. Notice how many aspects of development are affected: relationships, creativity, exploration, self-concept, initiative, inquisitiveness, knowledge, grammar, vocabulary, expressive language, social skills, storytelling and literacy, imagination, and thinking and reasoning.

Todd Risley's oft-repeated advice to parents and early childhood teachers was simple: Talk a lot! The extra talk is most likely to be the rich, playful, engaging kind that gets children talking and fosters their learning.

Table 1.1. The differences between play talk and business talk

Play talk	Business talk
Is responsive to child	Is adult-initiated
Is imaginative and often silly	Is serious
Is open-ended	Is goal oriented
Is encouraging	Involves fewer "affirmations"
Offers choices	Is directive
Asks and explores questions	Is largely made up of statements and commands
Describes objects and events; includes details	Is mostly short and to the point
Includes complex sentences	Uses basic sentence structure
Uses more colorful language, adjectives, rhymes, and word play	Is characterized by less embellishment and playful language
Uses richer vocabulary	Uses simplified vocabulary
Engages both partners	Can be a one-sided "conversation"
Involves information exchanges	Supplies little information
Involves stories that are told, retold, and often co-constructed	Has less of a narrative structure
Uses "decontextualized" language; includes talk about the past, future, the imaginary, and what may be	Focuses on the here and now, with little challenge to go beyond the immediate, shared context
Often models and supports reasoning, decision making, or problem solving	Provides clear answers and directions
Is likely to be more information-rich and intellectually challenging	Is less likely to evoke thinking

VIRTUOUS CIRCLES

Could it really be that simple? How can "just talking" make so much of a difference and have such a lasting impact?

For children, play talk creates an upward spiral. With more input and more opportunities for practice, they develop confidence and fluency as well as enhanced vocabularies. As their spoken language becomes more facile and sophisticated, they elicit more complex language from their adult play partners, which further fuels their language learning. Little children love big words—although they may be hard to pronounce, they are fun to repeat and usually impress the listener. And an impressed listener is likely to teach a child all kinds of things in a play talk conversation because, as with Sawyer and Josh, it's fun and rewarding for both of them.

When children enter kindergarten, those whose language is more sophisticated will be seen by their teachers as more mature and competent. Their rate of learning will be faster because they will be able to ask more interesting questions and comprehend more complicated answers. When responding to these children's sophisticated interests and vocabularies, teachers will provide more information, richer language, and more challenges. Facility in playing with sounds will give these children a head start on reading. And, of course, once they learn to read on their own, they will acquire new words and information from books and their learning will accelerate.

Facility with language—and especially with play talk—also supports social-emotional growth. The characteristics of play talk—responsiveness, exchange of information and opinion, playfulness, and especially affirmations—characterize and build the nurturing relationships that underpin social-emotional well-being. These positive, nurturing relationships give children the confidence to learn, explore, and persist in the face of challenge. Infants and young children who miss out on such relationships are likely to be compromised both in their ability and eagerness to learn and in their ability to form positive relationships in the future (ZERO TO THREE, 1992). Although these relationships are expressed and strengthened through nonverbal as well as verbal interaction, in a literate culture, words play an increasingly important role as children mature, especially in schools and other group care settings where language is the currency of social exchange.

The years between 1 and 4 are critical ones. Most children say their first words around the time of their first birthdays and start putting words together sometime between 18 and 30 months. Children ages 1 and 2 do most of their talking with adults, but by age 3 they are less dependent on adult conversation partners (Hart & Risley, 1999). Children increasingly talk to themselves, peers, toys, and even imaginary friends, as well as to parents and caregivers. Older children develop a range of relationships and interests, and their language is shaped by peers, books, and community experiences as well as by parents and teachers. Although some children will learn two languages in infancy and others will learn a second language when they enter child care or school, children's basic communication patterns and vocabulary-building trajectories are generally well-developed before they enter kindergarten.

Young children who can use their words to control their own behavior, avert or cope with frustration, and negotiate with others are less likely to act out aggressively or to withdraw from social interaction. Those who can use words playfully and tell good stories are generally valued by peers as dramatic play partners who can keep the play going and add elements that make it fun (Segal & Adcock, 1983). In the peer culture of preschool and kindergarten, where much of the interaction consists of pretend play, children who are good at talking tend to get more opportunities to hear and practice language.

In both the social-emotional and intellectual realms, early language advantages compound.

LOOK WHO'S TALKING

Hart and Risley's study took place in children's homes, and most of the adult talking was done by parents. But the communication techniques that the most successful parents were using are similar to those long recommended and used by early educators and child development experts. Although Hart and Risley were surprised by the amount of talk they recorded, the magnitude of the differences they found, and the strength of the correlations between parent communication style and children's verbal abilities, they were not surprised by the features of extra talk that were associated with positive child outcomes.

The analytic categories underlying Hart and Risley's definitions of business talk and play talk and their analysis of communication patterns grew out of a long tradition of child development research and practical knowledge that emphasizes responsive relationships, positive affect, mutual attachment, expansion of children's ideas to support and extend their learning, learning through play, and other developmentally appropriate practices. What is new, however, is the finding that *more talk makes the difference* because *more talk is richer talk.*

Similar findings emerged from another longitudinal study, the Home–School Study of Language Development (Dickinson & Tabors, 2001). This study was conducted in the Boston area by a team of Harvard researchers who visited toddlers from low-income households in their homes and then in their Head Start centers and followed their progress into elementary school and beyond. In this multifaceted investigation, Catherine E. Snow, David Dickinson, Patton O. Tabors, and their colleagues analyzed mealtime conversations in children's homes and looked closely at the communication techniques used by their preschool teachers during large group lessons and small group activities, as well as when they conversed with individual children or with pairs of children engaged in pretend play.

Like Hart and Risley, the Harvard researchers found large differences among families in the amount and style of communication with young children, although their sample only included low-income households. They also found differences among teachers, both in their pedagogical philosophies and in what they actually did in the classroom. They identified particular techniques—such as the use and explanation of rare words and the presence and active use of a writing center—that prepared 3- and 4-year-old children for success in kindergarten and first grade. They identified effective practices in both intentional, adult-initiated instruction and child-initiated, play-based learning. But their most consistent, overarching finding was the importance of "decontextualized language," talk that went beyond the here and now, beyond the immediate shared context of the conversation partners, to include the past, the future, the far away or imaginary, and the hypothetical or fanciful.

Decontextualized language is frequently present in play talk and is characteristic of storytelling, reflection, planning, and wondering. It is also, of course, the language of books. One of the reasons that reading aloud to young children plays such an important role in fostering literacy is that it exposes children to rich and complex literary language, often containing pleasing rhythms, rhymes, and alliterative patterns that attune their ears to the component sounds of words. This language is also likely to engage their imaginations as they try to picture what is being described and infer the meaning of unfamiliar words.

When parents and teachers use books as springboards for conversations, children both hear and practice decontextualized language. Whether a teacher or parent uses the structured and very effective techniques of "dialogic reading" pioneered by Grover Whitehurst (Whitehurst et al., 1994) to encourage children to recall story elements, interpret words and pictures, and make connections to their own experiences, or whether the child and adult simply talk about the pictures and make up a story of their own, the conversations are likely to be rich and enriching. As in other play talk conversations, there will be more questions and explanations, more exchange of ideas and opinions, more elaboration by the adult of the child's observations and ideas, more use of descriptive language and narrative elements, more provocations and supports for imagination and reasoning, and more opportunities to hear and practice new words and deepen understanding of word meanings than in business talk exchanges.

Reading to a child, individually or in a small group, gives a teacher something to talk with the child about. When the child and teacher can enjoy the book together, and when the dialogue it evokes is genuine and open ended, the shared experience can strengthen their relationship and may become a topic of future conversations.

Children today are likely to get the majority of their language input and practice in out-of-home child care settings. When these environments are language-rich—offering children a wealth of words and opportunities to use their words to ask questions, tell stories, solve problems, share information, imagine, and play—they build firm foundations for social-emotional health and later academic success.

AT A LOSS FOR WORDS

Unfortunately, too many of the settings in which very young American children spend their days are not language rich (Bardige, 2005). In many settings, either there is too little talking or too much of the talking is being done by the television. In either case, infants, toddlers, and young preschoolers are missing out on the responsive, interesting, emotionally affirming, vocabulary-building conversations of play talk, and the adults who are caring for them are missing out on the fun of just playing and the wonder of witnessing young minds emerge.

The National Institute of Child Health and Human Development (NICHD) longitudinal study of 1,364 children born in 1991 concluded that "positive caregiving" is "somewhat" or "very uncharacteristic" for more than 60% of American children between the ages of 1 and 3 (NICHD Early Child Care Research Network, 2005). The study looked at children at home with their parents, as well as those being cared for by relatives or in family child care homes or child care centers. Positive caregiving was observed with an instrument that included a nine-item Caregiver Language Checklist focused on supports for language development. Observers noted the frequency with which the caregiver 1) responded to the child's vocalization, 2) read aloud to the child, 3) asked the child a question, 4) praised or spoke affectionately to the child, 5) taught the child, 6) directed other positive talk to the child, or 7) had close physical contact with the child; or with which the child was 8) occupied (engaged in a task or in play) and 9) not watching television.

In determining the likelihood of positive caregiving, observers also considered the child's and the caregiver's affect (i.e., expressed feelings, especially toward each other) and age-appropriate supports for the child's exploration, social interaction, and learning. Not surprisingly, positive caregiving correlated well with other measures of the overall quality of the child care environment and was associated with higher scores on language and problem-solving measures given when the child was $4^1/_2$.

More television watching, in particular, was associated with lower scores on the language and problem-solving tasks. This is concerning in light of recent studies of toddlers' television and video viewing habits. In November 2003, the Henry J. Kaiser Family Foundation released a report based on a national telephone survey of a random sample of more than 1,000 households with children younger than age 6. The study found that

> In a typical day, 69% of all children under two use screen media (59% watch TV, 42% watch a video or DVD, 5% use a computer, and 3% play video games) and these youngsters will spend an average of two hours and five minutes in front of a screen (Rideout, Vanderwater, & Martella, 2003, p. 5).

Rather than being educational, as many parents and caregivers believe, this screen time seems to be detrimental to young children's learning. Back and forth, serve-and-return interaction is what builds a baby's brain—and no electronic device can match the capacity of an enthralled human partner to deliver it.

In early 2007, the Administration for Children and Families reported the results of a 17-state study of child care use by low-income families (Layzer & Goodson, 2006). Many of the children were being cared for by their parents' friends, relatives, or neighbors; others were in licensed or license-exempt family child care homes or centers. In the home-based settings, the researchers were pleased to find that

> Providers showed interest in and affection for children, supervised their activities and were responsive to their needs. There was little stress or conflict in the homes and few children were observed to be in distress (crying, listless or withdrawn). Providers encouraged and were involved in children's play (Layzer & Goodson, 2006, p. 2).

Still, in contrast to what would be expected in accredited family child care homes that met professional guidelines, the researchers noted that "reading activities were observed in only 37% of the homes. Compared with caregivers in center-based programs for pre-school children, family child care providers spent less time in activities that promote cognitive and language development" (Layzer &

Goodson, 2006, p. 3). The researchers highlighted their concern with the ubiquity of television. "In more than 40% of the homes, the television was rarely or never turned off. In the majority of homes, at least one child was watching television at each observation point" (p. 3).

Young children living in poverty or in families with low incomes face a variety of challenges to healthy development. They are at higher risk for nutritional deficits, exposure to lead and other toxins, inadequate or inconsistent health care, and chronic stress that can interfere with their learning and brain development. Supportive relationships and a lot of play talk are especially important, and parent–child programs that make this a focus are likely to have dramatic effects. National, multisite programs such as The Parent–Child Home Program, the Abecedarian Project, Even Start, AVANCE, Early Head Start, and Parents as Teachers, as well as many similar but less studied local programs, have demonstrated the power of language-encouraging play to diminish or prevent the achievement gap that low-income children face at school entry. The impact of a high-quality play talk intervention can extend into adulthood, with children who participated in the program being more likely to graduate high school and continue their educations than children from similar backgrounds who did not. Interest in such programs has been growing, as has state, federal, and private funding to support them. Still, these programs reach fewer than 10% of the low-income families whose toddlers could benefit from them (Bardige, 2005).

The more we learn, the more we see how much talk matters—for *all* young children. For American children from relatively affluent, English-speaking homes, the quality of child care they receive as toddlers can speed or slow their language development (Vernon-Feagans, Hurley, Yont, Wamboldt, & Kolak, 2007). For children of highly educated mothers who do a lot of effective play talking, the amount of talk their fathers do with them makes a difference, as does the quality of their child care. Indeed, a father's talk may add value precisely because it is more often about adult interests such as work or hobbies and thus more likely to be decontextualized and abstract and to include unfamiliar words and concepts that stretch children's vocabularies (Pancsofar & Vernon-Feagans, 2006).

In this age of cell phones, MP3 players, television, and multitasking, when high-quality infant/toddler care is both scarce and expensive, too many of our children are not getting enough playful, engaging conversation during their prime time for language learning. The experiences that they are missing out on are as critical for social-emotional development as they are for language, literacy, and intellectual growth.

T. Berry Brazelton, a baby doctor, parent educator, author, and child advocate who has been called "the nation's pediatrician," is concerned that the "irreducible needs of children" (Brazelton & Greenspan, 2001) too often go unmet. In the foreword to the author's 2005 book, *At a Loss for Words: How America Is Failing Our Children and What We Can Do about It*, Brazelton points out "the importance to each child not only of a strong language base, but also of the emotional background that it represents" (p. xi):

> We know that both intelligence and resilience are founded in emotional learning. Without the necessary emotional base that comes from a devoted environment, a child's intelligence is not likely to flourish. And in the early years, when the bases for emotional learning are laid down, children whose parents or caregivers are too stressed to talk or read to them are already at risk for their future. (Bardige, 2005, p. xi)

This need not be the case. In Brazelton's words, "[a] parent who talks to her child right from the first is fitting her child for a rich future" (p. ix). If, as a society, we can provide the family friendly policies, programs, and public supports that reduce the stress on parents and teachers and contribute to language-rich environments; if, as parents, grandparents, teachers, and devoted friends of young children, we can follow Todd Risley's advice to talk with them a lot, then we can indeed fit our children for bright futures.

"INTO THE DRINKING WATER"

As chief public health officer for the city of Cambridge, Massachusetts, Harold Cox chaired The Agenda for Children Steering Committee, which coordinated the city's efforts to support its youngest children and ensure that their early experiences would prime them for later school success.

He listened to the academic experts, who explained the importance of talking with infants and young children. Catherine E. Snow, who had chaired the National Academy of Sciences panel on Preventing Reading Difficulties in Young Children, described the importance of rich early language experiences for literacy in the early elementary school years and beyond. She stunned the policy makers with the Hart and Risley data, then presented preliminary results of her own research that found a strong link between early childhood vocabulary and 10th-grade reading comprehension scores (Snow, Porche, Tabors, & Harris, 2007).

Richard Weissbourd, author of *The Vulnerable Child* (1997) and architect of the Read Boston program, urged the city to focus its prevention and intervention efforts on getting parents and teachers to do more talking with young children. He argued that there may be nothing more important to children's school and life success than early language development, and there is nothing more important to children's early language development than adults who regularly talk to them in enticing, encouraging ways. He then pointed out that the city—and the nation as a whole—provided many different, often expensive interventions to help older children who were not doing well, but was doing "frighteningly little" to influence the everyday interactions between adults and young children that shape development and set the stage for later learning.

Following the Action Plan that the city developed after consulting with these experts, Cox oversaw new efforts to reach out to families of newborns, both in the hospital and through home visits, to connect them with a variety of local family support, child care, and parenting education resources, and to encourage them to talk to their babies. These efforts are described on The Agenda for Children web site and include the following:

- *Maternity Ward Visits:* Literacy Initiative staff visit new mothers on the maternity ward at the Cambridge Hospital to encourage them to talk to their babies. Staff explain that talking, singing, and responding to babies help develop the language and literacy skills that are necessary for learning to read.

- *Home Visits:* Staff visit the homes of families with babies (newborn to 15 months). They talk to parents about the importance of bonding and playing with their baby, provide information about social services available in the community, and if necessary, link families to these resources. In addition, staff "model" techniques that parents can use to stimulate their child's language development, such as playing rhyming games or singing songs together.

- *Talk Presentations:* In 2002, the Literacy Initiative launched *Let's Talk. . . It Makes a Difference,* a campaign to increase awareness about the importance of oral language development in young children. During Let's Talk presentations, staff teach parents simple techniques for interacting with their youngsters that will spur rich and elaborate conversations. All presentations are given in multiple languages.

- *Reading Parties:* Using modeling techniques, staff teach parents how to use age-appropriate books to develop their child's vocabulary and to help their child understand the correspondence between printed letters and their sounds. Parents also learn how to engage their child as an active participant during storytime. At the end of the party, parents are given free copies of the books used by the facilitator.

- *Interactive Literacy Activities:* Building on the reading party concept, staff model for parents how to have rich and elaborate conversations with their children during book-related activities. After reading a book to their child, parents learn how to extend learning through singing songs, arts and crafts projects (such as making puppets that recreate book characters), and other activities. Events are held in English, Spanish, Portuguese, and Haitian Creole. Venues include public housing complexes, libraries, churches, and hospitals (The Agenda for Children, n.d.).

With the Cambridge-Somerville Health Alliance, Cox supported a "book prescriptions" program in which pediatricians gave out books during well-baby visits, talked with parents about the importance of reading, and wrote prescriptions as reminders—following the successful model of Reach Out and Read developed in neighboring Boston and expanded nationally. The program's mission and approach are as follows:

> *Reach Out and Read* makes literacy promotion a standard part of pediatric care so that children grow up with books and a love of reading.
> *Reach Out and Read* trains doctors and nurses to advise parents about the importance of reading aloud and to give books to children at pediatric check-ups from six months to five years of age. A special focus is placed on children growing up in poverty. By building on the unique relationship between parents and medical providers, Reach Out and Read helps families and communities cultivate early literacy skills so that children enter school prepared to succeed at reading. (Reach Out and Read, n.d.)

Cox collaborated with early educators and others to initiate a series of playgroups for young children and their parents, held in the city's health clinic, housing projects, and Center for Families. These get-togethers focused on developing language and literacy through play.

He applauded the successes of a coalition that included the school department, libraries, family literacy and adult education programs, university professors, and early educators in providing intensive literacy training and classroom coaching to center-based and family child care teachers and in teaching the basic concepts to adults enrolled in basic education and English language courses.

He followed the ongoing evaluations of this work—much of which had been supported by two federal Early Learning Opportunities Grants—and saw not only the progress of children in learning both their home languages and English, the increased use by teachers of effective language and literacy facilitation techniques, and the increasing attendance of families at library story hours, parent forums, neighborhood reading parties, and citywide fairs but also the rise, over several years, in the reading scores of the city's kindergarteners and first graders.

Cox was fully convinced of the importance of talking with young children and of the power of simple interventions that supported their parents, caregivers, and teachers. But what really fueled his passion was a personal experience that showed how wide the language input and conversation gap could be—and the difference it could make in a young child's life.

On the way home from a conference, Cox happened to be seated near two parents with toddlers on a 3-hour flight. The first family talked incessantly. They talked about how the seat belt worked and why it was important to keep it fastened. They put the tray up and down, and talked about how it worked and why it needed to be in the up position and latched for take-off. They looked out the window and talked about the vehicles servicing the aircraft, the parts of the plane they could see, and the markers along the runway. In the air, they talked about their changing view of airfield, city, and ocean, the clouds they flew through and then looked down on, the speed of the aircraft and the distance they had to travel, the people they knew in the places they flew over, and the books and toys they had brought along. They made up stories together about the inhabitants of "cloud land," speculated about what the child's father was doing and what they would do when they got home, and reminisced about their recent visit with the child's grandparents. The 3-year-old talked almost as much as his mother—pointing out sights; asking questions; repeating new words such as "stewardess," "luggage," "taxi," "oxygen," "life vest," and "flight path"; telling stories or adding details to his mother's; requesting toys, books, and snacks; and occasionally singing a favorite song.

The second family remained silent for almost the entire flight! The 3-year-old dutifully allowed her mother to fasten her seat belt, played quietly with her doll and then her coloring book, ate her meal in silence, took a short nap, and spent a great deal of time quietly staring ahead—as did her mother. The only words Cox heard the mother say to her daughter were brief commands—the business talk of an airplane flight. He did not hear the child speak at all.

As he told this story to his colleagues, Harold Cox shared his own reactions. He had been tired, he said, and planned to sleep a bit on the plane and catch up on some reading. He wasn't thrilled to be seated next to nonstop talkers who, although polite, were difficult to ignore. But, as he listened to the avid learner happily chatting with his mother, he was drawn to their conversation. At the same time, he wondered about the silent child and her virtually silent mother. Were they always so quiet, or were they just being considerate of other passengers? Did cultural norms prevent the mother from engaging her child in conversation in a public place, did she believe that children should be seen but not heard, or was she simply unaware of how much her child was capable of learning and the important role she could play by engaging with her in play talk? In a voice filled with conviction, he exhorted his colleagues:

> We've been working to teach parents and teachers of young children how important it is to talk with them. But teaching individuals is not enough. As a public health professional, I know that we have to create a new norm. Somehow, we've got to get this into the drinking water, so that everybody talks to babies all the time—and gets them to talk back!

Cambridge is a diverse community. More than 40% of the children in its public schools come from low-income families, and more than 30% are from families whose first language is not English. Its public school families hail from more than 60 different countries and collectively speak more than 40 different languages. One of the strategies that The Agenda for Children has pioneered is the development of a multilingual cadre of "literacy ambassadors" who have gained expertise in talking with young children in ways that boost language, emotional resilience, literacy, and learning. These ambassadors reach out to their cultural communities, in the places where people naturally gather and at special events, to share their knowledge—in their home languages—and to connect parents, teachers, and caregivers with programs and supports that can enrich their conversations with the young children in their lives.

My hope is that this book will provide you with such resources and supports that you will not only be affirmed in your daily work and inspired to try new things but also that you will find many practical, easy-to-use suggestions that can make your direct interactions with children more fun. Whether you are a teacher, home visitor, adult educator, or doting parent or grandparent, I hope that you will use what you learn to support parents and other caregivers. Finally, I hope that you will become literacy ambassadors in your community, and that you will help get the play talk message "into the drinking water."

Baby Babbles

(Birth–1½ Years)

Baby Ana, just 2 days old, is meeting her doctor for the first time. "Hey, Ana," he coos softly as he lifts her from her hospital crib. Ana fusses as he carries her, but is gradually soothed by his voice. As he lays her down to examine her, she gets her fist into her mouth and sucks steadily. The doctor makes sure that her parents notice. "Look how she's taking over from me! She's already figured out how to soothe herself!" Ana's parents watch in awe as their newborn follows the doctor's talking face with her eyes, then turns her head toward the sound of a rattle that he shakes softly near her ear. When he holds her against his shoulder, they see her cuddle, suck her hand, and then lift her head a bit to look around. "What a great baby you have!" he tells Ana's parents as he winds up the examination. "Did you see how interested she is in the world around her?"

Before giving Ana back to her parents, the doctor once again holds her with her face near his and tells her in his gentlest baby talk what a great baby she is. "You call her," he says to her mom. "Let's see what she does." Ana turns toward her mother's voice and gazes at her face. "She knows me already, doesn't she?" "Yes she does," the doctor responds. "And I bet she knows her dad, too." Sure enough, Ana turns to her father, seeming to prefer his voice to the doctor's. "She knows you both," the doctor concludes, "and I can see that you and this very healthy, curious young lady are off to a wonderful start."

Most babies do well on the Neonatal Behavioral Assessment Scale (NBAS; Brazelton & Nugent, 1995) or its simpler relative, the Newborn Behavioral Observations system (Nugent, Kecfer, Minear, Johnson, & Blanchard, 2007), designed for use by home visitors, nurse practitioners, and others who support new parents. These assessments were designed to provide a "portrait" of a baby's strengths, adaptive responsibilities, and vulnerabilities. But these assessments do more than reassure anxious parents and grandparents. They provide opportunities for parents to see for themselves the remarkable communication and learning skills their baby already possesses. They help each parent to tune into the baby's particular patterns of relating to others and to his environment, so that together they can forge an alliance that will support the optimal development of a unique human being.

> "All children are born wired for feelings and ready to learn."
>
> —From Neurons to Neighborhoods: The Science of Early Childhood Development (National Research Council and Institute of Medicine, 2000, p. 2)

Call it chemistry, natural attraction, or falling in love—babies lure adults from the start, and adults who tune in are easily lured. Bonding begins when parent and baby see each other for the first time—and it's a two-way street. With their large eyes and sweet expressions, babies are as cute as they are helpless. Adults naturally soften in their presence, and soon baby and parent are gazing into each other's eyes and forging a connection.

If you talk to a newborn, she will likely turn toward your voice. If you are her mother or father, she may recognize your voice and turn toward it rather than toward someone else's. Most babies reliably recognize and choose their mother's voice by the time they are 1 week old, and will typically choose their father's voice over a stranger's at 2 weeks or before. Many parents discover this for themselves, of course. Even so, parents' eyes light up when a pediatrician or home visitor or grandparent who is holding their baby demonstrates how the baby turns toward his mothers or father's call. No matter how sophisticated they are, it's hard for parents to resist a newborn's charms, especially when it's clear that their baby knows—and chooses—them.

GETTING TO KNOW YOU

Maria is nursing 4-day-old Marisol, her first child. Marisol takes a couple of sucks, then pauses. Each time she pauses, Maria jostles or strokes her lightly and murmurs encouragement. "Have some more. You're just getting started. What a good baby you are!" Maria doesn't notice it, but each time she talks, or even makes an encouraging sound, Marisol lengthens the pause. While Maria is trying to get Marisol to keep eating, it seems that Marisol is trying to get her mother to keep talking.

Babies depend on adults for care and communication, as well as for food. The more attentive engagement they get, the more they learn to elicit.

The love affair between parent (or frequent caregiver) and child typically deepens over time. Parents and babies spend minutes at a time gazing into each other's eyes. The parent speaks in a high-pitched, sing-song voice, and the baby knows: She is talking to ME! The baby's limbs move in rhythm with her parent's voice, and she makes sounds of her own when the talking stops. Her expression mimics her parent's, and then her parent's mimics hers. Soon they are on the same wavelength—engaged in a subtle communication dance. They connect, communicate, take a momentary break as the baby tires, then they connect and communicate again.

By the time they are 3 months old, most babies have learned how to hook familiar adults and engage with them in back-and-forth inter-action. This process of increasingly synchronized mutual engagement, or "attunement," is the basis of a positive relationship. Attunement occurs with time between a baby and each of the important people in her life—parents and grandparents, siblings, and stable caregivers.

The newborn period is a time of rapid learning. As the baby adapts to life outside the warm and watery womb, he must learn to control his body movements, take in and make sense of information about his surroundings, and learn how his actions can affect those of objects and of other people. His brain is growing rapidly and its basic architecture or "wiring" of neural pathways is being formed. Each of his experiences creates or strengthens synaptic connections in his brain; collectively these early learning experiences shape the way his brain will function and thus provide a foundation for how he will learn and who he will become.

In a baby's early weeks and months, he depends on his caregivers to keep him comfortable and help him engage with his environment. Babies learn best in a calm, alert state, but their nervous systems are immature, and it's hard for them to stay calm and engaged on their own. Too much stimulation or excitement can cause a baby to grimace, stiffen, and twist away; to cry out in pain; to "lose it" and scream uncontrollably; or to shut down and go to sleep. Too little stimulation and the baby can tune out, look bored and listless, fuss, or try to soothe or stimulate himself. In extreme situations like understaffed orphanages, babies who receive very little stimulation or human interaction and who have few opportunities to explore an interesting environment or learn through their own activities develop undersized brains with too few connections. At the other extreme, babies who are chronically or severely stressed often become hyperalert and edgy. High levels of the stress hormone cortisol can damage babies' developing neural circuitry and interfere with their learning.

Adults who spend a lot of time with a baby—or who have learned what to look for—can read the baby's cues and know when she wants more and when she has had enough. They know how to talk and sing to the baby, as well as touch, bounce, and rock her in just the right way and at just the right time to engage or soothe her, bring her up, or bring her down. They know when a loud voice is too much and when it is fun, when a quiet voice is soothing and when even that is too much if it comes with eye contact or jostling, when a change of position provides an exciting view of something new, and when a backward tip or a sudden change in temperature will cause the baby to startle and cry.

Jack, who was born prematurely and spent his first couple of weeks in the neonatal intensive care unit, was a colicky newborn. At 3 months, he was still difficult to engage. Awakening from a nap, Jack would wail for his mother or father, then quiet when he heard their voices or footsteps. But, when either parent picked him up from his crib, he tended to go limp and avoid eye contact. If they persisted in trying to engage his attention, he often stiffened and tried to turn away.

Fortunately for Jack's parents, they had the support of an experienced home visitor who could help them see their baby's strengths—and their own. She commented on how responsive Jack's parents were to him and how he calmed at their approach. Together, they figured out that Jack needed time and physical support before he could engage them. Hanging in the air was stressful for him, as was a sudden approach or eye contact accompanied by speaking or touching. When his mother approached Jack more slowly, gave him more physical support, and waited for him to signal that he was ready for play, Jack could catch his mother's eye, smile in response to her smile, and even reach toward her face. As Jack's play skills and his parents' confidence increased, his limbs became stronger and his sensitivities began to abate. Without the support of a home visitor, this love story might have had a much less hopeful ending, with Jack's parents feeling like failures and growing increasingly distant while Jack increasingly missed out on the pleasurable exchanges necessary for his healthy development.

Although babies and adults are wired to connect with each other, the connections do not always go so smoothly. Some babies are fussy and hard to soothe, some are so sensitive that they have to be approached carefully and given lots of support before they can engage, and some are challenged in one modality (e.g., hearing or sight) but hyper-acute in another. Some babies are flexible by nature, but others are fearful or feisty. Babies also differ in their natural activity levels and in their rates of development. Some babies give clear signals when they need food or play or comfort or rest; others are much harder to read.

When adults try to engage and connect with a baby, most will instinctively slow down, watch intently, and respond to the baby's overtures. They talk to the baby—in regular words and sentences that express their understanding and affection, in "baby talk" and terms of endearment that the baby senses are meant especially for him, and in comforting lullabies and other special songs. They experience a rush of pleasure when the baby responds to them, and they adjust their level of stimulation to what the baby can take in at the moment.

An adult who is depressed or preoccupied or exhausted may not have the energy for these enjoyable interactions—or for the more demanding task of soothing a baby who is distressed. Similarly, an adult who is stressed or fearful or rushed may miss the baby's cues. The adult may speak too loudly, move too suddenly, hold too stiffly, or interact too intrusively, transmitting stress to the baby.

When the adult's natural rhythms match the baby's needs, connections are easier to make and sustain. When there seems to be a mismatch, early intervention can help strengthen the relationship. An expert's help is particularly valuable if the adult is feeling overwhelmed or if, for example, the baby is unusually sleepy or wakeful, particularly fearful or feisty, extremely laid back or hard to read, or very easily overstimulated.

Why Talk to Babies?

New parents often hear this question: "Why are you talking to that baby? She's much too young to understand." Their answers often reveal how much they have already learned about their child.

- "Look how she turns toward my voice. She knows that I am talking to her."

- "When I chat about what we are doing, it seems to relax him."

- "I notice that she pays attention, especially when people talk in my home language. I guess that's what she's been hearing."

- "Talking or singing to him relaxes me."

- "Look how animated she gets when I talk to her. It's like we're on the same wavelength."

- "When we talk, he's all eyes and ears. You can almost see him learning."

- "She may not understand what I'm saying, but she smiles anyway. She's so cute when she does that."

- "In Korea, we talk to babies in a special language that is easier for them to learn."

SHARING THE CARING

Many mothers go back to work when their babies are 3 or 4 months old. No matter how experienced the new caregiver is or how much they trust him or her, parents are likely to worry. Above all else, young babies need the security that a devoted caregiver who recognizes their individual, moment-to-moment needs provides. So the hand-off is likely to come with a lot of instructions, such as the following:

- "He likes to be held and rocked when he has his bottle."

- "Please don't overdress her—it makes her groggy."

- "He gets fussy in the late afternoon. Sometimes it helps to give him a ride in his carriage—even if it's just around the room."

But the most important instruction of all may be: *TALK TO MY BABY. It doesn't matter what language you speak, but baby talk is best. My baby thrives on one-to-one interaction. The more you give her, the better you two will get to know each other and the more fun you'll have together.*

THE TOWER OF BABEL

Babies have all kinds of ways of communicating. At first, they just cry, but soon their cries differentiate into a sharp one that means "Ouch"; an intense, rhythmic one that means "I'm hungry"; and others that mean "I'm bored," "I'm tired," "I'm really, really overtired," "I'm uncomfortable," and "I'm scared." With time, parents and caregivers learn to tell the difference and to respond accordingly.

Young babies also coo and babble as they "converse" with adults. Even when no one responds, babies enjoy playing with the sounds they can make. Vowels come first, then consonants, raspberries, and other sound effects. Babbling (individual consonant sounds and then strings of sounds like "da-da-da-da") starts at around 4 months and eventually turns into recognizable words.

Babbling is innate, and at first, babies the world over babble the same large repertoire of sounds. Over time, though, each baby narrows his babbling to the sounds that are used meaningfully in the languages he hears. If people around him all speak the same language, then by 9 months he will only be babbling the sounds of that language. In fact, he will no longer attend to subtle differences in sounds that are not meaningful in his language. By 10 or 12 months, he will be talking in a kind of gibberish or "expressive jargon" that mimics the cadences of statements, questions, and commands in that language, and he may also be saying a few recognizable words.

A baby who hears two languages spoken to her will follow the same pattern, gradually narrowing her babbling to meaningful sounds, speaking in bilingual expressive jargon, and learning words from both languages. But for a bilingual baby, the window for hearing and saying the distinct sounds of many languages is likely to remain open longer. As she begins to use words, her total vocabulary will likely keep pace with those of monolingual babies, but she may know some separate words in each of her languages as well as many in both (Genesee, Paradis, & Crago, 2004).

ATTACHING MEANING TO WORDS

For very young babies, language communicates feelings. Just as they communicate their own feelings through cries, babbling, and laughter,

Babble Games

Try these yourself or share some with parents and caregivers.

- Imitate the baby's babbling and enjoy her reaction.

- Record the baby's babbles and play them back to him.

- Catch the baby's attention and babble one sound repeatedly (e.g., "Buh-buh-buh-buh"). See if she will imitate you.

- Answer the baby's babbles by repeating them and then adding a new sound.

- Let the baby watch your mouth as you make distinct sounds.

- Babble with the baby while you both look in a mirror.

- Make silly sounds that get the baby to smile or laugh.

- Let the baby listen to a lot of different sounds: music, rustling leaves, people talking, the noise of a vacuum or washing machine (some babies find this especially soothing), bells, squeakers, and rattles. Talk about the sounds and the things that make them. Imitate a sound and watch the baby's reaction.

- Use the baby's sounds to get him "on your wavelength." As you talk to him (or even to someone else while looking at him), punctuate your conversation with his favorite sounds.

- Sing silly songs and gentle lullabies in your home language. Lullabies have calmed babies for ages; silly songs often are met with delight.

- KEEP TALKING. Babies need to hear real language as well as babbles. Talk about what you are doing, what the baby is doing, what happened yesterday, and what you want to remember to do today. Make language a part of all of your everyday baby care activities: bathing, changing, feeding, playing, soothing, and relaxing.

they respond to the feelings that others convey through language. When a mother calls, "I'm coming! I'll be there in a minute!" in a cheery, reassuring voice, her hungry baby is likely to stop crying, almost as if he understands the words. When an adult speaks sharply, babies too young to understand "No!" will startle, stop what they are doing, and sometimes burst into tears.

All around the world, adults speak to babies in the same melodies, using low, smooth murmurs to soothe; rising intonation to engage or direct attention; and short, sharp sounds to warn or inhibit. Babies key into tone of voice and cadence long before they can recognize individual words as units of sound that carry meaning (Eliot, 1999).

This universal baby talk, which psychologists call *parentese*, also contains features that help babies to hear where one word ends and another begins and to connect these words with meanings. Vowels are elongated, as are pauses between words, and key consonants are enunciated clearly. Sentences and phrases are short. Important words—mostly nouns, verbs, and endearments—are stressed and often repeated. The speaker often says the same thing several times in different ways.

Attentive adults also label things for babies—pairing an emphasized word with an object the baby is reaching for or investigating or naming an action as they help the baby perform it. "Here's your *bottle*," "*Up* you go." "*Wave bye-bye*." Babies listen—and learn.

A 2006 study by infant language researchers Shannon Pruden, Kathy Hirsh-Pasek, Roberta Golinkoff, and Elizabeth Hennon provided new evidence that children too young to speak are avid language learners. The 10-month-old babies in their study, who hadn't yet spoken their first words, learned the meanings of new words after hearing each *only twice*—as long as the researchers spoke in parentese and paired the word with an object that the baby was looking at or playing with.

Like parentese, traditional baby games also have features that help babies learn language. Classics such as Pat-a-Cake have a simple, steady rhythm and pair actions with words: "roll it" and "pat it." Bouncing games such as Pop Goes the Weasel and Trot, Trot to Boston have fun highlights that babies learn to anticipate—especially when "pop" always comes with a quick lift in the air, or "Watch out you don't fall IN!" is accompanied by a sudden but gentle drop between the bouncer's knees.

There are many ways to play Pat-a-Cake, and many versions of the words and gestures. In this one, the adult holds the baby's hands and claps them slowly for the first line, then faster for the second. He moves the baby's hands around each other on "roll it," claps them again on "pat it," holds them still, then moves them forward to "put it in the oven," touches them to the baby's chest "for Baby" and then to his own body for "me."

> Pat-a-cake, pat-a-cake, baker's man.
> Bake me a cake as fast as you can.
> Roll it, and pat it, and mark it with a *B*,
> And put it in the oven for Baby and me!

Pop Goes the Weasel lends itself to a knee-bouncing game. Seat the baby on your lap, facing you, and hold her under her arms. Bounce her up and down as you say the words. On "Pop," lift her high in the air. Start slowly with a gentle lift. When the baby can anticipate the lift (she may smile, tense her body, grab your arms, or give you a knowing look when you pause after 'fun"), you can go faster and make the lift more dramatic.

> All around the cobbler's bench
> The monkey chased the weasel.
> The monkey thought it was all in fun—
> POP goes the weasel.

Trot, Trot to Boston is played like Pop Goes the Weasel, except that you drop the baby between your knees on "in" instead of lifting him in the air. Again, you can start with a gentle drop and make it more dramatic as the baby learns the game and indicates his enjoyment.

> Trot, trot to Boston
> Trot, trot to Lynn.
> Watch out, Baby that you don't fall—
> IN.

"Hico, Hico, Caballito," an adaptation of a Christmas song from Spain, is used by many Latino parents to help their infants anticipate and cope with change while also enjoying rhythmic language. The baby is seated on the parent's lap, and the parent bounces the baby while chanting the rhyme. As the last verse is chanted, the knee-bouncing gets faster and faster. On the last "galope" the parent straightens his legs and the baby gets a sudden but gentle slide.

> Hico hico, caballito (Giddyup, little horsie),
> Vamos a Belén (Let's go to Belén).
> Que mañana es fiesta (There's a festival tomorrow)
> Y pasado también (and the day after, as well).

> Al paso (Walk),
> Al trote (Trot),
> Al galope al galope al galope!! (and gallop, gallop, gallop!!)

The following traditional knee-bouncing rhyme from Vietnam is fun in any language. As you say the first line, lift the baby's arm and shake it gently; do the same with the other arm on the second line, then bounce the baby on your knees as you say the third line and begin the fourth. Lift the baby high in the air on "up to the mountain" and then bring him back down to your lap.

Kia con ngua trang (Look—there's a white horse).
Kia con ngua hong (Look—there's a pink horse).
Nhong, Nhong, Nhong, Nhong (Galloping, galloping, galloping,
  galloping)
Ngua phi qua song hui (They fly up to the mountain and down
  to the sea).

Parents and caregivers can always make up songs and games of their own. These are especially fun (and helpful for building language) when they relate to what the baby is doing or seeing. For example, the traditional "This Is the Way We Wash Our Clothes" can become

This is the way we put on your onesie,
Put on your onesie, put on your onesie.
This is the way we put on your onesie,
So you can have some play time.

For a more invigorating workout, try moving the baby's arms and legs to go with the words of the following tune. If he likes the game, after a while he may learn to do some of the motions himself.

Wave, wave, wave your arms
Wave your arms together.
Clap, clap, clap your hands
Clap your hands together.
Kick, kick, kick your feet
Kick your feet together.

Using a baby's name makes any rhyme or song more personal. It also helps the child learn her name—and helps other children in a child care group learn it, too.

Here's a variant of the traditional "Jack Be Nimble":

Shawna be nimble,
Shawna be quick.
Shawna jump over
Your mama's broomstick.

Shawna can babble,
Shawna can call.
Shawna likes chasing
After her ball.

Similarly, a baby's own name can be substituted in the following traditional French lullaby. Its simple tune reflects the rhythm of gentle rocking, and its lyrics are easy to vary with a sibling's, caregiver's, or parent's own words.

> Fais do do, Pierrot mon petit frère (Go to sleep, Peter, my
>   little brother)
> Fais do do, t'auras du lolo (Go to sleep, and you'll have a treat).
> Maman est en haut (Mama's upstairs),
> Elle fait des gateaux (She's making cakes).
> Papa est en bas (Papa's downstairs),
> Il fait du chocolat (He makes chocolate).
> Fais do do, Pierrot mon petit frère (Go to sleep, Peter, my
>   little brother)
> Fais do do, t'auras du lolo (Go to sleep, and you'll have a treat).

IT'S NEVER TOO EARLY FOR STORIES AND BOOKS

Literary language—the language of books, folktales, nursery rhymes, poetry, and even simple stories—is different from ordinary talk. It uses longer and more complex sentences, with more adjectives and adverbs. Its rhythms are often distinct and memorable. It has style. Even very young babies who have no idea what the words mean may be captivated by its charms.

A series of studies done in the 1980s by Anthony DeCasper and Melanie Spence (DeCasper & Spence, 1986) revealed that even in utero, babies attended to a frequently read story and later preferred it to an unfamiliar one. The researchers chose a much-loved classic—Dr. Seuss's *The Cat in the Hat*—with a strong, easily recognizable rhythm, and asked mothers to read it aloud to their unborn children twice a day throughout the last 6 weeks of their pregnancies. When the babies were just a few hours old, the researchers assessed their story preferences by having them suck a special pacifier while listening to tapes of their mothers reading *The Cat in the Hat* or another children's story. Overwhelmingly, the newborns showed their preference for the story they had been hearing by sucking faster on the pacifier.

To the researchers, this was evidence that babies were hearing and learning before birth, and that they liked hearing a familiar voice reading a familiar story. Many parents, though, interpreted it as a way to make their babies smarter—by teaching them even before they were born. There is no evidence that reading Dr. Seuss books (or any other stories) or playing classical music (or any other kind) to unborn babies boosts IQ scores. However, there is ample evidence that even

The Books Babies Like Best. . .

- Are washable, chewable, sturdy, and easy to hold

- Have clear, colorful pictures

- Have pictures they can point to and name

- Show other babies

- Show familiar objects, actions, and routines

- Let babies feel different textures

- Have simple rhythmic or rhyming text—in their home language

- Don't need to tell a story

- Can be homemade—using picture albums with plastic sleeves

- Are fun for parents, too

- Will be read and played with over and over and over again

very young babies listen attentively to the songs, rhymes, and stories that their parents share with them and find the familiar sounds both riveting and soothing.

With very young babies, any book will do. They will listen to parents and caregivers read an adult book or a nursery rhyme, a letter or a newspaper article. Still, babies prefer books that sound familiar, just like frequently heard lullabies.

By 6 months, many babies will attend to pictures as well as words. They especially like photographs of other babies, as well as bright, clear, realistic pictures of familiar objects, people, and daily activities. Before their first birthdays, many babies will point to familiar objects or people in books and scrapbooks, follow a simple direction like "pat the bunny" or "look in the mirror," or make appropriate noises for several of the pictured animals. Some babies may also try to turn pages of sturdy board books or laminated photo albums. Of course, babies also like to pull, chew on, and bang the books.

Pediatricians and child development experts encourage sharing books with babies, both because babies enjoy the activity and because parents who develop the habit early tend to keep it up. Babies often come to associate books with special parent talk and cuddling time, and their delight can encourage parents to keep reading.

TELLING STORIES AND NARRATING THE WORLD

The Bardige boys grew up with their father's stories about the "Bald-Headed Chicken," and, when their own children were born, they carried on the tradition by sharing Bald-Headed Chicken stories with them. But each brother remembered the tradition differently and elaborated on it in his own way.

Art remembered the stories as fanciful and complex, and he waited until his kids were 2 or 3 to introduce them to the Bald-Headed Chicken. A teacher of science and math, he made up long stories that detailed the Bald-Headed Chicken's adventures with other farm animals, explained why chickens don't have teeth but other animals do, and even attempted to answer the question of why the moon sometimes appears in the daytime sky.

Gil's memories were mostly of the special closeness he had felt when his father told him Bald-Headed Chicken stories. He introduced the Bald-Headed Chicken to his firstborn when she was only 6 months old. "The Bald-Headed Chicken and Marissa are going for a walk. They are getting into the stroller. Okay, here they go! Bump, bump, bump down the stairs. The Bald-Headed Chicken and Marissa are going to the park."

Whether or not they use a story format, many parents enjoy narrating the world for their babies. They may take their baby on a tour of a room or outdoor space and keep a running commentary about what the baby is seeing and doing. When the baby shows particular interest by staring, reaching, pointing, or vocalizing, parents typically stop to engage the baby in a parentese conversation. "You found the light switch. We can turn it on and off. On…and off. On…You turned on the lights!"

GO, BABY, GO!

Ten-month-old Analese is "cooking" with her Dad. As he prepares supper, she plays with a stainless steel mixing bowl, a tennis ball, and a spoon. Her Dad shows her how to bang the spoon on the bowl, then gives Analese a try. She startles at the loud noise, but smiles when he comments, "What a loud bang! I think you're going to be a drummer!" After playing with the bowl and spoon for a while, Analese picks up the tennis ball and carefully places it in the bowl. She's fascinated by the way it rolls around, and she tries to "stir" it with the spoon. She picks the ball up and examines it closely, tries to take a bite, then drops it in the bowl. She lifts it and drops it several times, varying her approach slightly as if she is trying to figure out just how high she can bounce it without bouncing it out of the bowl. When Analese tries throwing, she misses the bowl entirely and the ball rolls away. She gets onto her hands and knees and begins to crawl after it, but the floor is slippery, so she shifts to a crab walk. Finding this mode of locomotion too slow as well, Analese sits on her bottom and scoots backward, pushing with her feet until she reaches the ball. Beaming at her accomplishment, she looks around to see if anyone noticed, and suddenly realizes that her father is out of sight. Just as she is about to cry, she hears a reassuring voice from around the corner. "What fast scooting, Analese! You got the ball! Can you bring it to Daddy?"

Newly mobile infants like Analese are often busy exploring their environments. As they venture farther and farther afield, they check back to make sure that a trusted adult is nearby. The adult's voice becomes a lifeline, assuring them that they are safe and connected, and thus enabling them to practice their developing motor skills.

Many parents call their mobile infants "young explorers" or "little scientists." Like Analese, these babies are busy learning how objects move and fit in space, what they can do with different objects, how to use objects—and people—as tools, and how to make interesting things happen over and over again. They are also learning how to move themselves through space and how to fit their bodies (or body parts) into defined spaces. As they lose and retrieve objects and as they move away from people and find them again, they are learning how to keep objects and people in mind or memory when they are out of sight. When adults comment on a baby's discoveries and share their delight in his triumphs, they encourage him to explore with confidence and zest and help him learn to persist at challenging problems.

The classic games adults play with babies are an important part of the "infant curriculum," supporting children's exploratory learning while building relationships, nonverbal communication, and language. Our endless variations of Peekaboo engage babies in keeping things in mind and making interesting things happen—as well as in playful conversation exchange. Games of chase such as I'm Going to Get You add the challenge of moving and maneuvering through space.

Many Ways to Play Peekaboo

- Cover your face with your hands while the baby is looking at you. After a second or two, rotate your hands to reveal your face while saying, "Peekaboo." If the baby smiles or laughs, smile or laugh back. Then repeat the game. If he is still interested after a few repetitions, try one of the variations below.

- Cover your face with your hands but pull them down (or lift your head) instead of opening them as you say, "Peekaboo."

- Uncover your face only partially as you say "Peekaboo." See if the baby will pull your hands to uncover your whole face.

- Cover your head with a blanket. Say, "Pee-eeek" and then pull it off on "aboo." See if the baby will pull it off after a few repetitions.

- Put a blanket over the baby's head and say, "Peekaboo." Can she pull it off? (In Spanish, this version is called "Sabanita," which means "Little Sheet." The game is traditionally thought of as a way to prepare the child for the mother's absence in the future: Things may not always be as she expects, but she will be able to take action to cope with change.)

- Hide behind a chair or around a corner. Say, "Peekaboo" as you pop out.

- Try whispering, "Peekaboo" as you reveal your face. How does the baby respond?

Turn-taking games such as rolling a ball back and forth while chanting something like "I roll the ball to Leticia . . . she rolls it back to me," highlight the back-and-forth qualities of conversation as they combine words and rituals with physical and spatial challenges. Show-off routines such as How big is Baby? So-o-o big! or Where is Daddy's nose? are fun for babies to learn because even partial success usually produces a delighted response from adults. And, of course, everything that fascinates a baby also creates an opportunity for adult connection and play talk.

TWENTY FUN THINGS TO DO WITH BABIES

Babies do not need expensive, elaborate activities to have fun and learn language skills. The following are simple activities that can be done with babies every day:

1. *Blow soap bubbles*: Use words to engage the baby's attention and encourage him to watch, reach for, and pop the bubbles. "Ready—set—BLOW! Look at all those bubbles! Can you catch one?"

2. *Give the baby a simple puzzle:* You might offer her a pot with a lid, a set of measuring cups or storage containers that fit inside each other, a shape sorter, or a ring stacker. As she tries to put the pieces together, use words to support her efforts. "You got the blue ring. Can you fit it on the pole? Almost. Push it over a little. You did it! Can you put another one on?"

3. *Show the baby how to use tools*: Use a stick to retrieve a toy that got stuck under a chair, make "music" by hitting an upside down pot with a spoon, or "paint" with a brush dipped in water. Give the baby many opportunities to use simple tools like these for his own purposes. As he does, use words to describe and support his efforts and praise his successes. "The ball went under the chair. Can you get it with the stick? That's right. Hit it hard. You got it out! Hooray!"

4. *Make baby toys*: Make simple shakers by partially filling plastic bottles of different sizes with water and screwing the tops on very tightly. Talk about all of the things the baby does with them—rolling, banging, shaking, tipping over, squeezing, carrying, dragging, hiding.

5. *Show the baby how to peek through a cardboard tube*: Try talking into the tube and letting the baby hear your voice. Then give her a turn.

6. *Ask the baby to give you something*: Hand the baby an object, then put out your hand and see if he will give it back. Say, "Thank you" (or "Ta," a traditional baby word in British and some African and Caribbean cultures, which is easy for babies to repeat), then hand the object back to the baby.

7. *Let the baby play with finger foods*: If the baby's parents are comfortable with self-feeding and playing with food, give her some interesting finger foods, such as banana slices, boiled edamame (soy beans), cereal Os, pasta of various shapes and lengths, or a slightly melted ice cube. Talk about the color, shape, and texture

of the food; the way it slides around the tray or sticks to the baby's hands; and what the baby does with it.

8. *Give the baby opportunities to experiment with cause and effect*: Busy boards, wind-up toys, jack-in-the-boxes, water wheels, and squeakers are classic toys that enable a baby to experiment with cause and effect. You can also make homemade toys that present babies with challenging problems, such as a bell to ring by pulling a ribbon or a pot whose lid needs to be lifted by the handle to find the surprise inside. Of course, a baby's favorite toy is likely to be the television if he can get to it, or anything else he can turn on by pressing a button.

9. *Have the baby look for hidden toys*: Hide a toy under a blanket; in a pocket, sock, or tote bag; or behind your back while she is looking. Ask the baby to find it, and see if she can. Try hiding something small (but too large to choke on) in the baby's pocket or up her sleeve. Tell her where it is and see if she can get it.

10. *Bring the baby a sturdy box or clothes basket*: Ask the baby if he can get inside. Can he put some toys in and get them out again? Can he tip the container over and bang it like a drum? Can he push it across the floor? Can he find you hiding behind it? Talk with him about all of the things he finds to do with the box. Use words to praise his efforts and help him solve the problems he creates for himself.

11. *Hand the baby an empty cup upside down*: See if she will turn it over and pretend to drink. Show her how you take a drink from the cup, then put it down and say, "All gone." Talk about what she does with her cup and what you do with yours. See if she will imitate your actions.

12. *Pair simple words with the gestures the baby uses to communicate*: For example, if the baby reaches out his arms to be picked up, say, "Up" as you lift him. If he shakes his head and pushes away the spoon at the end of a feeding, say, "No more" or "All done." If he puts his head down and closes his eyes for a moment, say, "Night-night." If he points to an object he wants or wants to show you, name it for him.

13. *Teach the baby some show-off tricks*: These can include having the baby wave "bye bye," give a high five, or play Show Us Your Shoe. Help her use these tricks to make connections with new people.

14. *Show the baby his reflection in a mirror*: Talk about what the baby in the mirror is doing. Does he realize that the baby in the mirror is

his reflection? If you put a hat on his head, does he reach for it or for the one in the mirror?

15. *Give the baby different kinds of fabric to play with*: Talk about how each cloth feels. Use sheer and opaque fabrics for Peekaboo games. Stuff a scarf or dish towel into an empty tissue box and let the baby try to pull it out. Give a special name to each blanket or fabric swatch that a baby likes to carry, stroke, or sleep with.

16. *Make some emptying and filling toys that will challenge the baby*: For example, let her put small toys or wooden clothespins into a bin or plastic container. When she has mastered emptying and filling, try a container with a narrower neck or with a lid that she can pull off. Increase the challenge by stringing large wooden beads on a piece of yarn or making a chain from plastic links for the child to put into a narrow-necked container or thread through a cardboard tube and pull out again. Talk about the different strategies she uses for getting things into and out of the container.

17. *Keep track of all the different ways that you can make the baby smile or laugh*: Most instances will involve both predictability and surprise. For example, some babies love tickles or tummy kisses—but only when they know they are coming and can prepare for them but aren't sure exactly when they will happen.

18. *Make an obstacle course for the baby*: Use pillows to climb over, low tables or tunnels to crawl under, furniture to pull up on and cruise along, and barriers to go around. Hide some surprises along the way—a toy to reach for, a picture hidden behind a cabinet door, or a favorite book peeking out from under a rug. Use words such as *up, down, over, under, along,* and *through* as you encourage the baby's exploration and describe his travels. Ask him to show the surprises he finds.

19. *Sit by the window with the baby and look out together*: Talk about all of the things you see. Point to different items or to exciting happenings, such as passing cars, barking dogs, or people walking by. See if the baby will point at things.

20. *Let the baby explore the effects of different tools for scooping, drizzling, stirring, and pouring water, soap bubbles, or sand*: Do this in a kiddie pool, bath tub, or sand box using cups, bowls, sieves, small watering cans with spouts, ladles, sponges, and pie plates to create interesting challenges for the baby. Talk about all of the things that the baby can do.

INCLUDING BABIES IN THE CONVERSATION

The teen parents and parents-to-be in a parenting class have been discussing the importance of talking with babies—and of taking advantage of everyday opportunities to expose them to language. The group leader asks volunteers to demonstrate some of the strategies they might use. She has brought a variety of props to support their role playing—board books, baby toys, a baby blanket, a doll, and a long-legged Bugs Bunny doll. She suggests a few scenarios that they might want to act out—giving the baby a bath, taking the baby on a walk, or sharing a book with the baby.

The first volunteer is a young and very proud father-to-be, and it's clear that he is well prepared for his language-supporting role. He chooses the stuffed rabbit as his "baby." Gently cradling it in one arm, he takes the rabbit on a walk around the classroom. "Hey, Baby," he says gently, looking into the rabbit's eyes. "We're going to go on a walk. I want you to meet all my friends. Here we go—out the door." After a few steps, he points upward. "Look. See those leaves up there—blowing in the breeze? And that bird singing a song for you—Hear it? Tweet, Tweet. Such a pretty red bird. I think it's a cardinal." Approaching one of his classmates, he bends to show the rabbit to his friend. "Here's Marcus, Baby," he says softly, and then speaks to his friend. "Hey—Bro. This here's my baby. He's cute, huh? And he likes to be talked to." He quickly turns back to the baby. "Baby—this is our friend, Marcus. Wave hi to Marcus, Baby," he says, while waving Bugs's arm. "That's right." Then, turning back to his friend, he says, "See how smart he is already?"

With a little prompting, the other teens point out the strengths of this performance. The young dad talked directly to his baby, looking him in the eye and speaking in a gentle, engaging voice. He showed things to the baby and gave him specific words for the things he was watching or listening to. He helped the baby make a friend, and he helped his friend include his baby in their conversation.

In some communities, babies are treated as conversation partners, even when they are out in public. Their parents—and other adults— look at them as they carry them around and address comments frequently to the baby, even when those comments are also meant for adult ears. "You're Mommy's big girl, aren't you? Should we tell Nana how you rolled over yesterday all by yourself?"

In other communities, babies go out into the world strapped to their mothers' backs, and much of the communication between baby and parent is nonverbal. In still others, babies are faced outward so that they can see what is going on and participate in the conversation, either as silent witnesses or by actively engaging with those around them.

There isn't one right way to include a baby in a conversation. In all cultures, babies cared for by responsive adults who are attuned to their needs develop secure attachments. Positive early relationships provide babies with a firm base for exploration and learning and the confidence to befriend new people and try new things. In all cultures, virtually all children will master the basics of at least one language by their fourth birthdays. At the same time, the children's early experiences with language will shape how—and how well—they will come to use their language(s).

Parents and caregivers may want to try some of the following strategies for enriching babies' social interactions and language-learning opportunities in the wider world:

- Introduce the baby to people you meet. Remember that he will take his cues about their trustworthiness from you, so make sure he sees that you are comfortable with them. Tell new people how the baby likes to be approached and what will make him smile. Help him draw them in with a wave or high five.

- Take the baby places where she can get to know other babies— child care programs and play groups, parks, library story hours or toddler rooms, or homes of friends and relatives. Set the stage for friendships by putting two babies together in a protected space. Give them similar toys—and see if they will imitate each other. Or, give them a toy that they can play with together, such as a large ball or roller, a scarf, or an overturned pot to bang on. Imitate their vocalizations to encourage more baby talk.

- Put the cell phone away when you take the baby on outings, so you can focus on what interests him and give him words for what he sees. If you need to take a long phone call, include the baby by giving him a toy phone of his own and by using an engaging voice to tell him what you are doing.

- Talk with the baby about where you are going and what is going to happen.

- Take older babies along to public events and celebrations. Give the baby a rattle or shaker and encourage her to join in when people are singing or cheering. Take your cues from the child about when she wants to participate and when the excitement is getting to be too much.

In a multiage setting such as a family child care home, providers need to find ways of supporting babies' pursuit of their natural infant curriculum while simultaneously engaging older children and keeping everyone safe, happy, and intellectually stimulated. Including the babies in the conversation can make this challenge easier. Here are some tricks that experienced providers use:

- Carry a young or tired infant in a sling, positioned so that he can watch the action and listen to the conversation, but turn away when he has had enough.

- Hold the baby on your lap as you read to older children, but let her crawl away or play with other (quiet) toys if she loses interest.

- Give the baby rattles or shakers and encourage him to join the fun when older children are singing, dancing, and making music. Let the baby ride in or push a stroller to join toddlers and preschoolers in a marching band.

- Hold the baby on your lap as you watch older children put on a dramatic performance. Clap the baby's hands at appropriate times, and encourage her to cheer along with you.

- Make a protected pen or corral out of low furniture or pillows, where you can sit with one or two infants. Comment on what the older children are doing as you watch them together.

- Schedule one-to-one time with each child. In addition, use diaper changing and feeding routines as opportunities to share favorite songs, rhyming games, and intimate conversations. Ask older children to help by getting a toy or book for the baby or singing a song or nursery rhyme with you.

- Show older children what the baby can do and engage them in helping to set up interesting challenges for him. Encourage them to talk to the baby.

- Help older children involve the baby in their play in appropriate ways. For example, they can offer her toy food from their pretend restaurant, let her ring the bell on their pretend train, or show her how to help with cleanup by wheeling trucks into a cardboard box garage or tossing toys into a bin.

- Teach older children how to tell when the baby has had enough.

- Talk with older children about all of the things the baby is learning. Help them make laminated books about his favorite activities that they can read to him.

- Include the baby in daily meals and special celebrations. Help other children to listen to the baby's babbles, repeat her sounds, and engage her in baby talk.

- At the end of the day, as you transition the baby back to his family, talk about all of the things he has done with his friends.

TALK WITH ME, BABY!

Speaking to more than 1,000 people at ZERO TO THREE'S annual training conference, Barbara Kalmanson (2006) concluded her address on "What Babies Teach Us" by playing an audiotape of a mother talking with her 8-month-old son. She translated some of the mother's words for those in the audience who didn't speak Spanish. The tape began with the baby screeching from his high chair, and his mother responding from across the room.

"Eee-eee-eek!" said the baby.

His mother's response encouraged him to keep talking: "Baby, what a big voice you have!"

Soon the baby began to babble. His mother imitated his sounds, and he repeated them. These cheerful exchanges continued for a while. Then the mother introduced a new sound, which the baby repeated, starting a new set of increasingly exuberant babble exchanges. Finally, the baby varied the game with a long string of babbles, which his mother did her best to repeat. Their mutual enjoyment of this game was obvious, and Dr. Kalmanson's audience laughed appreciatively at each of the baby's contributions. They knew that, long before he would speak either Spanish or English, this baby was learning the power of words.

First Words, First Stories

(10 Months–2½ Years)

Jennifer was not yet 1 year old when she crawled over to her great-grandmother's coffee table and, before anyone could stop her, carefully picked up her favorite item, the fragile china cat that she was allowed to admire but was not supposed to touch. "Cat," she announced in a clear voice. It was Jennifer's first recognizable word, and her great-grandmother was much too proud to take the cat away.

In many families, a child's first words are cause for celebration. Often these first words are names of family members—Mama or Daddy, or a nickname for a sibling or caregiver whose name is too long to say completely. Sometimes, the words mark items that especially intrigue a child. Jennifer loved her pet cat, and she was fascinated by her great-grandmother's china figurine. Sometimes first words stand for whole sentences that indicate what a child wants: "Ju-ju" for "I want juice," "Uppy" for "Pick me up," "Bankie" for "I need my favorite blanket."

Sometimes they are words of greeting or ritualized exchange, often accompanied by a well-practiced gesture—"Hi," "Bye-bye," "Ta" (thank you). And, especially if the child is older than 18 months, the first word may be an emphatic "No!"

Like Jennifer, many toddlers are labelers who build a large repertoire of words that name things that they want or want to call attention to. This is likely to include names for people who are important in their lives and words for foods; everyday objects; body parts; and things that move or make noise, such as "truck," "train," "dog," or "TV." Labelers often use a single word in multiple ways. For example, Aaron used his first word, "Ni-ni," which originally meant, "Nurse me," to mean "Mommy," "Help me," "I'm hungry," and "Pick me up." Nicky used "Vroom" to accompany his play with a toy car, to request a car ride, to point out a picture of a car in a magazine, and to ask if his Daddy had come home. Labelers may repeat new words they hear or ask for a name by pointing to a picture or object. They are likely to learn as many as 50 words before putting words together into two- or three-word sentences.

Other children use a more holistic strategy as they build their verbal repertoires. Rather than accumulating mainly individual words, they may learn a number of stock phrases, such as "Where is he?" "What's that?" "I don't like that," "My turn," "I want it," "That's mine!" and "Gimme five." Some children will even come out with whole sentences and then gradually pull out the separate words (Gopnik, Meltzoff, & Kuhl, 1999). Of course, like labelers, these toddlers may use idiosyncratic pronunciations that only those close to them understand. Their pronunciation becomes clearer over time as they try to make themselves understood by a wider circle of people.

In some cultures, parents use a special baby vocabulary to help children learn to speak. The baby words are easier for the child to say and are used only in private interactions. At the dinner table or in a more public setting, the child is expected to listen quietly to grown-up talk. Even in cultures and families in which the line between baby talk and grown-up language is less pronounced, parents tend to emphasize key words as they play with their babies in ways that facilitate word learning. The words parents use and emphasize for babies can influence later language development in subtle ways. In the baby talk used by Mandarin-speaking mothers, for example, verbs are more prevalent than they are in the baby talk of English-speaking mothers, in which nouns predominate. At 2, Mandarin-speaking children have a larger percentage of verbs in their vocabularies than do English-speaking children (Tardif, Gelman, & Xu, 1999).

No matter which vocabulary-building strategy children use, their early words and phrases are both attempts to communicate and markers of important events, feelings, and discoveries. They are likely to include announcements of success or failure (e.g., "I did it!" "All done," "Uh-oh," "Oopsie"), comments on the disappearance of an object (e.g., "All gone," "Where is it?" "Peek-boo," "Uh-oh"), and indications that they want to keep an enjoyable activity going (e.g., "Do again," "More," "Uh-uh-uh") or have had enough (e.g., "No," "No more," "Don't like that," "All done"). One of the earliest words for many Spanish-speaking toddlers is "Mira" (Look), which they use to call an adult's attention to an interesting object or event.

Interestingly, one of the things many young toddlers want most to communicate is their quest for new words. Indeed, researcher Katherine Nelson (1973) found that a word meaning "What's that?" was among the first 50 words spoken by most of the 18 toddlers she studied intensively, and among the first 10 words for 6 of them.

FROM GESTURES TO WORDS

"Sydney is an emphatic communicator," her aunt and frequent caregiver reported. "Even if you can't understand her words, there's no mistaking her meaning. When she's hungry, she pounds on the refrigerator and says, 'Cheee,' or she pats our seat next to the kitchen table and says, 'Yummy-yummy-yummy.' When she wants her bottle, she brings her hand to her mouth and says, 'Baba.' And when she's tired, she pulls me over to her stroller, tilts her head, and asks for 'Nanny-nanny-nanny,' her special blanket."

Although families celebrate children's early spoken words, expressive language may be rooted as much in gesture as it is in sound production and language comprehension (Bates & Dick, 2002). Most children use gestures with communicative and symbolic intent just before or along with their first words. Waving, pointing, nodding, shaking the head "No," reaching up to be picked up, banging on a table for "More," and holding out a hand to give or receive something are common toddler communications. Many toddlers on the verge of using spoken words will name objects with characteristic functional gestures, such as picking up a cup and pretending to drink or putting a comb to their hair. These gestures usually disappear when a child learns to say the words clearly, except when they are incorporated into longer pretend play sequences. In addition, many toddlers learn or invent symbolic gestures—licking an imaginary ice cream cone, flapping their arms like a bird, putting their hands together and opening them to indicate

"Book" or "Read," rocking an imaginary baby, pushing away to indicate "Enough" or "All done," clapping for themselves when they succeed at something, touching their lips when they want something to
eat. Children who talk very early may accompany their words with
gestures or skip the gesture phase altogether; children who show
marked delays in the use of communicative and symbolic gestures are
likely to be delayed in spoken language as well.

The movement to teach hearing toddlers "baby signs" or American
Sign Language, is rooted in these observations. Linda Acredolo, a child
psychologist who studied young children's language learning, noticed
that her own 12-month-old daughter invented several symbolic
gestures. Following her child's lead, Acredolo made this form of communication easier for her daughter by teaching her some new
gestures—or signs—paired with words. With her colleague, Susan
Goodwyn, Acredolo then set out to discover whether other children
were also inventing signs as they transitioned from babble talk to
speech. Most of the infants they observed invented at least one or two
signs between 12 and 19 months; furthermore, those who had used
more signs during this period developed larger vocabularies by 24
months. What would happen, the researchers wondered, if parents
paid the kind of attention to children's early gestures that they paid to
their first words? What if, like Dr. Acredolo herself, they actively
encouraged this form of labeling and communication?

Acredolo and Goodwyn recruited 103 English-speaking middle-
class families with 11-month-old babies and randomly divided them
into three groups. The researchers told the parents in the "sign training group" to pay special attention to their children's nonverbal communications, to pair their children's symbolic gestures with words and
to use them in communicating with them, and to teach their children
some new signs paired with spoken words. Parents received individual
instruction in ways to promote their particular child's use of symbolic
gestures, and watched films of babies and parents communicating with
signs. They received toys and books to help support their teaching of
eight signs that are easy for toddlers to learn: FISH, FLOWER, BIRD, AIR-
PLANE, FROG, WHERE IS IT? MORE, and ALL GONE.

Parents in the "verbal training group" received similar instructions
with regard to verbal communication—they were to pay special attention to their children's words, make a conscious effort to label things
for them, and teach their children some new words. They received
toys and books to help support their teaching of eight common toddler
words and phrases: *kitty, doggy, ball, shoe, boat, bye-bye, more,* and *all gone.*
The researchers did not give any special instructions, toys, or training
to the parents in the "no treatment group."

Every 2 weeks, the researchers interviewed the parents in the sign training and verbal training groups by telephone and asked about their children's use of words and/or gestures. Parents in all three groups brought their children to the laboratory six times during the time span between 11 and 36 months of age for play-based observations and a battery of language tests.

The parents in the study were a self-selected group; most were well-educated, and all were highly motivated to support their toddler's development. As the researchers interacted with the families over time, they saw that parents in all of the groups were using many effective strategies to support emerging verbal language, and their children were scoring well above the norm on the language measures. The sign training, though, appeared to add value. The children in this group learned an average of 20 signs, including the 8 that their parents had been told to teach. But they were also learning spoken words.

Whereas children in the two other groups developed spoken language at virtually the same above-average rate, those in the sign training group were learning even faster. At 15 months, their mean language-age scores were about 1 month ahead of the children in the other groups; by 24 months, they were about 3 months ahead. At 3, there was little difference between the groups on a language comprehension test, but the sign training group's mean language age on a picture naming task was 4½ months ahead of that of the no treatment group (Goodwyn, Acredolo, & Brown, 2000).

Being able to communicate to their caregivers through gestures or signs what they want or do not want is an obvious asset for babies—it minimizes their frustration and that of the adults who are trying to satisfy their wishes. Communication through gestures and signs also gives babies a new way of making things happen and a new set of accomplishments that bring proud smiles to their parents' faces. But why should it facilitate oral language?

One hypothesis is that as children learn and practice the gestures, they are learning the words as well. Just as stressing and repeating key words in speech helps children to learn them, pairing a word with a salient and interesting gesture makes it more memorable. Another hypothesis, one favored by the researchers, is that signing primes the communication pump because it is easier for toddlers to make signs than to say words. Success begets success. Children who are good communicators elicit more communication from their parents and teachers, and thus get more opportunities to learn more words, more signs, or both. In particular, the sign training may increase and elongate episodes of "joint attention," with adult and child focused together on a particular object, action, or idea that is associated with a word and its sign.

Knowing what it is that their child wants to "talk" about helps parents respond with on-topic words that build their baby's vocabulary.

Like the special baby talk used in many Asian communities, baby signs can make it easier for some babies to communicate with the important people in their lives. Using signs is just one of many, many strategies parents and caregivers can try who are eager to hear what babies have to say.

PRIMING THE LANGUAGE PUMP

Jada loved morning circle time at her family child care home. Before she could sit up, her provider would put her in her bounce chair, and Jada would kick happily along with the morning songs. Later, Jada would crawl over to sit on her provider's lap or that of an older child and join in by babbling along and trying to imitate the older children's clapping and other movements. She seemed to light up when her name was used in a group song. One day, when Jada was about 10 months old, her provider noticed that she wasn't just babbling—she was actually saying other children's names. Indeed, when her provider pointed to Daniel and asked, "Who's that?" Jada said, "Danny" quite clearly. It was one of her first recognizable words, and was soon joined by the names of all of the children in the family child care group. The children were thrilled that Jada had learned to say their names—as, of course, were Jada's parents.

All over the world—whether they are hearing and learning one language or more than one—most children who are typically developing say their first word between 10 and 15 months and have begun to put words together and amass significant vocabularies by the time they are 2. But the range of normal is wide; some children are speaking in full sentences as early as 12–14 months, whereas others do not say their first words until they are nearly 2.

Language is a hallmark of humanity, and children who spend time in a family or with other children will learn to speak with or without formal teaching and explicit language support. But, children who hear more words spoken to them in meaningful contexts, who hear more words of encouragement and play talk, and who are given more opportunities to participate in verbal exchanges and performances are likely to learn faster and to develop a stronger base for later learning (Katz and Snow, 2000). When they begin to talk is far less important than the richness of their communicative experience and word-learning opportunities.

Tips for Talking with Toddlers

- Respect the toddler's wariness of strangers and her need to be in control. If you don't know the toddler well or haven't seen her for a while, approach her slowly, looking just past her rather than directly at her. Give her a chance to reach out or follow you. Watch her face as you offer a greeting, and back off a bit if she seems wary. Put a toy on the floor between you. If she takes it, you can comment on what she is doing. If not, show her what you can do with it. Talk about what you are doing, then offer her the toy again.

- Talk to the toddler on his level. Squat down or sit beside him. Comment on what he is doing or seeing. Offer him an intriguing object, or join his play by playing along, providing appropriate words or sound effects. Make eye contact with him as you ask a question or make a suggestion.

- Respond to the toddler's efforts to keep the conversation going. Whether she uses babble-talk, gibberish, sound effects, gestures, signs, or words, give her the words for what she seems to be trying to say, and pause so that she can repeat the word more clearly.

- As you interact with the toddler, respond empathically to his emotional tenor. If he's excited by a game of rolling and catching a ball, play your part with exaggerated excitement. Your exuberant "You caught the ball!" is likely to be greeted with an equally exuberant laugh, babble, or attempt at speech. On the other hand, if a toddler is upset or fussy or just quietly reflective, a gentle, soothing voice is more likely to engage his attention and less likely to provoke a negative reaction.

- Provide a play-by-play description of the toddler's activity and perceptions, just as a sportscaster might comment on a player's actions. When the toddler looks at you with interest or chimes in with words or babbles, stop your narrative and give her a turn to talk.

- Use language to help the toddler interpret his world. When you see a puzzled or fearful expression, find a simple way to explain what is going on or what is going to happen.

(continued)

When the doorbell rings, explain that someone is at the door and wants to come in. Show the toddler the bell, and let him help you push it. When you pull the plug on the sink, explain that the water is going down through the pipe, all the way down to the ground.

- Use language to reassure the toddler and to prepare her for transitions. "I can't pick you up right now, but I can watch you go down the slide." "It's almost lunch time. One more slide, and then we'll go inside."

- Talk about a recent event that was special for the toddler. Use props or pictures to help him remember.

- Take breaks and breathers during conversations with the toddler. Most toddlers need simple, short sentences and plenty of time to take in the information and formulate a response.

- Sing favorite songs frequently, and encourage the toddler to join in. Listen for the point when gibberish turns into words. Pause before a key word in a song or rhyme to give the toddler a chance to fill it in all by herself.

- Respond to anything that sounds like a word and is used with communicative intent. For example, when a child who hears a plane overhead points to the sky and says, "Ane," you might answer, "I see the plane. The plane is high up in the sky."

- Give the toddler time to repeat a new word.

- Provide the toddler with many opportunities to practice using the words he knows. Read his favorite books over and over so that he can practice naming the pictures. Find a magazine or catalog with pictures of similar items that he can name with the words he knows.

- Use words to help the toddler name and manage her strong emotions. "That was a loud noise. It made you scared." "You're angry because Sam took your toy."

- Repeat the toddler's communication in words. If you are unsure, ask for confirmation, giving him a chance to repeat

> the word or gesture or to correct your interpretation. Use
> full but simple sentences.
>
> - Accompany language with gestures that the toddler can
>   copy. Clap "hooray," nod "yes," shake your head "no," or
>   wave "bye-bye."
>
> - TALK—AND LISTEN—A LOT.

This result, however, is not an argument for teaching vocabulary words to young children. No evidence demonstrates that pressuring babies to talk or deliberately teaching them to repeat words makes them talk earlier or end up smarter. Indeed, too much artificial teaching or drilling—with either words or signs—may interfere with the more natural, enjoyable, and often linguistically richer day-to-day interactions that sustain children's curiosity and build their emotional security and communicative confidence. At the same time, intentionally talking with young toddlers in playful, engaging ways can "prime the language pump" and sow the seeds for robust vocabulary development.

WHY ISN'T MY BABY TALKING YET?

Sateen lived on a military base, and for much of her young life, her father had been deployed in a war zone far from home. Sateen loved to chat with him on the telephone, producing long strings of gibberish that always elicited a delighted reaction. At 19 months, though, Sateen was still not using intelligible words, and her parents had begun to worry. They knew she understood language—she had been following simple directions such as "Sit down" or "Bring me your diaper" for months. She loved books and scrapbooks, and she could point to the pictures of animals, household objects, or relatives on request. One of her favorite books had a page with a mirror on it, and Sateen and her mom had developed their own game for that page. "Where's Sateen's head?" her mother would ask, and Sateen would respond by hitting the mirror with the top of her head. "And where is Sateen's tongue?" This time, Sateen's response would be to very carefully lick the book with just the tip of her tongue. Sateen was also good at pretending. She would put a block to her lips and take a "drink" and then give one to her favorite teddy bear. She was quite adept at communicating her wishes—pointing to things she wanted, shaking her head vigorously or pushing away when she didn't want something, patting the space beside her when she wanted her mother to join her on the couch, waving good-bye when she thought it was time for her to leave or time for someone else to go. So where were the words?

Sateen's parents soon realized that she was a holistic word learner who had been quietly amassing a collection of verbal routines. One day, Sateen picked up the telephone herself and sighed dramatically and very clearly—"Oh, man!"

There are many reasons why some children are slower to use words than others. Sometimes the problem is physical. A mild hearing loss, or even a series of transient episodes of not hearing well because of middle ear infections, can slow the onset of speech. So can weakness of the jaw muscles or difficulty coordinating tongue and lip movements. Some children are relatively late to achieve developmental milestones such as sitting, self-feeding, and walking as well as talking; others put so much energy into one realm that they seem to have little left over for others. A very active child, for example, may be running and jumping at 1 year but slower to talk than a less active sibling. And for some children, delayed speech is one of a number of signs that difficulties in relating and communicating or in developing an understanding of language should be assessed by a professional who can recommend early intervention strategies.

For a child like Sateen, whose sensory equipment is intact and who is on track in terms of physical and intellectual development, the reason may simply be that she can make herself understood more easily with gestures and actions than with words. A comprehensive communication behavior checklist—that looks at expression of emotion; use of eye gaze, gestures, and sounds; initiation of communication; and pretending, as well as at use and understanding of words—can help parents and caregivers to decide if further evaluation is warranted. Recommended resources include

- Communication and Symbolic Behavior Scales Developmental Profile Infant/Toddler Checklist (Wetherby & Prizant, 2001). This checklist focuses on specific communication and play behaviors and milestones that predict whether a child is likely to need extra support in developing language. It is available online in several languages at http://firstwords.fsu.edu/toddlerChecklist.html.
- *Ages & Stages Questionnaires*® *(ASQ): A Parent-Completed, Child-Monitoring System* (2nd ed.) (Bricker & Squires, 1999). Most children develop more rapidly in some areas than in others. For some

children, these patterns are stable; for others, they may change over time. The ASQ provides a comprehensive overview of development in all domains, and can help parents and caregivers understand a child's developmental strengths and areas of slower growth or possible delay.

ONE LANGUAGE OR TWO?

Contrary to what some believe, hearing two languages from birth does not create language confusion and is not likely to slow children's use of words. Fred Genesee, a Canadian researcher who has studied children growing up in bilingual households in the United States, Canada, and Europe, finds that once bilingual children start speaking, their total vocabularies tend to be the same size as those of their monolingual peers. Bilingual toddlers are likely to know basic words in both of their languages, but they may know some words exclusively in one language or the other. In families and communities in which adults "code-mix," or use phrases from two languages in a single utterance, children will do the same. If, however, a child always hears one language from one person or in one setting and another from a different person or in a different setting, she will tend to keep her languages separate and learn when each is appropriate to use (Genesee et al., 2004).

Parents may worry that they are putting their child at a disadvantage by using their home language. In fact, the opposite is likely to be true. Home language is an enduring connection to family and culture. The language the child has been hearing since before his birth is familiar and comforting to him, and easier for him to use than a new one. Parents who talk to their babies in the language that is comfortable for them as adults are likely to talk more and use richer language than parents who are trying to use a new language—or parents who limit their communications with a toddler because they fear that hearing two languages will confuse him. Toddlers whose parents talk with them in their home languages are thus likely to have more opportunities to hear and practice language; learn new concepts; and use language to question, investigate, and share discoveries.

Although learning two languages simultaneously or learning a second language in childhood may present some initial challenges, ultimately the child will gain. He will be able to draw on his knowledge of his preferred language as he adds new words in his other language. A large body of research suggests that learning a second language in childhood boosts both verbal and nonverbal IQ scores and helps children to think flexibly (Barik & Swain, 1976; Bochner, 1996; Cummins & Swain, 1986; Hakuta & Diaz, 1984; Harley & Lapkin, 1984).

When Ben was born, his parents thought long and hard about what languages to use with him. They both spoke English, and this was the language they used with each other. Ben's father, Manoj, who had grown up in Nepal, spoke several other languages as well, including Newari, his home language. Ben's mother, Jenny, spoke a little Newari and understood more, but the couple had long ago realized that her vocabulary was limited to basic household words and was not adequate for richer conversation. Aware of the benefits of early bilingualism and wanting to give Ben a strong connection to his extended family, Jenny and Manoj decided that they would each speak to him in their first language but would continue to use English with each other. This arrangement quickly broke down, however, as Manoj found it easier to imitate Jenny's English baby talk than to recall baby words and nursery rhymes from his own childhood. In Nepal, the women of his village had cared for all of their young children together; men and older boys were only peripherally involved. Ben's opportunity to learn Newari would have to wait until he could spend more time with his grandmother, aunts, and cousins in a setting where Newari was the dominant language, or at least until his English was strong enough to serve as a base for learning a second language.

EXTENDING THE CONCEPTUAL REPERTOIRE

Tyler, 18 months old, points to a neighbor's cat and says, "Goggie." Tyler's mom responds to Tyler by saying, "That's not a doggie, Tyler. It's a cat. A fat, black cat. Can you say 'cat?'" Tyler repeats, "cat," and his mother enthusiastically says, "That's right, Tyler! It's a cat. A fat, black cat with white feet." Tyler responds by saying, "Back cat."

Toddlers' early words are often all-purpose labels. "Doggie," for example, may refer to any animal with four legs and a tail; "juice" can be anything to drink or anything that is poured into a favorite cup; "red" may be the answer to any question about color. Gradually, with the deliberate or casual help of the adults in their lives, children learn to make the relevant distinctions.

Young toddlers are busy sorting out the world. As they endlessly put things into containers and dump them out again; gather up objects, carry them around, and put them down in new places; throw balls, socks, and anything else they can get away with; climb on people, steps, and furniture; and push the buttons that make their toys sing, the television talk, or the lights turn on and off, they are learning the concepts of *in* and *out, under* and *over, up* and *down, near* and *far,* and *on* and *off*. When toddlers line up their toys or put them into groups or "families," they notice likes and differences and begin to form categories (e.g., red things, animals, cows) and series (e.g., big, bigger, biggest). They learn that some objects are good for banging and making noise with, whereas others are good for rolling, pushing, or putting things into. They learn, over time, that some objects belong in the kitchen and others belong in the bathroom, that some things are okay to touch and others aren't, and that some things (and places) are theirs and some are "not for babies."

At the same time that toddlers are figuring out what goes where and what goes with what, they are also figuring out what aspect of what they are looking at corresponds to the word they hear, and how the words they hear relate to each other. Adults tend to help them out. We call an animal a "cat," then add that it is a "black cat." We contrast the black of most of the cat's body with the white of its feet. We may point out that cats and dogs are both animals, but that dogs have longer noses and bark. We may add that the black cat's name is "Midnight," or encourage the child to "Pet the cat gently." As we repeat the word *cat* in these varied verbal contexts, the child learns more about what the word means, how it is used, and how the concept of *cat* relates to other concepts such as *animal, pet*, and *dog*. Implicitly, we teach that Midnight is a cat and cats are animals, that petting is something you can do to a cat, and that black and white are names of colors that can describe cats. Toddlers' brains, it seems, are wired to learn these lessons.

The more such lessons parents and caregivers can offer to their children, the more toddlers will learn. And, of course, the best times to offer these lessons are when toddlers are paying attention and parents or teachers can build on the toddlers' interests.

FOLLOW THE CAR

When his mom drops him off at his grandmother's house, 14-month-old Jango makes a beeline for the spare bedroom. "You know where your toys are, don't you?" his grandmother asks as she follows him. "What would you like to play with today?" Jango pulls out the plastic dump truck she got him for his birthday. "You're going to drive your dump truck," she says, then pauses, awaiting his response.

"Drive dump tuck," Jango repeats as he pushes the truck across the floor. He stops and looks up at his grandmother. "Toys."

"Do you want some toys to put in your dump truck?" she asks.

Jango nods, and his grandmother hands him some small rubber animals.

"Would you like to drive these animals around and dump them out?" she asks.

Jango takes the animals and carefully puts them into the dump truck, one by one, then dumps them out on the floor, saying, "Dump out ammals."

"You dumped out all the animals!" his grandmother responds with enthusiasm. "You put them all in your big dump truck and dumped them out on the floor!"

Parents and caregivers who spend a lot of time with toddlers often adapt to their rhythm. They follow the child around, commenting on her investigations and discoveries. They stop talking when the child is intently engaged in solving a challenge, then use words as needed to help her keep going and celebrate her accomplishment. They develop a sixth sense about when the child is headed for trouble, and use words—and quick action—to head her off at the pass and redirect her activity.

The Follow the CAR (Comment, Ask, Respond) formula (California Institute on Human Services, 2003) capitalizes on this adult–child interaction pattern. The formula was developed to encourage interactive book reading, but you can encourage parents and other caregivers to use this formula in many situations. Whether an adult is reading a book with a toddler, watching him play with a toy, admiring the pine cones he has collected, joining him in watching the garbage collectors, or enjoying a rowdy game of chase, or helping him feed his teddy bear a bottle, this simple formula can enhance their conversations. There are just four steps, repeated over and over again.

1. Tune into what the child is focused on, and make that the focus of the conversation. **Follow the** child's lead.

2. Do one of the following: 1) **C**omment, 2) **A**sk a question, or, 3) if the child initiates the conversation or responds, even with just a single word or a gesture, **R**espond by acknowledging what the child said and adding a bit more. Turn a word or two into a whole sentence, add a bit of information, or share your opinion.

3. Wait. A young child may need up to 5 full seconds to put her comment, question, or response into words or meaningful gestures.

4. Repeat the cycle by following the child's lead.

USING SONGS, RHYMES, AND GAMES TO EXPLORE WORDS AND CONCEPTS

Most toddlers love nursery rhymes, and most parents and caregivers love sharing them because they enjoy the toddler's attempts to join in by bouncing, babbling, singing, and attempting to supply some of the correct words and motions. "The Itsy Bitsy Spider," for example, is universally popular.

Songs and rhymes also help toddlers to learn the names of body parts, animals, vehicles, and everyday objects, as well as concepts such as in and out, up and down, here and gone. Rhymes such as "Hokey Pokey" and "Where is Thumbkin?" that are popular with older children can be simplified for young toddlers to focus on the words and concepts they are learning.

Hokey Pokey (modified)
Put your foot (instead of "right foot") in.
Put your foot out.
Put your foot in, and shake it all about.
You do the Hokey Pokey, and you turn yourself around.
That's what it's all about.

Where is Thumbkin? (variation)
Where is belly button?
Where is belly button?

Here I am. Here I am. (Show belly button.)
And where is elbow?
Where is elbow?
Here I am. Here I am. (Show elbow.)

(Add verses with other body parts as children learn the game.)
And where is everybody?
Where is everybody?
Here we are! Here we are! (Jump forward.)

How are you today, now?
Very well we say, now.
Take a bow. Take a bow.

Children learning two languages can learn songs and accompanying gestures in both, with either literal or creative translation.

Una Boquita
Una boquita para comer (A little mouth for eating),
Mi naricita es para oler (My little nose is for smelling).

Mis dos ojitos son para ver (My two little eyes are for seeing).
Mis dos oídos son para oír (My two little ears are for hearing),
¿Y mi cabecita? Para dormir (And my little head? It is for sleeping).

My Little Mouth (creative translation of "Una Boquita")
My little mouth is for eating (Point to mouth and chew);
My little nose is for smelling (Point to nose and sniff).
My little eyes are to see with (Point to eyes or make
   "spectacles" with thumbs and index fingers);
And my ears hear storytelling (Pull ears forward).

My little head if for nodding (Nod);
I put it down for sleeping (Rest head on hands).
My two hands are for holding (Put hands together),
My special book for keeping (Open hands to make "book").

Other songs can be modified or extended to connect with children's
interests and experiences:

The Wheels on the Garbage Truck (variation of "The
   Wheels on the Bus")
The wheels on the garbage truck go round and round.
Round and round. Round and round.
The wheels on the garbage truck go round and round.
All through the town.

The lids on the garbage cans go crash, crash, crash.
Crash, crash, crash. Crash, crash, crash.
The lids on the garbage cans go crash, crash, crash.
All through the town.

The crusher on the back goes smush,
   smush, smush.
Smush, smush, smush. Smush, smush, smush.
The crusher on the back goes smush,
   smush, smush.
All through the town.

The children who are watching wave good-bye.
Wave good-bye. Wave good-bye.
The children who are watching wave good-bye.
All through the town.

"I'm a Little Teapot" is fun for toddlers to perform because they, too, tend to be short, stout, and frequently tipped over. For children who aren't familiar with teapots, here's another version of this classic:

I'm a Little Pitcher
I'm a little pitcher, short and stout
Here is my handle, here is my spout.
If you want a drink of water
Please don't shout.
Just tip me over and
Pour some out.

KEYING IN TO CHILDREN'S QUESTIONS

Even when they know just a few words or none at all, young toddlers still find many ways to ask the questions that are important to them:

"Does the spoon go in the garbage can with the dirty napkins?"

"Will Fluffy come back and play with me if I pull her tail?"

"Does dog food taste good?"

"How many toys can I carry at once?"

"What is at the very bottom of a box of tissues?"

"If I do something and you say "no," what will happen if I do it again?

"What is the name of this interesting object or person?"

"Where did Mommy go, and will she ever come back?"

Usually, toddlers ask these questions through active exploration, with an occasional glance at their parents or caregivers for permission to proceed or cues to solving the problem. Sometimes, toddlers ask their questions through pointing or gesturing, accompanied by a word or two, as, for example, when a toddler gazes out the window and plaintively asks, "Mama?" It's tempting to simply redirect a toddler when her exploration is leading to frustration or trouble. But these are also teachable moments, when a toddler's curiosity about how the world works can be satisfied with words accompanied by controlled demonstration:

"Dirty napkins go in the garbage. The spoon goes in the sink. Thank you."

"Fluffy doesn't like it when you pull her tail. Touch gently."

"Dog food is not for babies. Yucky."

"Do you want to put some of the toys in your tote bag?"

"I'm going to take out some of the tissues and save them for later. Your turn. You pulled out a tissue . . . . The tissues are all gone. Do

you want to look in the box? Should we put your toy inside and see if
you can get it out again?"

"Mama went to work. We'll see her after your nap."

USING POSITIVE, PROACTIVE DISCIPLINE

Learning to cope with being told "no" is a universal challenge of toddlerhood. Toddlers need limits—and may feel unsafe and out of control without them. They depend on adults to set clear, consistent
boundaries on what is acceptable at what time or in what circum-
stance—both for safety's sake and in terms of social expectations for
proper behavior.

At the same time, toddlers constantly test the limits. Much of their
out-of-bounds behavior is innocent. A child may pull a friend's hair,
throw sand on him, or roll a toy truck over his legs, then look expec-
tantly for a pleased reaction and be surprised to see tears or anger
instead. He may climb dangerously high, run toward a street, scribble
on a book, or throw a towel in the toilet—and expect everyone else to
be as proud of his accomplishment as he is. At other times, toddlers
know when they have broken the rules. "Uh-oh" is a common toddler
response not only to spilled milk but also to having done something that
he knows is not allowed. Knowing that something is wrong after the
fact, however, is not the same for a toddler as being able to avoid the
inappropriate behavior. Toddlers are just beginning to learn to predict
the consequences of their actions. It is often hard for them to stop themselves from taking something they want, investigating an interesting
object, or continuing an action they have started.

The usual parent or caregiver response to a young toddler's misbe-
havior is to remove the child from the situation, redirect her to a safer
or more constructive activity, and remove future dangers and temptations. As the child learns to understand the concept of *no,* words
become an important part of teaching the limits. At first, a simple "No!"
may be the most effective communication. For toddlers who are both
sophisticated in their understanding of language (even if they are not
yet saying words) and sensitive to adult disappointment, an elaborated
response can make the point without triggering a meltdown (e.g.,
"Please don't touch that, Honey. It's very fragile." "Stay on the sidewalk. Cars go fast in the street, and one could bump into you and hurt
you"). Although explanations like these may seem over the heads of
some 1-year-olds—and take way too long to say to keep others out of
trouble—this kind of positive guidance contributes to the development
of self-discipline, emotional security, and language.

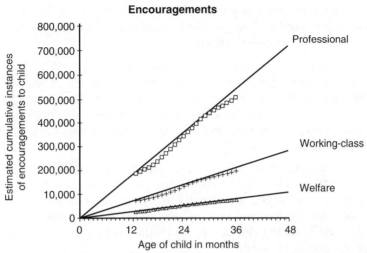

Figure 3.1. Cumulative instances of feedback containing encouragement addressed to the children in 13 professional families (squares), 23 working class families (plus signs), and 6 families on welfare (triangles), extrapolated from child ages birth to 12 months and 37–48 months. Encouragements were affirmations that repeated, extended, or expanded the child's utterances and expressions of approval of the child's behavior as "right" or "good." (From Hart, B., & Risley, T.R. [1995]. *Meaningful differences in the everyday experience of young American children* [p. 253].

In the Hart and Risley study (1995), the use of positive discipline techniques with 1- and 2-year-olds was strongly linked to vocabulary size at age 3. Indeed, when the researchers charted the number of words of affirmation and encouragement that the children had heard in their first years, the cumulative difference—and the widening gap it foretold—were striking (see Figure 3.1).

Telling toddlers "no" too often can limit their curiosity and willingness to explore; not saying "yes" enough can lead them to give up too easily on challenging tasks, as if they expect to fail or don't expect anyone to care if they succeed. But why should positive discipline make a difference for language development? It turns out that many of the limit-setting, trouble-avoiding, self-discipline–building, and conflict resolution techniques that parents and caregivers use with toddlers are also well suited to extending toddlers' conceptual and linguistic repertoires.

- *Offering choices*: "Do you want to wear your green shirt or your blue one?" Simple choices from among a few options allow toddlers a sense of control. They can also help to teach concepts, such as *green* and *blue*. At the same time, they encourage the toddler's use of language to express her choice.

- *Explaining reasons*: "We need to wear our jackets today because it's cold outside." Adults use more words and richer language when they explain something than when they simply tell a child what to do or just say "no." At the same time, the explanations help children to connect cause and effect.

- *Teaching words of self-control*: Words such as *hot, stop, wait, gentle, careful,* and *nice* help toddlers to avoid dangerous situations and handle fragile objects—and other people—with care. As they learn what is acceptable or safe and what is off limits, many toddlers say words such as these to give themselves directions. Language and self-control go hand in hand.

- *Acknowledging strong emotions and encouraging children to use their words*: "You didn't like it when Katie pulled your hair. It hurt, and it made you angry. Say 'That hurt, Katie. Please don't pull my hair.'" As children practice positive ways of expressing their feelings and handling conflicts verbally, they gain a new appreciation of the power of words.

- *Using words that help children anticipate what will happen and when*: "We can go to the park after lunch." "Grandma is coming to visit tomorrow." "When you wake up from your nap, we can read the book again." Delores Norton's longitudinal study of children growing up in resource-poor homes highlighted the importance of this practice (1993, 1994, & 1996). Children whose parents had routinely used such words with them as toddlers developed an expectation of predictability. Faced with challenging circumstances in later childhood, these children drew on their early coping skills.

- *Teaching polite words and practicing polite behavior*: Politeness is a core value in many cultures, and children—even quite young ones—are expected to treat adults with respect. Although the rules may be less strict in more child-centered families, words and phrases such as "please," "thank you," and "excuse me"—and their toddler-speak variants—can be powerful tools for gaining adult attention. Practicing polite behavior, including greetings, requests, exchanges, and good-byes, helps children handle new social situations with confidence.

- *Interpreting another child's facial expressions, body language, and behavior*: "Marcus is smiling. I think he wants to play with you." Helping toddlers to understand and connect with other children expands their opportunities for language-building conversations.

- *Making a game of it*: "Let's put the toys in the basket together. I'll put one in. You put one in. My turn. Your turn. We're filling the basket up very fast!" Games such as these put words to actions, give toddlers practice with turn-taking, and often become occasions for back-and-forth conversations that use specific language.

ABCS of Positive Discipline

- **A**nticipate problems. Toddler-proof the environment frequently, removing dangers and irresistible temptations. If more than one young child is present, provide multiples of popular toys or other toys and household objects that lend themselves to cooperative play. Feed children before they are really hungry, and help them rest before they are overtired. When children are likely to be tired, hungry, or stressed, provide relaxing activities with few demands.

- **B**e proactive and playful. It's easier for toddlers to start doing something than to stop doing something. Give them positive instructions, such as "touch gently" or "hold my hand." Prepare them for new situations by explaining what will happen and helping them practice what they will do. Offer reasonable choices: "Do you want to put your boots or your coat on first?" Teach turn taking, cooperation, and safety rules. Use humor, music, and pretend play to make things fun (e.g., "This is the way we clean up our mess. . . .").

- **C**alm yourself. Children pick up on stress and become more anxious and often more insistent on doing things their way. Never shake a baby.

- **S**caffold solutions. Provide just enough help to enable children to solve problems themselves. Encourage toddlers to "use their words" and teach them words and phrases such as "My turn," "Please," or "No hitting." Ask a question that helps a pair of toddlers work out a conflict or keep their building from collapsing.

- *Giving clear, explicit instructions*: "Put your cars away in the basket." Explicit language helps toddlers focus on the message, practice following directions, and learn specific vocabulary.

Positive discipline looks different in different families. Many parents will be uncomfortable with the explanations, choices, and indirect suggestions that come naturally to others. "How's that little child going to understand such complicated talk?" they might ask when they hear another parent giving a toddler an overly long explanation. "Why do those parents ask their child if he wants to put his toys away when what they really mean is 'Put your toys away now'?" In their home cultures, children learn appropriate behavior by observing what others do, but parents also instruct children and give them clear directions to follow.

FIRST STORIES

> One winter day, Kirsty, a 22-month-old who was just beginning to put words together, saw a fox trot past her living room window. Kirsty's mother pointed excitedly as it ran out of sight, then showed Kirsty the tracks in the snow. "See fox," said Kirsty the next morning. "Yes," replied her mother, "We saw a fox." "Feet," said Kirsty. Her mother elaborated. "Its feet made tracks in the snow," and Kirsty repeated, "Snow." Over the next several days, Kirsty told the fox story over and over again, helped first by her mother, then her father, and then her child care provider. Kirsty's few contributions—"See fox," "feet," and "snow"—were soon supplemented with "run," "fast," "tracks," "tail," and "red" as her story grew more elaborate.

Less noticed than first words, but equally exciting, are children's first stories—told through actions, grunts, and a few key words, with a lot of adult support and interpretation. Deborah Jervay-Pendergrass (2000) has identified key features of these "prenarratives" or "first stories." These early stories can be easy to miss, even when a toddler is trying hard to communicate. In their STORIES project, Jervay-Pendergrass and Brown (1999/2000) taught teachers to key into toddlers' first stories and extend their conversations.

Often, first stories are reenactments of memorable or exciting events, such as getting a cut or seeing a fire engine go by with its lights flashing and siren wailing. Sometimes, the child initiates the retelling by re-enacting the event. Jean Piaget (1952) described how his toddler daughter imitated a temper tantrum that she had seen a cousin throw days before. Similarly, toddlers frequently use toys or other props to reenact daily occurrences such as making and serving meals or going to sleep. By 2, most can play out a "story" with more than one step, such as pouring and drinking juice, giving a baby doll a kiss and then laying her down and covering her with a blanket, or driving a toy car into its garage.

Sometimes, a young toddler will string together a few words or signs to retell an emotionally important story all by himself.

> While Joey's father was away, his mother repeatedly reassured him that his dad would be home soon. "Daddy went on a long trip for work. I know you miss him. He'll be home in 2 days." When his father returned, Joey repeated the story. "Daddy. Work. Miss."

When Alan's older sister left on a bus for a week at summer camp, he sadly repeated, "Kayla. Bus. Camp," over and over again. When the family drove to the camp to pick up Kayla, Alan kept asking, "Where bus?" Only then did his family realize that, in Alan's 18-month-old mind, his sister had spent the week on a bus.

Adult listeners need to rely on their own knowledge, their shared experiences with the children, and environmental cues to give meaning to these early narratives (Jervay-Pendergrass & Brown, 1999/2000). Often, it is the adult who starts the story by reminiscing. "Should we tell Nana what you did today? Remember, we went to the park and you brought some bread. And who was the bread for? The ducks—that's right. You gave them some and they ate it up." As the adult tells the story, the child is invited to add key details. At first, the child's contribution may simply be attentive listening, the repetition of a word or two, or a one-word response to the adult's invitation. As a child's language grows, or as a favorite story is repeated over and over, the child's role in retelling the story expands as well. If she took part in the event, she may retell what she did or what happened to her. She may also add sound effects or key details, or act out a part of the story.

Susan Engel (1997) studied the factual storytelling patterns of mothers and their toddlers. She found that some mothers frequently reminisced with their young children, telling simple stories about what had happened and encouraging their toddlers to remember and to help retell the story. Other mothers seldom talked with their toddlers about the past. When they did, it was usually a brief conversation with a practical focus. For example, as they searched for a toddler's lost blanket, they might ask the toddler to remember where he had left it.

At 3½, the children who had more experience with elaborated reminiscing were more likely to initiate conversations about the past than those whose earlier conversations with their mothers had tended toward practical remembering. Those who had learned to reminisce were, not surprisingly, more adept at adding information and at keeping the conversation going.

The Hart and Risley (1995) study also picked up striking differences in the frequency with which parents talked with their babies and toddlers about the past—sharing narratives that went beyond the shared context of the here and now or the need to remember a past event in order to solve a present problem. The researchers coded the number of past-tense verbs that the children in their study heard and found that this—like the overall number of words and the number of affirmations they had heard—was highly correlated with vocabulary size at age 3 and beyond.

In many cultures, grandmothers are the tellers of family stories. Sitting on Grandma's lap, even a toddler knows that the stories she will hear will be about people in her family—the ones she knows well and some who may be far away or whom she has never met. As she listens to these special stories, the toddler begins to make connections between past and present. At the same time, she begins to learn the storytelling conventions of her culture—including how to talk about the past and how to engage an audience.

SHARING HUMOR

The *"Babies and small children love to hear the sound of laughter."*— Wakanyeja WoAwanka ("Caring for Our Sacred Children"; cited in Powell, 2005) quote comes from a manual developed by tribal coordinators in North and South Dakota to explain tribal values and traditions to non-native caregivers who might be caring for Lakota, Dakota, or Nakota infants and toddlers. But its wisdom is universal. Humor differs by culture, of course, but all toddlers learn to appreciate humor and to repeat any antics that get a laugh.

Typical toddler antics include

- Mimicking adults (e.g., "No-no-no-no-no") and imitating the routines that make them laugh (e.g., "I gonna getcha," "Tickee tickee")
- Doing something that she has recently learned is ridiculous, such as putting an apple on her head and saying, "Hat," pretending to drink from an upside-down cup, or feeding real cereal to a stuffed animal—with a knowing laugh or smile
- Wearing older people's shoes, hats, purses, or scarves, often with nothing else on but a diaper
- Making a big noise or a big mess
- Singing parts of favorite nursery rhymes and acting out the movements with exaggerated gusto (e.g., "All fall DOWN!")
- Trying to carry something that is much bigger than he is
- Imitating another toddler who is purposely doing something silly
- Dancing to music or performing for an audience, along with or in imitation of older children and adults

The circle game Punchinella capitalizes on a toddlers' emerging imitation and entertainment skills while letting every child participate at her own level. Acting as "Punchinella," a child stands in the center of the circle as others chant:

What can you do, Punchinella, funny fella
What can you do, Punchinella, funny one?

[Punchinella performs a simple action, such as jumping, turning around, scratching her head, or making a silly face. The other children then imitate it, chanting the following:]

We can do it, too, Punchinella, funny fella.
We can do it, too, Punchinella, funny one.

The game continues until every child who wants to has had a chance to be Punchinella.

Of course, parents and toddlers don't always agree on what's funny, especially when messes are involved. But behind the toddler's humor is an evolving understanding of the way the world works, a wish to please, and a rapidly growing ability to connect and communicate.

Tapping into toddler humor can be a great way to extend language. Encourage parents and other caregivers to highlight appropriate humor by joining in a game of All Fall Down, putting a joke into words and responding with appreciative laughter (e.g., "That's silly! Apples don't go on heads!"), or sharing a storybook in which a character engages in similarly outlandish antics.

BOOKS, BOOKS, EVERYWHERE!

Strapped in their booster seats, the toddlers at the Children Are to Be Seen Child Care Center were quietly waiting for their lunch. "These toddlers have learned to handle boredom way too well," thought the consultant who was observing that day. "They need something to do, and something to talk about." She asked the teachers, who were new to the field and hadn't had much training, if she could borrow a book, *Brown Bear, Brown Bear, What Do You See?* (Martin & Carle, 2007). "Brown Bear, Brown Bear," she began in an engaging voice as she pointed to the picture of the bear. "Can you help me make a noise like a bear?" she asked the children, who no longer looked bored and listless. "Grrrr," they repeated.

"And who is this?" she asked, pointing to the red bird. "I see a red bird looking at me. 'Tweet, tweet,' says the red bird." "Red bur," said the nearest toddler, as he reached out to touch the page. "Weet. Weet."

With their insatiable curiosity and notoriously short attention spans, young toddlers are not always kind to books. They want to grab, hold, drag, carry, poke, prod, and tear. And yet, for most toddlers, books and the stories they contain or prompt hold special appeal.

The Books Toddlers Like Best...

- Are sturdy and colorful

- Show clear pictures of everyday objects and routines

- Have distinctive covers. Many young toddlers learn to recognize favorite books before they can talk, and often bring them over to an adult to read.

- Don't have too many words. Although some 1-year-olds will listen for a while to a poem or story—especially at bedtime or while they take a bath—most will spend only a few minutes with a book before moving on to another activity.

- May have very simple repetitive rhymes or songs

- Include pictures and other elements that suggest things to do, such as textures to pat or stroke, favorite characters to find, sounds to imitate, flaps to lift, mirrors to look in, holes to peek or poke through, baby animals to pet or kiss goodnight, birthday candles to blow out, and pages that are easy to turn

- Include big, noisy things (e.g., garbage trucks, airplanes, or farm and zoo animals) or small, intriguing things (e.g., birds, bugs, butterflies, baby animals, balls)

- Provide opportunities to indicate and name familiar people, body parts, or everyday objects

- Provide opportunities to imitate actions (e.g., clapping, bouncing, jumping, waving, pointing) and routines (e.g., giving the baby a kiss, Peekaboo, "How big is Baby?")

- Illustrate simple concepts such as *big* and *little, in* and *out, up* and *down, day* and *night, lost* and *found*

- Tell simple stories about them—or children like them

- Are often homemade

- Help children learn and practice language, and may be the source of some of their early words, phrases, and songs

Parents and other caregivers have discovered many ways to share books with toddlers who are just learning to tell stories with words. Some toddlers—at some times—enjoy hearing a short poem or story all the way through, especially one with a strong rhythm or pattern. But most of the time, toddlers want to participate, at least by turning the pages, often before the adult has time to say the words.

Many classic books for young toddlers are designed to encourage their participation, with textures to pat or stroke, favorite characters to find, sounds to imitate, flaps to lift, mirrors to look in, holes to peek into or poke fingers through, baby animals to pet or kiss goodnight, birthday candles to blow out, and pages that are easy to turn. Whether a parent reads the story, makes up a story, or allows the toddler to choose which pages to play with and which pictures to name or talk about, the toddler plays an active role in the reading experience.

The *Conversation Books* by Joseph Sparling (2007) model a book-reading technique that his extensive research has shown to be an effective vocabulary and language builder. The technique uses the following steps:

- *See*: The adult directs the child's attention to a picture or detail and describes what she sees.

- *Show*: The adult asks the child to point to a picture or detail.

- *Say*: The adult asks the child to name the picture or detail or say something about it.

As the child masters these tasks, the adult can increase the challenge by sharing more information, asking the child to point to more specific details (e.g., the pink sock, two shoes, the tip of the monkey's tail), or asking questions that require more than a one-word answer.

TWENTY FUN THINGS TO DO WITH YOUNG TODDLERS

1. *Turn everyday items into fun toys*: For example, turn a laundry basket or cardboard box into a "car" or "boat" and give the child a ride. Talk about where you are going.

2. *Point out and name the sights on a walk:* Walks can include looping around the block or even just around a room. Stop to pick up a pebble or a small toy, pet the dog gently and feel her soft fur,

smell the flowers, open a cabinet to see what's inside, investigate anything that intrigues the child, and talk to everyone you know.

3. *Help the toddler practice greetings and farewells:* Help him to greet people with a word, wave, or handshake. Encourage him to say, "Hello" to his favorite things and places when he enters a room or say, "Bye-bye" to them when he leaves or "Good night" to them at bedtime.

4. *Make the toddler's stuffed animals talk:* When a toddler will let you hold one of her favorites, treat it like a puppet and make it engage her in conversation and play. "Want to see me jump? Jump! Jump! Jump! Way up high! Boom! I fell down. Can you give me a kiss?"

5. *Go on a pretend shopping trip:* This activity is especially fun for a toddler who likes to collect or carry things. Give him a large tote bag, a toy cart or wagon, or a stroller, and help him fill it with favorite objects as he travels around a room. Name each object together as he places it in the bag or cart.

6. *Introduce the toddler to painting and drawing:* There are many fun and not-too-messy ways to do this. For example, on a sunny day, give the toddler a bucket of water and a large brush and join him in painting the sidewalk. Let him finger paint on a high chair tray or washable placemat, using yogurt or pudding. Tape a large piece of paper or a shopping bag to the refrigerator and use non-toxic markers to decorate it. Talk about the pictures the toddler is making and the tools he is using. Note that he is writing—or drawing or painting—just like big people do.

7. *Introduce the toddler to flashlights:* Toddlers are often fascinated by flashlights, and with a little help, a toddler may be able to learn how to turn one on and off. Show the toddler how to shine the light down (so it doesn't go in anyone's eyes), highlighting different objects. Name each object together as the toddler shines the flashlight on it. You might also talk about concepts such as *light* and *dark, on* and *off,* and *up* and *down.*

8. *Plan a picnic:* Talk together about what to bring, and involve the toddler in the preparation. Be sure to pack some of the food or snacks in a basket or pail that she can carry. Bring along some books as well, especially those with food themes, such as *Eat Up, Gemma* (Hayes & Ormerod, 1994), *The Very Hungry Caterpillar* (Carle, 1994), and *Green Eggs and Ham* (Seuss, 1960), so that you can compare the foods you brought to the food in the books.

Decide together where to spread the blanket and what to eat or read first. After the picnic, encourage the toddler to fill her picnic basket with appropriate toys and books for a pretend picnic. (On a rainy day, you can have your picnic inside!)

9. *Encourage the toddler to help out with chores:* Toddlers love to be helpful, even when they aren't very good at it. You can give the toddler a damp rag or sponge and let him help wipe the table or turn on the vacuum cleaner and hold the wand as you vacuum together, or give him the job of putting out the spoons. Many toddlers are eager to fetch a bottle, blanket, or pacifier for a sibling or peer.

10. *Encourage the toddler to play dress up:* Collect some old clothes and accessories that the toddler can use to dress up in. Toddlers often particularly enjoy scarves, hats, shirts with nameable pictures, shoes and boots, purses and tote bags, ties, and anything that can be used as a cape.

11. *Encourage the toddler to participate in cooperative activities:* Although 1-year-olds may have difficulty sharing favorite toys, they often enjoy simple cooperative activities. With a same-age or somewhat older peer as a playmate, the toddler can learn the fun of cooperation and turn taking by playing with a see-saw or rocking boat, a riding toy built for two, a wagon that one child can sit in while another pulls, a ball that is relatively easy to catch and throw, or a simple walkie-talkie made by attaching two paper cups to opposite ends of a rope (one child talks into his cup while the other puts hers over her ear and listens).

12. *Make the toddler a family photo album:* The album can include pictures of family members, pets, close friends, special experiences, and favorite items or activities that are safely laminated or encased in sturdy plastic sleeves. "Read" the album with the toddler frequently, talking about the pictures and asking him to find particular pages or details. Bring it along on outings to new or potentially stressful places (e.g., the doctor's office, the grocery store), and encourage the toddler to look at it whenever he misses his parents.

13. *Pretend to talk on the telephone with the toddler:* A toy telephone (or a real one that is unplugged or has its keyboard locked) is a terrific toddler toy. Some toddlers enjoy babbling or talking into the telephone, with or without an imaginary audience. Others are more interested in pushing the buttons. In either case, the play

is even more fun when an adult gets involved. "Hi, Chandra. This is Mommy calling. Do you want to have some lunch?" "Let's call your friend Big Bird. I think his number is 1-2-3."

14. *Introduce the toddler to different walking surfaces:* Walk with the toddler barefoot over different surfaces, such as a smooth floor, a soft carpet, a squishy pillow, tickly grass, or a bouncy mat. Talk about the different ways that different surfaces feel. Encourage the toddler to try different ways of walking, such as tiptoeing, marching, jumping, taking giant steps, or walking like an elephant.

15. *Play Follow the Leader:* Toddlers who have mastered walking and running will enjoy joining a few peers or older children in a game of Follow the Leader—as long as the course is not too challenging and doesn't involve any tricks or climbing that are beyond their capabilities. Games involving starting and stopping (e.g., Red Light, Green Light), falling down (e.g., Ring Around the Rosie), being caught and released (e.g., London Bridge), or imitating motions (e.g., Arroz con Leche; Punchinella, or a simplified version of Simon Says) provide toddlers an opportunity to show off their new motor skills and, at the same time, learn new words and songs.

16. *Try sliding different small objects down a slide:* Select a collection that includes both things that roll and things don't, such as a ball, a toy car, a stuffed animal or doll, a blanket, and a book. Talk about which objects slide down fast or slow, which objects go far, which need a push, and which get stuck. Ask, for example, if the car slides better on its side, back, or wheels.

17. *Give the toddler a puzzle to put together:* She might enjoy a simple inset puzzle or shape sorter, a set of large snap-together beads or interlocking blocks, or a toy that comes apart into a few pieces and can be easily reassembled. You can also create your own puzzles by printing digital photographs on large mailing labels, affixing them to cardboard or heavy tag board, and cutting out a simple shape or making two or three interconnecting pieces. Use language to support the toddler's efforts to assemble the puzzle. "Where does that piece go?" "Look—here's a circle shape, just like that piece." "Try turning it around." "It fits! You did it!"

18. *Start a toddler marching band:* Give a small group of toddlers simple rhythm instruments—such as two pot lids, a pot and a wooden spoon, a shaker made by filling a cup or can with rice and sealing the top, a bell or baby rattle, or a set of chop sticks—and start the

music. Lead the band around the room as you sing, shake, and bang together.

19. *Encourage two toddlers to play together:* Give two young toddlers each a similar set of toys, such as a hat, a small ball, a spoon, and a pot with a lid. Watch to see if they play together or if they imitate each other's play. After a few moments, comment on what each child is doing separately or on what they are doing the same or together.

20. *Do something silly:* For example, put a cup on your head or pretend to nibble on a block as if it were an ear of corn or other piece of food. Give the toddler similar props and see if he will imitate you. Carry on a nonverbal conversation by imitating the toddler's antics and encouraging him to imitate yours. Or, talk about what you are doing. "I put the cup on my head. Boom. It fell off. I put it back on again." Repeat the action and comments, and see if he will imitate some of your words.

Too Much TV?

As a "literacy ambassador," Amerech reached out to newly arrived families in her community. Because she shared their cultural background, Amerech knew that these parents would look to her as an authority and would appreciate her lessons and demonstrations of "what to do" to help their children succeed in a new country. She had found the information empowering and expected that they would as well.

"I come from a culture where children are not allowed to speak to adults, children are not allowed to look in the eyes of adults or express their feelings to adults. Children are taught to put their heads down and listen to adults. At the same time I love my culture, my country, my family. My country has many beautiful things I cannot forget about. For example, children are taught to respect people and to love their friends. But, I do feel very angry when I think about the barriers to communication that affected my childhood and my adult life.

At the end of the program's first year, Amarech shared what she had learned with the policy makers overseeing her city's early childhood language and literacy initiatives:

"I did the talk and reading presentations with Ethiopian families and their children. The families were excited by what they learned. Most of the Ethiopian families told us that they would keep talking to their children. They told us no one had taught them or shown them what to do before. They promised to help their children to talk and to teach their children by helping them to read. I showed them how to do this by working together with their children and playing with their children.

One of the parents told us that . . . she lets her baby watch 10 hours of television a day, almost all day long! We explained that when children watch TV for many long hours, they can have many problems including attention deficits. Other parents told us they do the same thing. When we asked them why they let their children watch TV for long hours, they told us no one had told them it was a bad thing to do."

Television is a feature of American homes across the economic spectrum, and it is often on when young children are present. Toddlers know intuitively that this talking object is important in their family. Furthermore, the television responds when they push its buttons—turning off and on or changing the pictures and words. Many parents who are learning a new language themselves find that television shows and subtitled movies support their language learning, and so they keep the television on as much as they can. Some families gather around the television; others use it to keep young children quiet while adults do chores or take a much needed break, or to give their children a needed break. Some use it for "company" or background noise. And many believe that educational programs and videos are good for their children's intellectual development.

When it comes to toddlers, however, most experts advise keeping screen time to a minimum. With their keen emotional radar and powers of imitation, toddlers may be disturbed by violent or emotionally intense adult shows and cartoons, or they may pick up inappropriate language and behavior, without understanding the story. But even when a program's content is developmentally appropriate, the presentation may be too stimulating. Too much exposure to attention-grabbing media may interfere with young children's development of the ability to entertain themselves, to form their own images in their minds, and to deliberately focus their attention on a task. A 2004 study by researchers at Children's Hospital in Seattle (Christakis, Zimmerman, DiGiuseppe, & McCarty) found that toddlers' television exposure is related to attention problems at age 7 and that the risk increases with more viewing time. Equally important, time spent watching television or educational videos is most likely time not spent interacting with people. No matter how cleverly a television show or recorded video engages a child and gets her to talk or sing along, it can't respond to her communications and expand her emerging language. Indeed, a study by the same researchers (Zimmerman &

> "I arrived in a home with the TV on (thankfully at least to a children's program) and while using the images on the TV for language stimulation, I explained to the father that just like you don't learn to play football by watching it on TV (you have to play the game), his son was not going to learn to talk by watching TV. I think he 'got it.'"
>
> —Linda Lilly, Chief of the Division of Speech Language and Hearing,
> Baltimore County Department of Health

Christakis) published in 2007 ignited a firestorm of controversy with its finding that increased viewing of baby "brain-building" videos by children between 8 and 16 months old was associated with significantly large *decreases* in the number of words that parents reported their children understood.

Given that television is a part of most families' lives, however, there are some positive ways to turn children's attention away from the television toward other things. If a child asks to watch a show such as *Thomas the Tank Engine*, for example, suggest that you read a Thomas book or other book about a train together, instead. Parents should limit their own viewing, as well, so that they model other behaviors such as being involved in physical activities and reading, and of course, talking more.

The American Academy of Pediatrics (2008) recommends *no* television for children younger than age 2.

THE CHILD CARE CHALLENGE

Tina, an experienced family child care provider with a degree in child development, had always taught preschoolers. She used both Spanish and English with her largely Latino students, and their parents had consistently reported that their children did well in English-speaking classrooms in kindergarten and first grade. The few children whose families spoke only English learned enough Spanish to carry on basic conversations and understand Spanish picture books. Knowing that she was a good language teacher, Tina did not hesitate when she was asked to care for two 1-year-olds.

It didn't take long for Tina to realize that her training and experience had not prepared her to teach toddlers. The 1-year-olds seemed happy enough at first; they liked to join the older children in singing and dancing and got pretty good at moving, clapping, and babbling to the beat. They enjoyed throwing balls in the yard, squishing playdough, and making random marks with crayons. They quickly became great friends, and smiled when they saw each other. But pretty soon they developed a favorite game—chasing each other around the house and pulling things off the shelves and tables, especially whatever the big kids were using. It seemed to be the only thing they wanted to do, and Tina found herself running, too, just to keep some semblance of peace and order.

"Dump and run. We know that game very well," the experienced providers responded when Tina shared her problem in a workshop at a national family child care conference. They also had many suggestions to help Tina build a more balanced program that could channel the toddlers' energy into exciting and productive learning.

Here is a sampling of their advice:

- Plan a mix of active and quiet activities that suits the children's activity levels and rhythms. Some toddlers focus best on quiet activities after a period of active play; others focus best in the morning or right after lunch.

- Try lowering the level of stimulation. Put out just a few toys at a time, close some blinds or dim the lights, be sure that the television and radio are off, and engage the older children in relatively quiet, focused activities.

- Set limits, and explain them in simple terms. "We walk in the house. We can run outside." "That big crash hurt my ears! Let's put those books on a low shelf where they won't fall down." "Devon needs those pieces for her puzzle. You can use these pieces."

- Help the older children understand that the toddlers just want to be part of the action. If they take something that the big kids were using, they will probably put it down in a minute or two to investigate something that looks more exciting. Help the toddlers participate in big kid activities in their own way—by using similar toys or materials or playing a simple dramatic role such as "patient" or "passenger."

- Give the toddlers jobs that are within their capabilities—fetching an item needed for a project, task, or game; helping to put toys into a bin; making a decoration by scribbling on a piece of paper; pushing the stroller or pulling the wagon; or holding the class puppet during morning circle.

- Introduce simple imitation games such as "Simon Says" and "Punchinella" and encourage the toddlers to participate in their own ways.

- Use language-building strategies with the toddlers. Get the older children to help you by "translating" what the toddlers are saying, using comments and questions to encourage the toddlers to use their words, and responding to the toddlers' communications by adding a bit more.

At its best, high-quality child care for toddlers who are beginning to use language supports each child in all areas of development. It builds on children's interests—including their growing interest in other children. Daily routines balance active and quiet play, predictability and variety, child-initiated activities, and teachers' offerings or suggestions. The children are engaged and focused as they attempt new challenges or consolidate emerging skills. At the same time, there is a feeling of relaxed spontaneity. The children and adults enjoy being together, and amazement, invention, contemplation, and connection are routine parts of their days. Prompted by items that catch a child's attention, they talk, sing, question, explore, test, marvel, pretend, fetch, and reminisce. Music is used intentionally—not as background noise—and television is absent.

Adults speak to children often about what they are doing. Intriguing objects and activities prompt children and adults to ask questions of each other. Pictures of children's activities, family members, and favorite objects encourage labeling and stories. Pretend play materials and songs encourage word play, whereas quiet spaces with a few interesting objects foster intimate exchanges. Knowing that frequent reading with infants and toddlers boosts their language and cognitive development (Raikes et al., 2006), infant care teachers read with children several times a day and encourage parents to do the same.

Adults show genuine interest in what children think and feel by engaging them as conversation partners—even when the child's side of the conversation consists of coos, babbles, and gestures. Rather than formally instructing, good language teachers offer comments, open-ended questions, and information that extend a child's idea—and give the child time to respond. As they talk and play with individuals and small groups, they find many opportunities to support . . . development.

[Child care] teachers provide guidance as children learn to manage their own feelings and to be members of a group. They help children to regulate their emotions and behavior, gradually modifying their support as children mature. They help children prepare for new experiences and transitions, and encourage self-control by setting clear, consistent limits and having realistic expectations. They help toddlers to put strong feelings into words and to use their words to frame and resolve conflicts in positive ways. As a result, children hear many more "yeses" and words of deserved praise and encouragement than "nos." (ZERO TO THREE, 2008)

Whether care is offered in a home or in a school-like setting, in a mixed-age or same-age group, a high-quality environment for toddlers is safe, clean, and uncluttered. It offers interesting spaces and objects to explore, and is intriguing without being overstimulating or overwhelming. Books, decorations, play materials, daily routines, activities, and outings give children and adults a lot to talk about. Most important, the group size is small enough and the adult/child ratio high enough for each child to get to know the others and to have many one-to-one conversations throughout each day with an adult who knows her well. Families and caregivers work together to help each child feel at home in the group and feel good about who she is, what she can do, and the language(s) she is learning to speak. Children who experience such high-quality care at 1 and 2 are likely to have a language advantage when they are 3 and 4 (NICHD Early Child Care Research Network, 2005).

AWESOME!

Typically around 16–18 months, but sometimes as early as 1 year or as late as 2½, toddlers' vocabularies take a dramatic jump. The child who took 6 months to learn 40 or 50 words is suddenly learning 9 new words in a day. This spurt is often associated with (or soon followed by) the emergence of another amazing skill—the ability to put words together into meaningful two- or three-word sentences that the child may never have heard: "My doggie," "Want juice," "Daddy go car," "Mama all gone."

Language researchers have come up with a range of explanations for these seemingly miraculous transitions. Some have postulated a "language instinct" that primes a child's brain to pick up or invent grammar and to learn both what words refer to and how they are used (Pinkner, 1994). Others argue that the bulk of evidence points to an interaction between the language input a child hears and the child's efforts to make sense of what he is hearing and to communicate with the important people in his life (Gopnik et al., 1999; Hoff, 2006). Some point to an associated spurt in brain development in the area associated with word memory and retrieval, although it is unclear whether this is the cause or the result of an increased word-learning rate (Eliot, 1999). And some researchers claim that the image of a "spurt" is misleading. They note that, for most children, the word learning process gets faster over time, sometimes in spurts and plateaus, more often with steadily increasing speed. We may simply be seeing an initially slow word learning pace that keeps speeding up (Bloom, 2000).

It may be that at a certain point, children accumulate a critical mass of early experience with words, concepts, and successful verbal communication that makes using words an effective means of self-expression. As they work to make themselves understood with words and listen to what people say in response, they figure out more and more about how their language works. For labelers, putting words they know together to create two- or three-word patterns may create an upward language learning spiral. "Wannit" becomes a frame in which they can substitute a variety of words or phrases that tell what is wanted: "Want juice," "Want uppy," "Want go car." They can also vary the first part of a sentence such as "Want juice" with utterances such as "More juice" and "My juice." Similarly, children who focused on learning stock phrases and sentences learn to vary them—"I want juice please" becomes "I want more juice" or "I want a cookie." The more words and phrases children know and use, the more aware they become of these combinatory possibilities and patterns. And, as they begin to recognize and construct patterns, they find it easier to learn new words from their linguistic contexts.

Bob McMurray (2007), a researcher at the University of Iowa, developed a computer model that predicted the word spurt based on a few simple assumptions:

- Children learn words over time through multiple hearings and rehearsals.

- Children learn many words at once.

- Common words used frequently in speech addressed to the child will be learned first.

- Words that a child hears more rarely will take longer to learn because exposures will be more widely spaced.

McMurray claimed that complex explanations for the increase in children's vocabularies were unnecessary.

Whatever the explanation, word learning rates accelerate at some point for all children, but they accelerate more rapidly for some children than for others. And that's the important point. Children's early experiences with language build a reservoir of fuel that powers a language lift-off. Once children's word learning takes off, success begets success. The more words they use, the more opportunities they are likely to get to learn and practice new words, and the steeper their learning curves will be.

> It was Angelo's second New Year's Eve, and his parents decided to celebrate by taking him out for an early pizza dinner. The local Greek restaurant was quiet, and the waiters fussed over Angelo, who had come prepared with bottle, books, blanket, and a bagful of Christmas toys. Before long, though, Angelo looked up and noticed the red velvet ribbons overhead, festooned with sparkling lights and shiny green ornaments. "Uppy, Dada. Uppy," he insisted, pointing to the ceiling. His father obliged, gently lifting Angelo from his high chair and hoisting him up until a streamer was just out of reach. "Touch gently, Angelo," he said quietly. "One finger." Angelo's saucer eyes widened further as he stretched out his index finger and carefully stroked the streamer with it. "Feel how soft the ribbon is," Angelo's father continued. "Sof wibbon," Angelo repeated. "It's a velvet ribbon," his Dad added. "Isn't it awesome?" "Belbet wibbon," echoed Angelo. "Awesome."

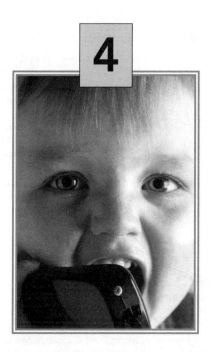

Off Like a Rocket

(1½–2½ Years)

Doctor (to mother):	"You've got a very healthy toddler, and she seems to be developing just fine. But I'm wondering how her language is coming. She hasn't said a thing during this whole examination. Does she talk much at home?"
Toddler:	"I can talk. You're a pediatrician."

At some point between the ages of 1 and 2½, toddlers figure out how to put words together, and their language takes off. They become hungry for words, constantly asking, "Whazzat?" and repeating new words they hear. Each day—and often many times a day—they amaze their teachers and parents with new words, clever observations and questions, and stories of past events that the adults may have forgotten.

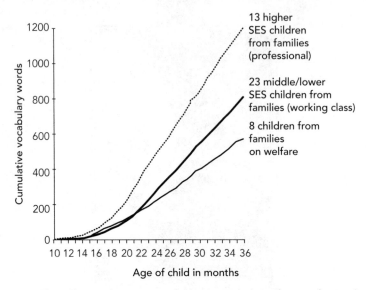

Figure 4.1. The widening gap in young children's vocabularies from professional, working-class, and welfare families across their first 3 years of life. (*From* Hart, B., & Risley, T.R. [1995, p. 47].

The Hart and Risley study (1995) traced 42 children's growing vocabularies from their first words until their third birthdays and graphed the averages for children of different socioeconomic backgrounds (See Figure 4.1). As the graphs reveal, word learning pace accelerated for all groups in the period between 16 and 24 months.

Once children begin to use words as a primary means of communication, their language learning increases exponentially. Those on a faster learning trajectory have an ongoing and increasing advantage. In order to catch up to the leaders, children who started out more slowly would have to dramatically increase their learning rate.

At the same time that their language development is zooming ahead, children are developing a new sense of themselves as individuals who can express opinions, make choices, and do things all by themselves. For some families, the period between about 18 months and almost 3 years is the time of the "terrible twos"—when a child's need to assert his identity keeps the whole family on edge. "No," "Mine," and "Me do it" dominate the toddler's side of many conversations, and temper tantrums are a common—though not always predictable—occurrence. For other families, this is the most wondrous period of child development, when their baby truly "becomes a person." Each day is filled with surprises as the child picks up new words, puts them together in new ways, and says and does a myriad of things that show unexpected insight, empathy, and creativity. In most families, of course, the "twos" are occasionally "terrible" and often "terrific"—the one constant is that the children keep their parents and teachers on their toes.

The amazing if sometimes rocky or "testing" period when language growth takes off is also a time when the language input that children receive and the practice it stimulates really matter. The amount of talk; the use of rare and interesting words; the exchange of information through open-ended questions or comments that expand on a child's simple observation; the use of books and photographs as springboards for conversation; and habits of positive, proactive, playful discipline all make a difference to a child's language learning. And, because 1- and 2-year-olds are doing most of their talking with adults (rather than with friends, toys, themselves, and the imaginary conversation partners they will later be able to create), what parents and caregivers do to elicit and enrich conversation and support healthy social-emotional development has both an immediate and long-term impact.

> A mother of a 2-year-old explained after participating in a literacy workshop,
> "In my home country, I didn't talk to my child. My place in the family was to cook and clean; my in-laws did all the talking. Now I know how important it is for me to talk to her. My in-laws aren't here. I can't read her stories, but we can look at a book together and talk about the pictures. In our home country, she was told not to ask questions. But here? Here I see that she will need to learn to ask questions, just as I will."

During this period, everybody counts. When parents are providing rich language experiences, the quality of a child care setting can still make a difference. When the child care program is full of interesting things to talk about and many opportunities to talk with interested adults, what parents do to support and encourage conversation still matters. When talkative, solicitous mothers are engaging toddlers in many conversations, father talk can still add value. Indeed, when mothers tend to keep a conversation focused on a child's interests, fathers who talk about their own work or hobbies with their 2-year-olds add an important dimension. Like little sponges, children who have learned to put words together soak up all of the language input they can get. The more they talk, the more people talk to them and the faster they learn.

FROM WORDS TO TELEGRAPHIC
SPEECH TO SENTENCES

It is important to look beyond vocabulary in order to understand children's suddenly rapid acquisition of language. Children are not just learning words. They are also learning how to combine words into meaningful phrases and sentences; how to add markers to words that indicate how they are used (e.g., *word* + *s* = *words; use* + *d* = *used*); how to form new words from known words and word parts (e.g., *lunch* + *box* = *lunchbox; meaning* + *ful* = *meaningful*); and how to use sequences of words to ask questions, issue commands, and tell stories. At the same time, they are learning their culture's largely unspoken rules about when to talk and when to listen, how children talk to adults and peers, and what is appropriate to say in particular situations.

Children's first word combinations have a grammar of their own. Word order tends to be derived from fully formed sentences, but past tense and plural endings; articles such as *a* and *the*; and other grammatical markers tend to be omitted, along with pronouns such as *I* and *you* and connecting words such as *are* or *did*. Children often ask questions with rising intonation but not in special forms, and most "sentences" are only two or three words long. Like 20th century telegram writers, these toddlers are including only the essentials, leaving their listeners to mentally flesh out the full message.

As children learn more and more of the fillers and the implicit grammatical rules that govern placement and usage, their sentences become longer. "Mommy?" becomes "Where Mommy go?" and then "Where did Mommy go?" In addition to filling in the elements that the rules of their grammar require, children learn to add descriptive words to phrases and to combine phrases or sentences to create longer sentences. In the United States, some developmental psychologists use *mean length of utterance,* or average sentence length, as a rough measure of children's progress in mastering the grammar of their first language(s) or dialect(s).

Dialects, both standard and nonstandard, are governed by rules of pronunciation, word formation, and grammar. Toddlers who primarily hear a nonstandard dialect in their homes and communities will learn the rules that characterize that dialect, even if they are hearing a different dialect on television or in occasional educational settings such as library story hours. Traveling in a wider social orbit, adults are more likely to shift between dialects as the situation demands. Fluent adult speakers of African American Vernacular English, for example, may routinely use sentences such as "He run slow," "That Damitra book," and "We don' got no more" when talking with family and friends, although they may also use the Standard English forms in more formal contexts.

Just as certain sounds may be ignored by children whose first languages don't contain them, the standard dialect's grammatical markers such as the –s on a singular verb or the 's on a possessive noun will be ignored by toddlers who are learning to speak a dialect that marks these grammatical relationships in other ways or not at all. Instead, these children will gradually learn to add the words, endings, and other markers that are important in their primary dialect.

The quality of children's language experience may affect the speed at which they master the basics of sentence formation, but it rarely derails their ultimate achievement. Almost all children will learn to speak grammatically—according to the usage rules of their linguistic communities—by the time they are 4 or 5 years old (National Research Council and Institute of Medicine, 2000). Groups of children who are not exposed to a fully developed language will often invent one. Such groups include

- Children whose parents speak a pidgin language (a proto-language that combines elements of two or more languages and is likely to sound like telegraphic speech to speakers of either one). The children often develop a creole (a blended language with its own grammatical rules and markers) within a generation.

- Deaf children who have not had the opportunity to learn sign language but who learn signs that they use with each other. These children will collectively develop a true sign language.

Children who are learning two languages simultaneously will go through the same developmental phases in each, moving from single words to two- and three-word combinations to telegraphic speech and eventually to fully grammatical sentences. Those whose families, teachers, and playmates code-mix—using two languages interchangeably (often within the same utterance)—will do so as well. They will use the grammatically appropriate word order for phrases in each language and gradually add the appropriate grammatical markers. Unlike many individuals who learn a second language later in life, those who learn two languages as toddlers will process the grammatical markers and function words for both languages in the same areas of their brains (Kim, Belkin, Lee, & Hirsch, 1997).

Researchers describe grammar as a robust capacity because its development is hard to disrupt. Only children with rare genetic disorders or severe conditions that make them unable to communicate with either words or signs fail to develop this aspect of language (National Research Council and Institute of Medicine, 2000).

Tips for Talking with Toddlers and Twos

- Watch the toddler at play, wait to see what she will do, and ask yourself what she is trying to accomplish. What story is she telling? What is she trying to discover or figure out? What is she trying to communicate by her behavior?

- Find a way to enter the child's play world. You might play beside him and then link your play to his, make a comment or ask a question about what he is doing, or talk to or for a toy that he is using as a pretend companion.

- Talk about anything that interests the child—or that interests you.

- Name objects and parts of objects for the toddler, and explain their uses and relationships. "Let's tighten the strap on your shoe. Can you push it down so the Velcro will stick?"

- Acknowledge the toddler's contributions to the conversation, then build on them by adding more information or asking a related question.

- Expand telegraphic speech into natural sounding sentences. Don't just repeat what the child is saying; rather, add a bit more to spark her response.

- Don't correct grammar or pronunciation. Respond to what the child meant to say, rather than to how he said it.

- If you are not sure of what the child said or meant, ask her to repeat it. If it is still not clear, you might put your best guess into words or ask her to show you. If you just pretend to understand, you may miss the opportunity for a genuine exchange.

- Remember that even 2-year-olds who can use full sentences may still be learning how to carry on conversations. Be flexible and patient when the child responds with silence, abruptly changes the subject, or chatters on without regard to your responses.

- Use specific language, including some unusual, interesting words; onomatopoeic words (words that sound like their meanings); and other words that are fun to repeat.

- Ask questions that offer choices (e.g., "Would you like to put your coat on yourself or should I help you?"), support problem solving (e.g., "Do you think we could reach the ball with this, or do we need something longer?"), solicit ideas and opinions (e.g., "What flavor would you like? What should we get for Mommy?"), extend the child's pretend play (e.g., "Where is this train going?"), or prompt investigation (e.g., "What do you think would happen if . . . ?").

- Use fanciful language and playful approaches to add interest to ordinary routines. "Hey, hand. Are you hiding in that sleeve? Come out, come out wherever you are!" "Shh. The fairies are sleeping."

- Wonder with children. "Do you think an animal might live in this hole?"

- Think out loud.

- Don't monopolize the conversation. Give the child many chances to chime in, and stop when he loses interest.

- TALK—AND LISTEN—A LOT.

Vocabulary, verbal flair, and functional use of language are much more dependent on experience. Children who are read to a lot or who hear poetic language in nursery rhymes and bedtime stories are likely to learn unusual words and phrasings and to incorporate these into their own stories, patter, and pretend play. Children who spend a lot of time talking and playing with adults who encourage and try to satisfy their curiosity are likely to comment on interesting or unusual events, ask all sorts of questions, and offer their own explanations for things they observe or learn about. Children who frequently hear and practice polite greetings, requests, invitations to join in play, and other ways of initiating or interrupting a conversation become adept at social routines. This helps them to be comfortable with new people and to make friends easily. Children who have many, many opportunities to engage with adults in recalling experiences and making up fanciful stories will learn to use their words to weave narratives of their own. As all of these children learn to hook adults into telling them stories, joining their play, and answering their questions, they will get still more language-learning opportunities.

Many people think that the best way to talk to young children is to use only short sentences and simple words. They don't realize that little children love big words—both because they are hard but fun to say and because people are impressed when they use them. Longer sentences are likely to contain more interesting words, along with more contextual clues to their probable meanings. And, of course, interesting words—when used naturally in meaningful contexts—stretch vocabularies.

The trick is to build on what the child knows and is curious about, not to bombard her with esoteric vocabulary words that have little connection with her interests or experience. So much is new for 1- and 2-year-olds that almost any discussion or explanation or shared fantasy play is likely to introduce new words and concepts.

"Watch, wait, and wonder—then find a way to join the play."

FROM THINKING OUT LOUD TO INNER SPEECH

Two-year-old Andre used his new words to remind himself how to stay out of trouble. "Mama papers. Don't touch." Betty, an early talker and late walker, gave herself instructions as she mastered walking: "One foot, the other foot." Chandra recited her father's reassurances over and over to comfort herself when he left her at her child care center. "Daddy come back. Daddy come back SOON." Darrel told himself how to fix everyday problems. "Uh-oh. Milk pill. Need ponge." Elena accompanied her doll play with a running narrative. "Here bankie. Night-night. Wake up. Get bottle. Night-night."

Language provides toddlers with a powerful new tool for organizing their behavior—they can use language to give themselves instructions, repeat a comforting mantra, or state a simple plan. Sometimes, it seems as if toddlers are driven to talk—even when no one is listening. Language researchers who taped young children's nighttime talk were surprised at how much time these newly verbal children spent practicing words, phrases, and telegraphic sentences (Brown, 1973; Nelson, 1989).

By age 3, most children have learned how to keep a conversation going—if they choose to—and how to carry on a conversation without a partner's help. They will talk to and for a puppet or doll, begin a conversation by asking a question or making an announcement, and even talk to their hands or feet if there's nothing to play with and no one is listening.

Toddlers also talk to themselves. When faced with a problem, they can frame the question, state a guess or hypothesis, or give themselves step-by-step directions. They will repeat and memorize a short list of items or instructions or a fragment of a favorite song, poem, or story. And, although much of their self-talk is spoken or whispered, they are also developing a capacity for inner speech. They can use their words not only to communicate but also to think silently—to reflect and plan, reason and synthesize, wonder and imagine.

Most 2-year-olds are just beginning to develop the ability to use language in these ways. They rely on partners to support and encourage their thinking by offering questions, information, and extensions of their ideas.

Consider the following two conversations:

Andrew:	"Here comes the big truck. Watch out everybody, big truck coming."
Father:	"Sorry big truck, you have to slow down. You are coming to the tollgate. Here's your ticket, Mr. Truck Driver."
Andrew:	"Thank you, Mr. Man. Zoom . . . zoom, going up the mountain. Oops, flat tire."
Father:	"Hmmm . . . that flat tire looks pretty serious. We'd better find the jack and jack up your truck."
Andrew:	"Here's the jack. Fix the tire."
Father:	"Let's hurry. Looks as if you've got ice cream in your truck. We don't want it to melt."
Andrew:	"Yeah—got lots of ice cream and chocolate ice cream, strawberry and more ice cream."
Father:	"You're making me hungry. How about giving me an ice cream sandwich while we repair this flat tire. (Segal & Adcock, 1985, p. 127)"

Child:	"Here comes the big truck. Watch out everybody, big truck coming."
Adult:	"Where is the big truck going?"
Child:	"Up the mountain."
Adult:	"What's up on the mountain?"
Child:	"Trees."
Adult:	"What's the truck going to do?"

Child: "Zoom . . . zoom."

Adult: "Where's the truck going now?"

Child: "Zoom . . . zoom."

In the first conversation, the adult knows the child well and responds to both his words and his enthusiasm. The conversation flows easily, with each exchange building on the previous one. Child psychiatrist Stanley Greenspan (Greenspan & Salmon, 1996), who works with children with autism spectrum disorders and other communication challenges, describes such conversations in terms of interlocking "circles of communication." Each new idea, question, or comment opens a communication circle, which each response closes or completes. The circles form an interlocking chain when each response invites a related response.

In the second conversation, the circles don't interlock, and some are not even completed. The child is dependent on the adult to keep the conversation going, but the adult's attempts are less successful than in the first example. The child's limited verbal facility is only part of the issue. The disconnects occur when the adult's questions fail to engage the child, and, as a result, the child's responses give the adult very little to build on. Instead of a discussion, the conversation feels like a short-answer quiz.

TWO-YEAR-OLD LOGIC

As a first child of older parents, James was used to getting his way. When his mother weaned him shortly before his second birthday, he soon tired of being a "big boy" and insisted on being nursed. His mother patiently explained that she had no more milk for him; her breasts were empty. But, with impeccable toddler logic, James had a ready solution: "Go to store. Buy milk. Fill up Mommy."

A few days later, James went with his child care class on a field trip to the fire station. He was particularly interested in the fire axe that was hanging high up on the wall. "Whazzat?" he asked his teacher.

"It's a fire axe," she explained. "Sometimes, the firefighters have to break down a door so they can get to a fire. This axe is the tool they use."

"See axe," James demanded.

"You can look at it from here," his teacher responded, "but I can't get it down for you." The solution was obvious to James. "Tell fireman get ladder. Climb up. Get axe."

Carly, age 2½, is busy making block enclosures and setting up rubber animals inside them.

"What are you building?" her teacher asks.

"A zoo." Carly answers brightly. "I'm making play pens for the animals so they can play together."

"And who is in this pen?"

"Rhinoceros and stegosaurus and triceratops. They're friends. And a cow and a giraffe."

Knowing that Carly loves dinosaurs, both as toys and in books, the teacher is curious about the thinking behind Carly's arrangement. "I thought stegosaurus and triceratops were dinosaurs."

"Um—hmm."

"Could we see dinosaurs in a real zoo?"

"Um-hmm."

"I thought you told me dinosaurs were extinct."

"No more dinosaurs hanging on the brink," Carly chants, quoting from one of her favorite books, *Ten Little Dinosaurs* (Schnetzler & Harris, 2000). "They all disappeared in a geologic wink . . . Poor little dinosaurs, all extinct."

"Where did all those poor little dinosaurs go?"

"To the zoo."

As toddlers like James and Carly master language, they learn to string together not just words, but ideas. They notice likes and differences, and use words to make links between disparate objects that share functions, names, or key characteristics. They can follow—and give—multistep directions. Their logic may be their own, but the steps are in order and the ideas connect.

Many of the songs, books, hand and finger rhymes, and spontaneous stories that adults share with toddlers help them practice step-by-step thinking.

The Itsy-Bitsy Spider

The Itsy-Bitsy Spider went up the water spout.
Down came the rain and washed the spider out.
Out came the sun and dried up all the rain,
So the Itsy-Bitsy Spider went up the spout again.

With a little creativity, adults can adapt traditional songs to help toddlers remember multiple steps and reinforce causal links.

This Is the Way We Wash Our Hands (Variation)
This is the way we wet our hands, wet our hands,
    wet our hands.
This is the way we put on the soap
To make a lot of soap suds.

This the way we rub our hands, rub the fronts, rub the backs.
This is the way we rub our fingers
And cover our hands with soap suds.

This is the way we rub off the dirt, rub off the dirt, rub off the dirt.
This is the way we rub off the dirt
With lots of bubbly soap suds.

This is the way we rinse off the soap, rinse off the soap,
    rinse off the soap.
This is the way we turn off the tap.
'Cause now our hands are all clean.

Similarly, when adults wonder aloud about whether it will rain, or why the sky is dark, or what they need to bring along on an outing, they invite children to think with them. This gives adults an opportunity to evoke and extend the children's logic, and also to model theirs. Even the simplest plans, when shared with a toddler, become opportunities to build language and reasoning skills.

ADVANCES IN PRETEND PLAY AND IMAGINATION

Visiting their cousins for their Nana's birthday celebration, the not-quite 2-year-old twins, Hannah and Ramsey, were very excited. The whole family had gathered and, as the youngest ones, they were the center of attention. Their older cousin had a doll house with real furniture, and she showed them how to open the toy oven's door. Soon, Hannah was busy making pretend cookies and serving them to everyone except her sister, who had found a set of trucks and was busily driving them "all around the town." As Hannah served each adult in turn, they all played along, commenting on how delicious the cookies were, thanking Hannah profusely, and asking for more. Ramsey waited until Hannah's back was turned, then quietly snuck over to the doll house and ate an entire batch of pretend cookies, one yummy bite at a time.

Just as they are learning to combine words and sequence ideas in conversations, 2-year-olds are learning to string together multiple steps in their pretend play. They will pick up a toy telephone, say, "Hello," jabber for a bit, then say, "Bye," and hang up. They will load a toy truck with sand or blocks, drive it around, deliver its contents to a new location, and drive it back to its garage. No longer content just to eat a pretend cookie, they will now go on a pretend shopping trip and unpack their play food, bake invisible cookies in a toy oven, and enjoy an imaginary tea party with an adult companion or even with a friend. Favorite sequences will be played out over and over again.

Many toddlers come to associate particular play routines with particular places or people. At the library, for example, they greet the gerbil, then get a book and "read" it to their stuffed rabbit. At the park, they climb on the toy train, shout, "All aboard!" and drive to the zoo where they visit the giraffe. At the pediatric clinic, they make spaghetti on the play stove while they wait for the doctor. When Aunt Carrie comes to babysit, they get out the toy farm and make the farmer give each animal a big serving of hay.

Just as language helps toddlers to organize their own behavior, it can help them play together. For 2-year-olds, playing together usually means doing the same thing or following a leader's direction. One child calls, "Monster gonna get us. Run fast!!" and everyone runs. Or a child invites a friend to help build a tall castle. "Get more bricks," and his friend happily complies. As they approach 3, children learn to play complementary roles, such as doctor and patient, waiter and diner, store clerk and shopper, or parent and child.

At first, toddlers will play out the salient parts of a process, repeating those that are most fun to act out, regardless of real-world constraints. They might, for example, pass out imaginary cookies, pour some imaginary tea, and then eat their own cookies, although they never took any. They are not likely to mind if their playmates take a drink before their cups are filled or after their tea has been declared, "All gone."

With practice, 2-year-olds become adept pretenders. The shopping excursion that once involved picking up an old purse and walking around the room while repeating, "Goin shopping" now requires car keys and a shopping list, a bag or cart to fill with groceries, and a doll or human to collect the money. Whereas Teddy Bear's doctor visit once involved a silent listen with the stethoscope and a shot or two followed by Teddy Bear crying and being comforted, he now needs a thorough exam and a full explanation of why shots are necessary.

Pretending with a 2-year-old or with a small toddler group is a wonderful way to enhance both vocabulary and functional language use. Adults can get involved in many ways:

- *Set the stage and supply props:* A box can serve as a table, stove, or store counter, or be opened and turned on its side to make a doll house, a barn, or a garage. A dress-up collection—with scarves, hats, costume jewelry, ties, vests, capes, shoes, purses or brief cases, and boots—can support everything from "going to work" to being butterflies, firefighters, or dinosaurs. You can also create theme boxes, with collections of props such as party hats, cards, and candles for a birthday party; Band-Aids, empty plastic bottles, and a toy stethoscope for a doctor or veterinarian visit; pails, shovels, shells, and a towel for going to the beach; and impromptu collections that relate to a child's interests, upcoming or past experiences, or favorite storybooks.

- *Initiate the play:* Call the child on a pretend telephone, invite her on a pretend trip to the beach or the grocery store, turn an ordinary cleanup chore into a game of basketball or a race to get the cars to their garages, ask what her doll would like for breakfast.

- *Ask a question or make a comment that helps children put words to their play:* "Oh, no. Snoopy fell down. Did he hurt his knee? Does he need a Band-Aid?"

- *Follow the child's directions:* Get the things she asks for, eat the food she serves, clap and cheer for the performances that she asks you to watch. When the directions are nonverbal, put them into words as you comply.

- *Add a bit more to the child's game:* Play your role with enthusiasm, and take the action one step further. Ask for some cheese to sprinkle on the delicious pasta, hand the conductor your ticket to stamp, point out the stellar sights as you zoom through space, ask if the camel is thirsty or if the car needs some gas.

- *Inject humor:* "I know what this spaghetti needs! Do you have any chocolate sprinkles?" "I'm glad you're going shopping. We need eggs, bread, and dinosaur food."

- *Help children pretend together:* You might suggest a cooperative task such as making dinner for the dinosaur family, putting on a dancing show for you and their dolls to watch, putting out an imaginary fire, or going fishing.

MONSTERS THAT LURK IN THE DARK

Fascinated by the tadpoles in a pond she was visiting with her parents, 2-year-old Nora leaned over too far and fell in. Her father rescued her quickly, but the experience was still frightening. "Don't like dark water," Nora kept repeating. "Nora scared."

Nora still seemed upset when her mother shared the story with their home visitor the next week. "How can I help her?" Nora's mother asked. "I don't want her to be afraid of the water."

"Try replaying the story with her at bath time," the home visitor suggested. "Show her how to make a Nora doll fall in the water and have a daddy doll rescue her. Make the Nora doll cry or say that she is scared, and have the daddy doll comfort her. Then give Nora a chance to play Nora or to play the daddy. After a while, you can extend the story. Have the daddy and Nora dolls go for a happy swim—just like the tadpoles—but with their heads above water!"

Nora's mom followed this advice and found that Nora loved the game. Soon the Nora doll was happily swimming with Froggy and Rubber Ducky and even diving under the "dark water." By the next summer, when Nora started taking swimming lessons at the local YMCA, she had forgotten the trauma.

A two-year-old's ability to connect ideas and imagine what might happen can lead to new fears. The memory of a frightening or painful experience can make a child reluctant to go to a particular place, or even one that is similar. A dark room may suddenly be home to nameless terrors—imaginary monsters may lurk in a closet or under a bed. A child may worry that the cow will jump over the moon and come crashing through her bedroom ceiling, that the sweat that runs down her body on a hot day is a sign that she is melting like an ice cream cone, or that she will be sucked down the bathtub drain along with the soap bubbles.

Language can enhance fears, but it can also help alleviate them. A child who can say, "Go away, big green monster" (Emberley, 1992); tell a friend that "There aren't any real lions around here, only in the zoo"; or explain to his parents why he is worried about going to a friend's house all by himself has developed important coping skills.

ADVANCES IN STORYTELLING AND RETELLING

Nicholas was 2½ when his father took him to his first movie. Nicholas didn't understand it all, but he was entranced with the larger-than-life cartoon characters, the music, and the crowd of children and parents. On the way home, his Dad helped him to review the story and rehearse what he would tell his mother. Nicholas condensed it to its core. "Pinocchio tell a lie. Pinocchio nose grow." (As he said this, Nicholas put his hand on his nose and then stretched out his arm to indicate how long the nose had grown.) "Pinocchio tell de troof." (On "troof," Nicholas quickly bent his arm and hit his nose to indicate that it had returned to its regular size.) Nicholas was so delighted with his mother's response that, for the next several days, he repeated this performance whenever anyone came into the house.

Children like Nicholas are beginning to understand that actions have purposes and consequences. The stories they tell or retell are not just a series of observations or unrelated events. One thing follows from another. Although there may be gaps in the action or logical impossibilities, there is an emerging sense of sequence. Children at this age are starting to realize that most stories have a beginning, a middle, and an end. Those who have been read to a lot or who hear many family stories often pick up the literary conventions that mark a story's beginning or ending. "When I was a born baby . . . ." 2½-year-old Sam would frequently begin, before prompting his mother to retell his favorite story about how his big brother had slipped while carrying him down the stairs but managed to keep him safe (Engel, 1997). When Jason and his mother used miniature figures to retell a story from one of his favorite books, Jason added an ending of his own. "So they put on their hats and their mittens and went outside to play Kooshball."

At this point in development, children especially like to hear stories about themselves. They enjoy retellings of events they remember and also like to hear about when they were little babies. A baby book or family scrapbook provides treasured opportunities to retell such stories and talk together about all the ways in which a child is growing up and all the new things she can do. With a little help, children can put three or four pictures of a recent event in order and use them to tell a story. "Me and Rashid got lots of blocks. We made a big, big castle. Then the truck came and knocked it down. CRASH!"

Many toddlers like to take small family photo albums to child care to talk about with their teachers and look over at naptime. Home–school journals, in which both parents and providers can make notes about a child's experiences and accomplishments, are another way that parents and teachers can keep each other informed about the stories that toddlers may want to hear or want help in telling.

BOOKS AS SPRINGBOARDS
FOR CONVERSATIONS

For the third time that day, Aileen agreed to the 2-year-olds' request to read *The Rainbow Goblins* (De Rico, 1994). It wasn't really a toddler book, but it was the children's favorite. The illustrations were gorgeous. The story as written was a bit violent, but the pictures were sufficiently ambiguous that Aileen could easily change the words. The book told the story of seven greedy goblins, each with his own color, who set out on a journey to eat the rainbow. They were supposed to be evil characters, but Aileen left that part out. Instead, she gave each goblin a unique voice and some unique gestures and sound effects to go with his unique color. She also used special voices to mark the highlights of the story—whispering for the secret plans, suspenseful for the impending thunderstorm, exaggerated slurps for gobbling the colors, awed at the rebirth of the rainbow. But the children did much of the reading and acting out by themselves.

"I wanna be Red," announced Alex. "I'm the leader. March. March. March. Everybody follow me."

Jody chimed in, "I'm Yellow. I'm the craftiest. What's crafty?"

Each time Aileen read the story, the children found something new to imitate, retell, or ask about.

On their last home visit, Mandy had brought Jamal *Blueberries for Sal* (McClosky, 1948), which they had read it together. For today's visit, Mandy brought a set of blocks. Jamal, who had been reading *Blueberries for Sal* all week with his grandmother, chose the blue one. "I'm little Sal," he announced. "This is my blueberry. Kerplink!"

Books play many roles in the lives of 2-year-olds. They can be familiar friends, providing comfort and relaxation at bedtime or naptime, during times of stress or long waiting periods, or whenever a child needs a break for "refueling." Books are often sources of amusement or inspiration—and may give children like Jamal ideas for active and imaginative play that continues beyond the book.

Some books are filled with pictures of interesting things that toddlers love to name—all kinds of road-building machines, trains and planes, pretty flowers, sea creatures, or creepy-crawlers. As parents and teachers add more information about the pictures in the books, a child's curiosity is piqued and her expertise extended. She may want to see real life examples, get other nonfiction books from the library, and incorporate her growing knowledge into pretend play routines.

The Books 2-Year-Olds Like Best

- Have colorful illustrations that are easy to identify and talk about

- Feature characters who behave like 2-year-olds and share their feelings

- Often tell reassuring stories about characters who are lost and then found, who run away and return, or who misbehave and are forgiven

- Introduce interesting words

- Contain words and phrases that are fun to say, such as "Kerplink . . . kerplank . . . kerplunk" (*Blueberries for Sal* [McClosky, 1948]), "And the big thing just said 'Snort'" (*Are You My Mother?* [Eastman, 1960]), or "I do not like them, Sam-I-Am" (*Green Eggs and Ham* [Seuss, 1960])

- Have distinctive covers so that children can find their favorites

- Have parts that children can imitate in pretend play

- May use literary language, such as "In the great, green room there was a telephone..." (*Goodnight Moon* [Brown, 1991]), "And they went out together in the deep, deep snow" (*The Snowy Day,* [Keats, 1962])

- Show many kinds of animals, sharks, dinosaurs, trucks, trains, houses, or members of other interesting categories

- Help children to be "experts" on favorite topics

- Have easy-to-follow patterns, sometimes with a twist at the end

- Often use literary conventions to mark the beginning (e.g., "Once upon a time . . . ") and the ending (e.g., "Good night.")

Some books are tailor-made for helping toddlers cope with strong feelings. A boy named David loved the book *No, David* (Shannon, 1998), about a child who was always getting into trouble and being told "No!" Finicky eaters, and those who have recently learned to enjoy more varied foods, can relate to books such as *Eat Up, Gemma* (Hayes & Ormerod, 1994), *Bread and Jam for Francis* (Hoban, 1964), *Gregory the Terrible Eater* (Sharmat & Aruego, 1989), and *Eating the Alphabet* (Ehlert, 1994). Adults can read the stories in such books as they are written or can vary the story to match an individual child's issues or attention span. Either way, books can help children put their own strong feelings into words and find ways to cope with the world's demands that preserve their dignity and emerging sense of self.

Indeed, parents and teachers will find that different kinds of books lend themselves to different kinds of conversations. Some provide opportunities for toddlers to show off their knowledge or join in the fun of reading by chiming in with the refrains they know. Some lend themselves to questions that ask children to look closely, describe details, or make inferences about what a character is doing and why. Adults can expand children's sentences and observations, acknowledging correct answers, adding a bit more, and correcting any misconceptions. "You're right. That caterpillar doesn't want any more food. His tummy is so full that it hurts!" "It looks like a horse, but I think it's supposed to be a cow. See, here's its udder, where the milk comes out." Many books provide opportunities to strengthen toddler logic by linking stories to other books and to real-world experiences. And some, of course, will spark conversations about upsetting or recurring issues.

TAMING THE TERRIBLE TWOS

"A language-focused home visiting program primes children for success in preschool and beyond," the program representative explained, as she tried to convince the governor's aide to increase the line item in the state budget. "It's not just language and literacy that are affected, but also social-emotional development. A child who can use her words is less likely to act out or be aggressive."

"I know," the young staffer replied. "I have a 2-year-old. She was always hitting her 8-year-old sister—I think just out of frustration. Like a lot of second-born children, I guess, she didn't talk as early as her big sister did. Just last month, she finally started to put words together and now—all of a sudden—we have a peaceful house again! I'm sure it's not anything we did—it's just, like you said, that now she can use her words."

Once toddlers can use their words to express their wishes and emotions, to reassure themselves when they are worried or scared, or to remind themselves of the proper ways to behave, they often become happier and easier to live with—at least most of the time. A gentle and well-timed reminder from an adult or older sibling can often help a frustrated, angry, or insistent toddler to use his words rather than hitting, screaming, or dissolving into tears.

No matter how good toddlers are at using their words, it isn't easy to be 2. You want so badly to do the things you see big people do, but you just aren't tall enough or strong enough or fast enough or good enough at remembering what to do first. People are always making you wait, or sit still, or share, or take "just a little"—and you aren't good at any of these things. Your puzzle pieces are supposed to go together, but sometimes they just won't. Your clothes are too tight or too scratchy or your favorite ones are in the wash. You try hard to be helpful and make people happy, but your "help" isn't always appreciated.

Mercer Mayer captured this perfectly in his book *Just for You* (1998), a favorite with toddlers and parents alike. Little Monster, the hero of that story, keeps trying to be helpful. She tries to carry the groceries, but the bag breaks. She tries repeatedly to clean up the messes she makes, but each attempt somehow leads to a bigger mess. She tries her best not to splash in the bathtub and soak the whole room, but her imagination and activity level just won't be contained. "There was a storm," she explains. Of course, Little Monster's efforts are both exasperating and endearing, and eventually she does find a way to do something "just for you" that every parent can truly appreciate.

Toddlers are beginning to understand the consequences of their actions, even if they can't always anticipate or control them. Many parents find that when their children are just beginning to put words together, it's best to keep explanations simple and to quickly redirect a toddler from a dangerous, annoying, or inappropriate activity to something more acceptable. "Sand is not for throwing. Say, 'Bye-bye, sand.' Time to play on the grass. You can throw your ball."

As children demonstrate the ability to link actions and consequences in their play and to use language to organize their behavior, parents can shift to more complex explanations and enlist their children's reasoning. "Sand is not for throwing. The wind can blow it into people's eyes. That hurts. What can we do with the sand that is safe and fun?" Although it won't avert every power struggle, this kind of guidance and discipline builds the child's competence—in acceptable behavior, self-regulation, and language.

Caleb hated transitions. He didn't want to stop playing with his
puzzles to eat lunch, or leave the table when lunch was finished, or
put down his books or blocks to put on his jacket and go outside,
or come in when outside play time ended. A 2-minute warning was
helpful, but not always enough. When she could, Caleb's caregiver
offered him simple choices: "Should we wash your hands at the
table or at the sink?" "Do you want to get your jacket or do you
want me to get it?" She knew that Caleb would be more likely to
comply if the choice was his—and also that he would be using his
words to express his choice or, on occasion, to propose a third
alternative. But sometimes Caleb simply refused to choose.

Fortunately, Caleb and his caregiver shared an off-beat sense
of humor. One day, when Caleb was being particularly recalcitrant
about getting ready to go home, she wrapped his jacket around
him. "Okay, Caleb. I'm turning you into a rolling pin. Roll, roll, roll
the dough." As she rolled a now giggling Caleb back and forth,
she gently tucked his arms into his sleeves.

Caleb's parents used a different but equally effective technique.
When Caleb resisted their efforts to prepare him for a change or
kept asking for more time long after the 2 minutes had elapsed,
they knew there was no point in reasoning with him. However, they
could reason with Garfield, the stuffed cat who accompanied Caleb
everywhere. "Garfield," Caleb's mother would say, "It's time for you
to go to child care. I know you don't want to be left behind today.
Your friend Sunshine will be there, and you can play with the
dinosaurs together. Do you want me to carry you, or do you want
Caleb to?" Most of the time, Caleb would quickly get into the act,
and help get Garfield to child care.

Intent on their own agendas and determined to assert their identities, toddlers often resist changes that they do not initiate. But most
are easily intrigued by humor or fantasy. With the tension diffused, it
is easier to find a compromise that both they and their parents or
teachers can accept.

Dr. Marilyn Segal, a pioneering infant psychologist and parent
educator, developed a sure-fire cure for her grandchildren's temper
tantrums. As soon as the children were old enough to imitate her
words and actions and appreciate her silliness, she taught them the
"right" way to have a tantrum. Making it clear that this was a game,
she led them step-by-step through the process, exaggerating the
motions and sound effects until the children could no longer contain
their giggles. The children loved the game. When a tantrum loomed
over a minor issue, their Nana would help the child put her complaint

into words. "Grump," she might say. "I hate having carrots on my pasta plate. I think I'll have a temper tantrum. First the arms . . . ." As long as the child was not in acute distress, the threatened tantrum would dissolve into shared laughter. The following poem, which is fun to act out together with a loud "whoooop!" for the scream, was written by Dr. Segal, with some help from her grandchildren and their parents.

How to Have a Temper Tantrum
How to have a tantrum
Is something every child should know.
If you don't know, I can teach you.
I'm a temper tantrum pro.

With my kind of tantrum, there's nothing to fear
I can do it without even shedding a tear.
Are you ready to try a tantrum now?
Then listen up! I will tell you how.

First wave your arms up in the air
With all the power you can spare.
The next thing to do is to stamp your feet.
Stamp so hard you break up the street.

Then after that you can gurgle and rumble
Shout "grump, grr-rump," and then start to grumble.
When you can't grumble for one minute more
Give one last grr-rump and fall on the floor.

Now let out a really ear-splitting scream

Just as loud as a whole football team.
Scream so loud that you're certain to scare
All of the people everywhere.

Then be real quiet for a second or two
To make sure that somebody's watching you.
You'll know that your tantrum was perfectly done
When you get the attention of everyone. (Bardige & Segal,
    2005, p. 27)

For real tantrums, the ones that reflect intense frustration or distress and that a child cannot control, Dr. Brazelton's advice has stood the test of time:

> It's often wisest to simply make sure he can't hurt himself, then walk out of the room. Soon after you leave, the tantrum or violent behavior is likely to subside. In a while, go back to him, pick him up to contain and love him, and sit down in a rocking chair to soothe him. You want him to know that you care, that you understand, and that tantrums are not something to be ashamed of or punished for. When he's able to listen, try to let him know that you can see how hard it is to be two or three and to be unable to make up one's own mind. But let him know that he will learn how and that meanwhile, it's okay.
>
> Brazelton & Sparrow, 2006, p. 278

USING LANGUAGE TO LEARN

- "What's that man's name? Where is he going? Why don't you know?"
- "Can I drive the bus?"
- "Does Corduroy miss his Mommy?"
- "Where's Little Sal's Daddy?"
- "Why is that boy crying?"
- "Why are you washing the pot?"
- "What's gonna happen?"

Children's questions are gifts. They let us know how children see the world and how we can enhance their understanding. They give us opportunities to respond to a child's interest and also introduce new words and concepts. Probably the best way to encourage them is to show interest, and to respond with straightforward answers that encourage further discussion.

Remember—with young children, especially—questions don't always start with *who, what, where, when, why,* or *how.* Children may ask their questions with a gesture, such as pointing accompanied by a quizzical look, a statement that ends with rising intonation (e.g., "Mama mad?") or a request for confirmation (e.g., "The moon comes out at night, right?"). Often, questions are asked through actions—such as holding up a broken toy or mixing different color paints to see what will happen.

Two-year-olds' questions are likely to be related to an immediate situation. They want to know the names of the people and objects they see around them or in their storybooks, as well as where they are going, what they are doing, and why. They want help in understanding how things work, how they can do the exciting things that they see big people doing, and how one event is related to another. They want to know whether the people, animals, and imaginary friends they encounter in the real world and in storybooks and videos have families and feelings and experiences like theirs and, if not, why not. As adults answer toddlers' explicit and implicit questions, they help them to "read the world" (Rosenkoetter & Knapp-Philo, 2006).

Adults can also ask children questions in many ways—by asking directly, by pointing out something interesting, by sharing our own curiosity and wonder. The most interesting questions—and those that build language—are the ones whose answers the questioner doesn't know in advance and really wants to learn. They are the questions that go beyond quizzing (e.g., "What color is that?") or issues of compliance (e.g., "Did you put your toys away?") to really engage thinking and curiosity.

- "What would you like to play today?"
- "Why do you think your friend is crying? How can we help him feel better?"
- "Why do you think it gets dark at night?"
- "Where do you think that airplane is going?"
- "What do we need for our tea party?"
- "Where do you think Spot will hide next?"
- "Who did you play with at child care today? What did you do together?"
- "Whose sock is this? Can you find another one that matches it?"
- "How do you think we can make this toy go?"
- "That looks like some sort of seed pod. Where did you find it? Do you think it came from a tree?"
- "If you were a very hungry caterpillar, what would you want to eat?"

LANGUAGE-RICH CHILD CARE PROGRAMS

The 2-year-olds in Miss Rachel's classroom have been reading the classics. Goldilocks and the Three Bears gave them a chance to work with mathematical concepts. As they played out the story with stuffed animals—giving the biggest bear the biggest bowl, the biggest chair, and the loudest voice—they arranged objects by size, worked with sets of three, recognized and created patterns, and practiced counting one object at a time. They read several different versions of the story, but in the end preferred their own—with Goldilocks becoming friends with the bears but learning some manners and knocking before entering.

They've moved on now—to The Three Little Pigs. Again, they've read several versions of the story (with some editing by their teacher, so that none of the pigs get eaten and the wolf escapes unscathed) and talked about the similarities and differences among the versions. They've made their own books, using stickers of pigs and wolves and pasting real straw and twigs onto their drawings of the houses. Of course, some children decided that there should be more than three pigs and that they should build a house or a village together. Some put walls around the village to keep the wolf away; others had the pigs make the wolf a birthday cake that they could all share.

As they worked on their books, Miss Rachel encouraged the children to explore the materials. Was straw soft or scratchy? Strong or brittle? Could they blow away a piece of straw or hay? Could they make a twig move if they blew really hard? Or if two children blew together? What about a brick? But the children didn't stop there. They tried to make model houses from the straw and twigs, but didn't get very far. They took turns showing off their strength as they hefted the heavy brick, then decided to build a house with the cardboard bricks in their block area. Their teacher helped them to lay out the foundation for the house. When they ran out of cardboard bricks, she helped them figure out how many they would need to borrow from another classroom to make it tall enough to stand up in. Miss Rachel then brought in a large carton so that the children could design and build a more permanent house. They decided to make it a rainbow house, and worked together to paint it in many colors.

When the house was finished, the children used it to reenact their own version of the story.

"Little pigs, little pigs, let me come in," said the wolf as she knocked gently.

"Not by the hair of my chinny chin chin," one little pig
responded.
"Please?" asked the wolf sweetly.
"Okay. You can come in. Want some birthday cake?"
"I'll huff and I'll puff and I'll blow out the candles."

Two-year-olds thrive in language-rich environments. No matter the setting—whether at home or at child care, in a center, family child care home, Early Head Start program, or a community play space—a language-rich environment includes people who are fun to play with. The group is small enough for the children to get to know their child and adult playmates well. Children's questions and discoveries are encouraged, taken seriously, and greeted with delight. Adults expand on children's ideas and seek ways to further challenge their thinking.

In settings such as these, adults and children do a lot of talking. Books; planned activities; and the objects, stories, and questions that children bring from home spark investigation, pretend play, and extended projects—all of which fuel information-rich, back-and-forth conversations among children and adults that build children's language and communicative competence.

Conversations occur in small groups or one to one, with a lot of time for toddlers to formulate their ideas and put them into words. Intimate spaces foster quiet exchanges, and more open places support active play and larger group activities. Continuity and predictability are balanced with challenge and surprise. Familiar objects, arrangements, routines, and activities invite children to play out favorite themes, deepen their knowledge, and practice using words they know. Unusual objects and arrangements, new books, outings, and visitors prompt the children to investigate and to ask new questions and also introduce words and ideas that stretch children's vocabularies. Songs, stories, objects, and caregiving routines that are culturally familiar support children's emerging identities and help them feel at home in the group. New foods, art materials, musical forms, and other unfamiliar experiences pique their curiosity and extend both language and coping skills.

There are "many right ways" (Modigliani & Moore, 2005) to create a language-rich child care environment. Some things are constant: warm relationships; interesting things to talk about; interested people to talk with; and a group that is small enough so that every child can explore at her own pace, develop enduring friendships, and have relaxed conversations with adults many times throughout each day. Other things vary: whether the children are all about the same age or range across several years; whether the setting looks like a classroom, a playground, a home, or some combination of these; whether the things the children are playing with are natural objects, home-made creations, household materials, or store-bought toys; and whether only one language is spoken, read, and sung or whether language-building activities take place in more than one language.

And some things that are becoming increasingly common in young children's worlds would be kept to a minimum or absent altogether from language-rich child care environments. In such an environment there wouldn't be much idle waiting or aimless wandering or standing in line quietly. The television, if one is present, would be off most of the time. If providers do show brief videos or children's television shows, they will be used like storybooks—to spark conversations and follow-up activities. There would not be a lot of recorded music, either, unless it is played at a child's request or used as part of a group activity or to signal a change of pace. Instead, children and adults will be singing, dancing, and playing instruments, putting their own motions and words to familiar rhymes and tunes, and enjoying inventive word play. Language-rich environments do not have a lot of worksheets or flashcards or "educational" toys that can only be played with one way to produce a correct response. Adults ask some of the questions, but the children themselves ask many of them, either with words or through gestures and play. Curious, receptive, observant teachers will be building on those questions to expand children's language and prompt further exploration.

Two-year-olds like to imitate each other, so several children may be playing with similar toys or making the same art projects. Still, the teachers will not be marching children through a set curriculum, so focused on completing one activity and setting up the next that they miss the opportunities for real conversation.

READING, WRITING, COUNTING, AND PROBLEM SOLVING

As a family child care provider with a degree in child development, Laurie was determined not to teach her 2-year-old daughter the alphabet. "There's too much emphasis today on pushing," she explained to the other parents. "Two-year-olds are interested in things they can touch, see, and do. We do lots of talking and reading and scribbling and hands-on investigation. Letters don't mean a lot at this point." One day, however, Laurie's daughter returned from a weekend visit with her grandparents singing the

ABC song. Soon Laurie discovered that some of the other 2-year-olds were singing it as well. Laurie realized that the alphabet was an important part of these children's culture—especially for those who had older siblings in kindergarten or first grade. She was surprised, though, when on one of their walks around the block, one of the children stopped and pointed to the letters on a manhole cover. "Look," the child said with excitement, "it's the alphabet." The other children repeated reverently, "The alphabet." Then, quite spontaneously, they all joined hands and sang the alphabet song.

Teachers like Laurie understand that instruction in ABCs and phonics is premature for most 2-year-olds. Just as it makes little sense to teach esoteric words and factoids to young children outside of the meaningful contexts of direct experience, stories, and picture books, it seems reasonable to hold off on teaching the components of written language until children have learned that print represents spoken words and words are made up of identifiable parts. But that doesn't mean that 2 is too early to introduce children to many forms of print—books, lists, messages, labels, captions, and even individual letters and alphabet displays.

Two-year-olds who see the important adults in their lives reading and discussing books, letters, magazines, labels, and advertisements and writing checks, notes, to-do lists, appointment schedules, and e-mails want to imitate these activities. Computers, calculators, and telephones—which combine letters and numbers with buttons that can be pushed—are likely to be irresistible. And, if reading is defined to include identifying books by their covers, finding favorite cereals on grocery store shelves, recognizing other "environmental print" such as store logos and stop signs, and reciting memorized lines or even whole books while turning the pages appropriately, then many 2-year-olds are adept and eager readers. Similarly, if random keyboarding and the little squiggles and chicken scratches that many 2-year-olds append as a signature to their scribbled artworks or proudly identify as "letters" count as "writing," then many children are writing by their third birthdays.

Two-year-olds who play with alphabet blocks or ABC books may learn letter names, just as they learn the names of other objects and pictures, but it will likely be several years before this knowledge is of much use to them. What they are learning about speaking, listening, reading, and writing as they share books and conversations with responsive adults and imitate valued adult activities is of far greater importance.

Amina had only a few years of schooling as a child. Although she had learned to speak English in her adopted country, her reading of even the simplest texts was halting at best. When a home visitor arrived with a book for Amina's 2-year-old daughter, Ayana, Amina's first reaction was panic. Would she be expected to read to her daughter already? Couldn't she just wait for her daughter to be old enough to learn to read in school? Amina listened closely as the home visitor explained that reading aloud on a daily basis was one of the most important things parents could do to help their children learn to read. Holding Ayana on her lap, Amina listened intently as the home visitor read the simple, repetitive text and encouraged Ayana to repeat some of the words. Both Ayana and Amina urged the home visitor to read the book several times.

On the next home visit, Amina showed the visitor how she and Ayana read the book together, exactly as they had been shown. But she declined to read the new book, insisting that the home visitor do it. It took several months for Amina to feel comfortable enough with the home visitor to admit that she had been memorizing the books. Surprised and deeply moved, the home visitor assured Amina that her enthusiastic "reading" and her commitment to helping her 2-year-old develop a love of books and stories were exactly what Ayana needed.

What is true of literacy is also true of math. Numbers, like letters, are the tip of an iceberg whose subsurface mass is far greater than its more obvious protuberance. Toddlers who hear number names in counting songs and ordinary conversations and see numerals on elevators, telephones, door frames, and picture-book pages may learn to recognize number words as such, to recognize some numerals, and to count forward or even backward by rote. Basic concepts of size, sequence, quantity, one-to-one correspondence, and measurement are learned over time through direct play, active problem solving, and related conversation.

Miss Rachel's students—who matched the biggest bed with the biggest bear, gave each bear a chair and a bowl of porridge, and figured out how many blocks they needed to borrow to complete their house—were working with the mathematical concepts underlying counting and arithmetic. Similarly, when toddlers figure out how to make block towers and bridges that don't fall down, traverse interesting obstacle courses, find the right-sized wrench to tighten a bolt or a stepping stool that will enable them to reach a high shelf, put together a simple puzzle or sort the family socks, ride a tricycle or scooter, or use sand molds to make a castle, they are developing concepts of size, weight, direction, sequence, pattern, experimentation, and problem solving that are at the core of mathematics and science.

Adults can help by using mathematical vocabulary in their ordinary conversations with children:

- Number and quantity words such as *one, two, twenty-five, half, few, several, many,* and *hundred*

- Size words such as *tall, fat, tiny, huge, long, wide, heavy, skinny,* and *gigantic*

- Space and direction words such as *near, in, under, above, around, left, straight, middle,* and *where*

- Comparative words such as *more, very, worse, bigger,* and *fastest*

- Shape words such as *square, circle, round, oval, zigzag, squiggly,* and *triangle*

- Measurement words such as *inches, quart, pound, temperature,* and *liter*

- Time words such as *when, now, soon, yesterday, tomorrow, after, then, year,* and *minute*

- Problem-solving words such as *match, fit, figure out, count, add, take away, how much, why, even,* and *enough*

Adults can also help by being alert to what children are trying to figure out or accomplish and available to help when the problems children encounter or create become overly challenging or frustrating. Telling a child what to do is usually less helpful than coaching him by helping him describe the problem, asking leading questions, noting partial successes, suggesting next steps or alternative ways to frame the problem, or demonstrating a key step without solving the whole problem for the child. Often an older sibling or friend will be able to help by showing the toddler a trick or making the problem easier.

Can You Help Me Fix My Wagon?
My wagon's wheel is wobbly
It's not exactly tight.
Will you help me fix it?
Can you help me make it right?

I wonder why it wobbles
And what we need to do.
Can we fix it with a hammer?
Does it need an extra screw?

When we have fixed my wagon
We both can sit inside.

It will be so exciting
To take a wagon ride. (Bardige & Segal, 2005, p. 168)

Of course, one of the best ways to support budding scientists and mathematicians is to set the stage for exploration, encourage them to talk about their approaches and discoveries, and share their delight when they achieve their goals or produce unexpected outcomes.

TWENTY FUN THINGS TO DO WITH OLDER TODDLERS AND TWOS

1. *Play a memory game:* Place a few small items on a table. Then ask the child to close her eyes while you hide one or two in your hand. See if she can guess what you are holding. Then let her take a turn. At first, she may think your ability to figure out what she is holding is magic, but after a while she will realize that you can tell what is missing by looking at what is left. Try using items that are all the same and asking the child to tell you how many you are holding.

2. *Play a guessing game:* Put a small item in a bag. Ask the toddler to reach in and try to guess what the item is without looking at it. Ask leading questions to support his thinking: "What does it feel like?" "Is it hard or soft?" "Does it have wheels?" "What do you think it's made of?" "What else do you notice?"

3. *Make Jell-O together:* Read the directions one step at a time and talk about each step. Talk about what happens as the powder dissolves and as the Jell-O cools and begins to set. Try making different colors and using cookie cutters to cut out different shapes. Make up fun names for your creations: "jiggle wiggle worms," "twinkly winkly stars," "cherry-berry yum drops," "green goop."

4. *Experiment with sounds:* Use your voices to make loud sounds and soft sounds, high sounds and low sounds, long sounds and short sounds, fast sounds and slow sounds. Make rain sounds by squeezing water from a sponge onto different surfaces. Imitate other sounds such as popcorn popping, dogs barking, buses going by, and footsteps approaching. Make simple instruments by using wooden or metal spoons to hit pot lids, aluminum pie plates, oatmeal boxes, or empty and water-filled plastic bottles. Fill different containers with rice or beans to make shakers. Talk about all of the different sounds you can make.

5. *Experiment with different consistencies:* Try making different consistencies of sand or mud in a sand box, water table, kiddie pool, or large bin or at a beach. Introduce different tools for sifting, molding, digging, stirring, building, carrying, shaping, sprinkling, soaking, splattering, and poking. Use sticks or small objects to write or draw or to adorn your creations. Use words such as *sticky, gooey, damp, powdery, thick, runny, slippery, lumpy, fill, shape, pat, decorate, bury,* and *tunnel* as you plan and play together.

6. *Wash things:* Give a toddler bins or pails of soapy and clean water and let her wash toys or doll clothes, or engage her in washing large items such as riding toys with soapy water, rags, and a hose. Add tools such as spray or squirt bottles, sponges, wash cloths, scrub brushes, towels, and a clothes line. On a sunny day, make rainbows in the hose spray or watch drops and puddles evaporate. Use words such as *scrub, rinse, drip, drop, splash, squeeze, wring, wipe, dirty,* and *shiny* as you talk with the toddler about what she is doing.

7. *Create a "gas station" for tricycles and other riding toys:* Most 2-year-olds aren't fussy about realism—you can use a hose, jump rope, or empty watering can to fill the "gas tanks," a turkey baster or cardboard tube to put "air" into the tires, and plastic tools or even unsharpened pencils to "check the oil," "tune up the engine," or "repair" anything that is broken. When favored riding toys are in short supply, many children are happy to take a turn as the "gas station attendant," with a little adult support.

8. *Fingerpaint with shaving cream or whipped cream:* With these materials, children can safely fingerpaint on a table or tray—or even on their faces and bodies—without making too much of a mess. A small amount of food coloring can add to the fun as a toddler works individually or with others to mix different colors. As you observe a child or fingerpaint with her, describe the shifting patterns you see and encourage her to do the same: "Here comes a long, wiggly snake." "Here comes a bunny—hop, hop, hop." Remember that for 2-year-olds, the fun is in the process, not the final result.

9. *Make playdough:* Let the toddler help with the process by pouring in the flour, salt, and water, deciding what color food coloring to add, stirring the batter, and kneading the dough. Give the toddler balls of soft dough, and encourage him to roll them flat, using a cylindrical block or a small rolling pin. Give him some small (nonswallowable) objects such as old keys, jar tops, plastic

letters, toy trucks and animals, cookie cutters, craft sticks, shells, pebbles, and large beads. Show him how to use these objects to make impressions and designs in the playdough, to cut out different shapes, or to decorate playdough cakes. Help the toddler use his words to ask for objects he wants, talk about what he is doing, and tell others about his creations.

10. *Make books, collages, and mobiles:* Help the toddler with these projects by cutting pictures from magazines, catalogs, calendars, greeting cards, product labels, and advertising circulars; pasting them onto construction paper or index cards; and then stapling or tying the pages together or hanging cards from a coat hanger. Encourage her to choose pictures related to a theme, such as "my favorite things," "things to eat for breakfast," "farm animals," or "my favorite color." Talk with the toddler about the pictures she selected, and help her find others that she would like to add. Be sure to encourage the toddler to share her books or artistic creations with family and friends.

11. *Make doll furniture:* Use diaper boxes, tissue boxes, or other cartons to build beds, chairs, cradles, boats, kitchen appliances, or carriages for dolls and stuffed animals. Join a toddler in pretend play and conversation as he takes care of his babies.

12. *Go on a hike:* Pack up a wagon or backpack with snacks and with plastic bags, pails, or other containers for collecting interesting objects and a journal or camera (real or pretend) for recording interesting sights and experiences. Sing traveling songs. Hunt for rocks, seeds, shells, bugs, different colored houses or flowers, or shapes such as triangles, squares, circles, and octagons. Stop to watch people at work. Make up stories about the real or magical creatures that live in the rocks, trees, sidewalk cracks, roof tops, or under the ground. When you return, help the toddler make a collage or scrapbook so that she can tell others what she discovered on her hike.

13. *Meet the people in your neighborhood:* Introduce the toddler to the shopkeepers, neighbors, crossing guards, and pets you know, and encourage familiar people you meet to talk with him. You may need to translate for children whose pronunciation is still idiosyncratic, but try to let them speak for themselves.

14. *Make a playhouse or fort:* Help the child make a playhouse or fort out of a large box, by blocking a corner with a chair, or by draping a blanket over a table. Encourage her to stock her special place with pillows and with favorite books and toys. When you

pay a visit, be sure to knock or ring the doorbell and to bring a "special delivery."

15. *Read an animal book together and act out the animal motions it describes:* Good animal books include *Pretend You're a Cat* (Marzollo & Pinkney, 1997) and *From Head to Toe* (Carle, 1999). Practice making the animal's noises. Give the toddler a chance to act out motions on cue, and also to say some of the words while you take a turn acting out the motions. Have your own animal parade with others, with each person being a different animal. You can enhance the parade with animal hats (a headband with ears works fine, and is easy to make). Talk to each animal in ways that encourage further pretending. "Hi, Cat. Yes, I heard you meow. Does that mean you want some milk? Here. Lap it all up! You were very thirsty! Do you want some more?"

16. *Make a stage for performances:* It can be as simple as a low platform, mat, or throw rug. Supply some simple clothing that children can use for dance or circus costumes, with a nearby mirror so that they can check out their regalia. Put on a CD, sing a song, or encourage the children to make their own music with voices and/or instruments. Be sure to clap when the performance is done and then ask for an encore.

17. *Help children act out a simple, familiar story:* Often this is easiest when an adult takes the narrator's role, cuing children when to play their parts. "The three bears go into the kitchen. Father bear looks in his bowl and says . . . ."

18. *Explore shadows:* Encourage a toddler to watch his own and others' shadows as you take a walk on a sunny day. Can he step on your shadow? On his own? What does the toddler's shadow do when he walks frontwards or backwards or turns around? Do other things, such as trees and cars, have shadows? What happens to his shadow when he stands in a tree's shadow? Use a flashlight to explore shadows indoors.

19. *Plant a garden:* Radishes, marigolds, and beans germinate fairly rapidly, and children can start them in paper cups or directly in the garden. Children can plant fast-growing herbs such as mint, parsley, basil, and chives in a window box or container or along a path and pick them to flavor their mud pies and tea party drinks. As you involve children in the digging, planting, watering, checking on growth, and harvesting, you can talk about what the plants need to grow and all of the ways that people

help them. Encourage the children to look for changes in their plants and talk with you about what they see.

20. *Talk about when the toddler was a baby:* Just out of babyhood themselves, most 2-year-olds are fascinated with infants. Capitalize on this interest by reading books about human and animal babies; telling stories about when the toddler was little; talking about all the things that she can do that babies can't; playing with baby dolls or baby stuffed animals together; and, if possible, giving her carefully supervised opportunities to interact with real babies. When a baby is around, enlist the older child's help in figuring out what the baby wants; getting things for him to play with; engaging him in simple, back-and-forth routines that are fun for them both; and recognizing when it is time for the baby to take a rest.

A WEALTH OF WORDS

"Travis, why are you making me do all the work?" his caregiver asked one day when Travis was being particularly demanding. Travis responded without missing a beat, proudly (mis)using his newest word: "Cause Travis is being generous."

Words are "brain food" for 2-year-olds. Having rich, engaging conversations with all of the important people in their lives helps to build the vocabularies, information stores, and neurological connections that they will draw on as they face more complicated problems; weave more elaborate stories and imaginative play scenarios; and, over the next 3 or 4 years, learn to read.

In the period between 18 months and 3½ years, children rapidly acquire words, concepts, language patterns, and the ability to use language in a variety of ways for a variety of purposes. Home visiting, child care, and parent–child programs that target language during this time have had remarkable, long-term results. Comprehensive programs that combine approaches can add still more value.

For children in low-income families, children whose parents have had little education, or children with moderate developmental challenges associated with difficulties at birth, programs such as the Parent–Child Home Program, Parents as Teachers, AVANCE, Even Start, the Abecedarian Project, the Infant Health and Development Program, and Early Head Start have reduced or erased early disadvantages. In a host of longitudinal studies, graduates of these programs have achieved average or above test scores at school entry and in the elementary grades. Those who have been followed into adulthood have graduated high school at similar rates as more privileged peers, and often have gone on to succeed in higher education (Bardige, 2005). For middle-income children who are typically developing, a small but intensive study (Vernon-Feagans et al., 2007) showed that child care quality had a notable effect on language development. Language developed faster—both in terms of vocabulary and in terms of grammatical complexity and functional usage—for children in higher quality child care programs with fewer children per teacher, better trained teachers, and more one-to-one conversation than for children of similar background whose child care was of lower quality. For toddlers of all backgrounds, higher quality child care that is richer in language supports is associated with higher achievement in the early elementary school years.

The toddler years are the time when children first fall in love with words. They learn that some words can impress, others can shock, and still others can provoke laughter or defuse a conflict. "Magic words" such as *please* and *"Scooz me"* make it easier for them to get what they want, whereas words and phrases such as *mine, my turn,* and *go away* protect them from losing what they have or getting what they don't want. They learn that some words have special functions, such as counting or naming colors, and they often recognize a word as a color or number word before learning its precise meaning. Their favorite books, songs, and family stories are filled with words that sound pretty and are fun to repeat.

"Aram Sam Sam" is a nonsense song from Morocco, enjoyed by children throughout the world. The words are often accompanied by simple gestures—clapping on "ram sam sam," rolling hands on "guli guli," and putting hands up beside the face on "rafi."

Aram Sam Sam
A ram sam sam, a ram sam sam
Guli guli guli guli guli ram sam sam
A ram sam sam, a ram sam sam
Guli guli guli guli guli ram sam sam

A rafi, a rafi,
Guli guli guli guli guli ram sam sam
A rafi, a rafi,
Guli guli guli guli guli ram sam sam

"Down by the Station," written by Lee Ricks and Slim Gailand in 1948 and widely adapted, is fun for toddlers who are enamored by trains and like to shout out sound effects. Many toddlers enjoy the challenge of getting their tongues around the interesting word *puffer-bellies.* As they learn to say this word, they can also practice puffing like little round-bellied steam engines.

Down by the Station
Down by the station
Early in the morning.
See the little puffer-bellies
All in a row.

Hear the station master
Sounding out his warning
Chug chug. Toot toot.
Off they go!

The following song was created by a 2-year-old word lover—with some help from his mother—as they raked leaves and played together in the piles. It's easy to add to, or to adapt for puddles, mud, or snow.

Playing in the Leaves
I'm raking all the leaves.
I'm shaking all the leaves.
I'm taking all the leaves.

I'm jumping in the leaves.
I'm thumping in the leaves.
We're bumping in the leaves.

I'm blowing lots of leaves.
I'm throwing lots of leaves.
It's snowing lots of leaves.

I'm singing in the leaves.
I'm swinging in the leaves.
I'm flinging all the leaves.

We're playing in the leaves.
We're swaying in the leaves.
I'm staying in the leaves.

Songs like "If You're Happy and You Know It" and "Shake My Sillies Out" (Raffi, 1988) are easy to extend and adapt with words that capture a toddler's strong emotions: excited, worried, curious, playful,

angry, tired, proud, grumpy, fidgety, sorry, sad, hurting, fearful, confi-
dent, calm. A song like "Shake My Sillies Out" also prompts word play.
As children use made-up words such as *sillies* and *waggles* and invent
similar ones such as *saddies, twitchies,* and *grumpies* to add to the song,
they are also learning about how words are put together and practicing both sound and grammatical patterns.

If You're Happy and You Know It (Variation)
If you're happy and you know it, clap your hands.
If you're happy and you know it, clap your hands.
If you're happy and you know it,
Then your face will surely show it.
If you're happy and you know it, clap your hands!

If you're angry and you know it, stomp your feet.
If you're angry and you know it, stomp your feet.
If you're angry and you know it,
Then your face will surely show it.
If you're angry and you know it, stomp your feet!

If you're excited and you know it, jump for joy.
If you're excited and you know it, jump for joy.
If you're excited and you know it,
Then your face will surely show it.
If you're excited and you know it, jump for joy!

It's fun and often easy for children to learn new words that are
inserted into the well-rehearsed patterns of their favorite songs and
nursery rhymes. Similarly, toddlers enjoy learning lots of words within a category—such as vegetables, earth-moving machines, sharks, or
crayon colors. It is not unusual for a 2-year-old with a special interest
to be able to identify exotic animals or many kinds of sports cars and
to know some words that will be foreign to most adults.

The more children learn about the sounds, meanings, and uses of
the words they know, the easier it will be for them to learn similar
words when they encounter them in speech and, later on, in writing.
The more words they know, the more likely they will be to notice and
learn from such similarities and the easier it will be for them to learn
new words. Engaging eager toddlers in conversation, storytelling, and
word play builds learning patterns that accelerate language development and prime children to be successful readers. Equally important,
it enables parents and teachers to appreciate and support toddlers'
unfolding minds and wonderfully individual personalities.

"What color are my eyes?" Dr. Sherry asked his 2-year-old patient. Knowing that this child was verbally precocious and enjoyed showing off his knowledge, the doctor was a bit surprised when Brenan didn't answer, but he was careful not to show it. He could see that Brenan was thinking, so he waited . . . and waited . . . and waited. Finally, Brenan solemnly announced his conclusion: "Turquoise."

When Professor JoAnne Knapp Philo told this story at a national infant/toddler conference, she ended with a reminder to listen closely and patiently to what 2-year-olds have to say. "If we don't give them enough of a chance to respond," she explained, "we may miss the gems."

What Will They Think of Next?

(2½–5 Years)

On the way to the ice cream store, Marin, not quite 4, amuses herself by talking with her Oscar the Grouch puppet. "We're going to get some ice cream, Oscar. I'm getting chocolate with Oreos." Then, speaking for Oscar, "That's yucky, Marin. I'm getting spinach with green sprinkles and mud sauce."

Marin's mom joins the game: "Spinach ice cream with green sprinkles and mud sauce? Doesn't sound too tasty to me! I wouldn't like to eat mud!"

Noticing that they are approaching a stop sign, Marin asks, "What about signs, Mom? Do you like to eat signs?"

"I don't know about signs. I think they might be a little too crunchy for my teeth."

"What about traffic lights?"

"Oh, those are scrumptious—mint, butterscotch, and cherry—my favorite flavors."

"What about cars? Do you like to eat cars?"

"Well, that's a bit of a challenge. They're very tasty, but if I ate a whole one, my tummy would get so full that it might explode! Maybe I could split one with Oscar. Do you think he'd like that?"

By age 3 or 3¹/₂, most children can make themselves understood by adults and peers. They may still mispronounce some sounds, use pronouns such as *I* and *him* incorrectly or not at all, or make systematic errors that show that they understand the rules of grammar but have not yet mastered all of the exceptions (e.g., "We goed to the store.") They may still have trouble putting their thoughts into words or making their tongues keep up with their brains, and so they may hesitate or stutter, especially when they most want to get the words out. Still, they can talk to themselves both aloud and silently, use sentences of four or more words, use words to describe particular objects and events, and ask several different kinds of questions. They rely on language as their primary means of communication.

With their rapidly expanding conversation and storytelling skills, 3-year-olds become relentless questioners and constant pretenders. Language becomes a means of investigation, as children not only ask questions but also make predictions; construct explanations; formulate hypotheses; and try out words, ideas, and roles. Pretending is more than "just playing"—it is an essential way of making sense of the world, practicing new words and concepts, expressing ideas and feelings, dealing with emotional upsets, and making friends.

By age 4, most children are competent conversationalists. They know how to engage a conversation partner, take conversational turns, and contribute enough to keep the conversation going. They can stick to a subject—or change it if they choose. They can report or question matter-of-factly or use their words to pretend and be silly. They speak differently to different people and on different occasions— whispering in church, using their politest words and voices with unfamiliar adults, speaking Chinese to one parent and Vietnamese to the other, or using English at school but a combination of Spanish and English at home.

They can also speak differently *as* different people. As Oscar, Marin used a gruff tone of voice as she expressed her preference for spinach ice cream. Most of their speech is clear enough and most of their grammar and word usage are conventional enough so that the adults and children who they interact with on a regular basis can understand them. They use language to describe and explain, wheedle and convince, discover, invent, and—especially—to pretend.

Children like Marin, who routinely learn interesting words as they engage in language play with the important adults in their lives, are likely to command large vocabularies. As the ice cream store conversation reveals, Marin's mother is an adept language teacher. Responding to her daughter's playful questions, she naturally included interesting words such as *tasty, crunchy, scrumptious, butterscotch, challenge,* and *explode* as she built on Marin's ideas. Her mother's willingness to accept and build on Marin's increasingly outlandish premises made the game fun for both of them. If you asked Marin's mother, though, she would say that she was not intentionally teaching, just enjoying her daughter and trying to keep her happy.

Three- and 4-year-olds who know many words and can use their words effectively in conversation and pretend play enjoy a social as well as cognitive advantage. They are fun for other children to play with because they can come up with interesting ideas and keep a story going. At the same time, they can pick up ideas from other children and from the surrounding environment and weave them into their play. Their facility with words enables them to ask interesting questions and to offer comments and suggestions that prompt their teachers and playmates to provide them with more information, ideas, and imaginative directions.

Books, oral stories, silly rhymes and word play, props, playmates, and real-world experience all fuel children's pretending. Preschool play is further enriched when adults accept children's invitations to get involved—not just as an appreciative audience or bringers of needed props or readers of stories to act out—but as participants in the creation of imaginary worlds. Through playful engagement with adults and older children, preschoolers stretch their vocabularies, learn and practice more sophisticated sentence structures, enlarge and deepen their understanding of how the world works, and hone their ability to construct both reality-based explanations and fanciful stories. At the same time, they learn the verbal forms of their community's oral and written traditions— forms for storytelling; factual reporting; word play; humor; negotiation; description; questioning; giving directions; and presenting evidence, interpretations, and conclusions. As they play with peers and younger children, or alone with dolls, toys, construction materials, and ordinary household objects, they practice their languages and hone their performance skills.

Tips for Talking with Young Preschoolers

- Respect young preschoolers' needs for uninterrupted play, alone or with a peer—but join in when you are invited or when a child gives you an opening.

- Make a connection. Comment on or ask about something the child is doing, playing with, wearing, or investigating. You can join her pretend play game by taking on a role, talking to a doll, or asking about the story she is creating.

- Share interesting information. Offer an observation or explanation that expands on the child's idea or connects his experiences with yours.

- Respond to the tone of the child's communications as well as the literal meaning. Is she being fanciful, inquisitive, silly, earnestly serious, matter of fact, playful, or distressed?

- Ask some open-ended questions that make the child think.

- Encourage the child's questions and answer them succinctly. Give him a chance to ask if he wants to know more.

- Simplify your explanations but not your vocabulary. Use concrete examples and analogies to help the child relate abstract ideas to things she has touched, seen, or experienced.

- Let the child's curiosity or fanciful creativity spark your own.

- Pay full attention.

- Introduce interesting words as you build upon the child's ideas.

- Help the child see how objects and ideas relate to each other by using words such as "alike," "similar," "opposite," "therefore," "but," and "since" and categorical terms such as "furniture," "vehicles," "shapes," and "tools." This is particularly helpful to second language learners, as it supports them in connecting what they know in one language with what they are learning in another (August, Calderón, & Carlo, 2002).

- Model kind, polite language and appropriate ways of speaking in different situations.

- Don't correct the child's grammar; pronunciation; or choice of vocabulary, language, or dialect. Instead, respond to the meaningful communication in your own words, using correct terms.

- Use the language(s) or dialect(s) in which you are comfortably fluent and can explain complex ideas, play with sounds and words, and expand the child's vocabulary.

- Support all of the child's languages or dialects by responding to what he says and means to say when he uses his preferred language or attempts to speak a new one; incorporating his favorite words and phrases into your conversations; sharing books, poems, and songs in all of his languages and dialects; and providing frequent opportunities for him to converse with peers and adults who can enrich his use of the language or dialect in which your fluency is limited.

- TALK—AND LISTEN—A LOT!

THE MAGIC YEARS

Three-year-old Arran couldn't wait to get outside. It was a beautiful, bright fall day, and his father and big brother were already outside raking leaves into a big pile just right for jumping into. As his mother helped him put on his coat and shoes, Arran composed a poem that captured his anticipated delight.

It's not the leaves
Your father raked for you
It's the sun of the morn.

It's not your swing set
That flies you high in the sky
It's the sun of the morn.

When they wrote the poem down later, Arran's mother helped him add a final verse:

It's not the clouds
It's not the trees
It's not the flowers and the leaves
It's the fun in the sun of the morn.

For most children, the achievement of basic proficiency in their first language (and often a second language or dialect as well) coincides with a flowering of creativity. Their understanding of language, storytelling, and symbolism allows them to enjoy and create pretend stories and to imagine things that couldn't possibly exist. At the same time, their rudimentary understanding of the laws of physics and the nature of space and time makes it difficult for them to know for sure where reality ends and fantasy begins. In their minds it is still possible to take the "biggest" half, blow the clouds away, or cause an event by wishing it. Animals can talk—at least if they are magic or live in faraway places or long ago times. Fairies can fly and grant wishes, and children can become superheroes who save the day. Developmental psychologist Selma Fraiberg's (1996) term "the magic years" captures not only the magical thinking that is characteristic of young children but also the magical inventiveness that so delights their parents and teachers.

THE HUNDRED LANGUAGES OF CHILDREN

- Alvin carefully lines up knives and forks and "drives" a salt shaker over his "roads" and "bridges."

- Myla asks her mother to buy some extra bananas for her invisible friends: Ackie, Mimi, the babies, and their sisters.

- Wearing his favorite towel cape on his shoulders and brandishing a wooden spoon sword, "Super Justin" scares away "bad guys" and rescues a truck that was falling off of a kitchen counter "cliff."

- Naina, who has never been to school, seats all of her dolls in a row and gives them a "reading lesson."

- With a little help from his older brother, Kevin turns a broken ping pong ball into a football helmet for his toy frog, complete with his favorite team's logo.

- Mia proudly picks several radishes from the garden and mixes them with water, leaves, and a sprinkle of sand to make "soup" for her family.

- Two 4-year-olds—a girl and a boy—were playing together and wanted to play different games. In this version of a common dilemma, the girl said, "Let's play next-door neighbors." "I want to play pirates," the boy replied. "Okay," said the

girl, "then you can be the pirate that lives next door."
(Gilligan, 1993, p. 9)

Creativity comes naturally to preschoolers. As they play with words, objects, people, and all kinds of "stuff," they seek out new ways to use materials and find joy in expressing themselves in unique ways. In fact, the attributes that developmental psychologists and educators identify as characteristic of highly creative children (Eliason & Jenkins, 2003) describe many children between the ages of 2½ and 5. These children

- Have the ability to perceive unusual and broad relationships, unconstrained by conventional categories

- Have a different time–space perspective

- Have a keen sense of humor and an eye and ear for the ridiculous or outlandish

- Ask a lot of questions

- Enjoy first-hand investigative activities that provide the opportunity to probe, explore, discover, and create

- Show great ingenuity and imagination

- Are eager for adventure

- Are often persistent in reaching a goal

- Use elaborate language and often express themselves in unique ways

In Reggio Emilia, Italy, a town that has become world renowned for the quality of its preschools and the amazing artistic productions of its preschoolers, teachers intentionally nurture the sense of wonder and multifaceted creativity that they see as characteristic of young children. Teachers observe children closely at work and play to see what they are exploring and where their interests lie. Then, with the curiosity and care of scientists, the teachers set about to discover what the children perceive, understand, and are eager to master. They offer children "provocations"—interesting materials, experiences, and challenges that will get them thinking, exploring, and building. They help the children to represent their ideas in "the hundred languages of children" (Edwards, Gandini, & Forman, 1998)—words, drawing, clay, dance, map making, song, block building, drama, and a host of other media. As teachers talk with children about their creations, they often urge the children to look again. What features of a real or imagined object did they capture in their drawing or sculpture? What might they want to add or change to better represent what they are trying to show?

Many preschools, elementary schools, and arts education programs in the United States have adopted a "Reggio model" or a "Reggio-inspired" curriculum.

ADVANCES IN PRETEND PLAY AND STORYTELLING

Three-year-old Kylie loves to play doctor. She begins by donning her "white coat" (an old shirt of her father's) and gathering her "doctor stuff"—a toy otoscope, thermometer, and stethoscope and an empty vitamin bottle that she uses for "medicine." "Is anyone sick?" she calls hopefully.

"I think I might be sick," her father responds.

"Let me see," says Dr. Kylie. "I need to feel your head and take your temperature to see if you have a fever."

"Oh, yes," Kylie continues after some forehead feeling, temperature taking, and ear checking. "Your face is all red and so is your ear. And you have a bad temperature. Here's some medicine. Do you feel better yet?"

"Yes," her father replies. "I think I do. But you'd better listen to my heart and breathing with your stethoscope, just in case. I might have a touch of bronchitis."

Dr. Kylie listens intently to her father's heart, lungs, back, and tummy with her toy stethoscope. "Yep. You got brackitis. Here's some more medicine. Feel better now?"

"Oh, yes. Thank you," her father replies.

"Okay, bye," says Kylie.

Five minutes later, Dr. Kylie is calling for her next patient. "Anybody sick?" Her father obligingly repeats the play, this time complaining of a sore throat.

After several episodes, Kylie asks her father a question that has been puzzling her. "Remember when we were watching Toy Story? That mean boy, Sid, said he was a doctor when he was doing surgery on his toys. But he didn't have any doctor stuff, so how could he be a doctor without his stuff?"

At their family child care center, 4-year-old Sasha convinces 2-year-old Jenna to play doctor with her.

Sasha:	"I'll be the doctor and you be the patient, okay? Let's pretend that you are really, really sick and I'm going to take care of you and make you all better."
Jenna:	"Okay."
Sasha (in her doctor voice):	"Oh, Jenna. I'm sorry you're not feeling well. Lie down on the examining table so I can make you better." (Jenna lies down and looks expectantly at Sasha.)
Sasha (in her normal voice):	"Pretend you have a really bad earache. When I look in your ear, you cry and say, 'Ouch!'"

Both Kylie and Sasha are accomplished pretenders. They know the doctor script, and can use appropriate props, words, gestures, actions, and tone of voice as they enact the role. Like most young 3-year-olds, Kylie enjoys playing the same game over and over with minor variations. She has a firm conception of what doctors do and how they behave. They are supposed to be nice, not mean, and they always wear their "doctor stuff." Kylie's father's part is scripted as well—he is supposed to complain of illness, point out a specific part of his body that needs attention, submit to the exam, take his medicine willingly, and feel better. But Kylie also gives her father openings for creativity: He can come up with a variety of complaints and request a variety of treatments. As Kylie's father plays his role, he introduces words and play ideas that expand Kylie's vocabulary and enrich her understanding.

Sasha, at 4, is not only adept at playing doctor but also able to coach a younger friend in playing her game. Although her plot is similar to Kylie's, Sasha creates a more elaborate emotional drama. She and her partner need to agree not only on what roles they will play but also on how they will enact these roles. As the play progresses, Sasha periodically steps out of the pretend frame to instruct her partner. Because her partner is a compliant younger child, Sasha can dictate the topic and direction of her story; she doesn't need to negotiate roles or take her partner's pretend words and actions into account as she would with a peer who wanted to express her own ideas.

As children practice pretending, their plots become more complex and their play more sophisticated. A game of "doctor" may involve an ambulance ride to the hospital for an operation or a cast for a broken leg. Pirates may set out on a long sea voyage, rescue a man overboard from hungry sharks, take time out to create a treasure map, and then hunt for their buried treasure. Favorite games are enhanced by new props, variations introduced by different partners, and the questions and suggestions of observers who may be called on to supply a needed prop, fix a costume, or referee an argument about the direction of the story.

New games may be sparked by storybooks or real-life experiences, overheard conversations, interesting new props or new combinations (e.g., toy dinosaurs in the sand box, a fire hat in the play kitchen), or children's questions and concerns. With settings ranging from ancient castles to futuristic space ships; from deserts to rain forests to polar ice fields; from mountain tops to ocean depths; and from everyday homes, schools, stores, and basketball courts to elaborate fantasy worlds, children play out stories of work and play, family relationships, dramatic rescues, good guys versus bad guys, discovery, and celebration. Parents and children lose each other and are eventually reunited, strangers are befriended, babies are cared for, and hurts are healed. Intrepid explorers make amazing discoveries and inventors create powerful new gadgets, magic potions, and all kinds of delicious or useful concoctions. Clever children build forts and cities, make game-winning sports plays, take turns winning imaginary video games, and earn thunderous applause as stars of stage and screen. Heroes, victims, and monsters die and magically come to life again; the small and weak overpower the big and strong; the youngest child succeeds where older ones have failed.

Mature pretend play—involving planning, gathering props, negotiating roles and storylines, and dialogue—has multiple benefits for preschool-age children. It exercises their imaginations, social skills, and coping strategies, and engages their resourcefulness. It promotes intellectual and social flexibility, provides an outlet for expressing strong feelings, and fosters emotional resilience. It builds friendships. It is compelling—and fun—and can help develop empathy, humor, and self-confidence. It engages children in conversations that go beyond the here and now, building language and providing the foundation for literacy. As friends collaborate to co-construct the story they enact, they push each other to convey their ideas with words, at times stepping out of the story context to explain a direction or agree on a next step. As they enact roles and adapt to their partners' responses, they learn to understand and appreciate different points of view. Children who speak different languages may learn each other's language as they pretend together, beginning with stock phrases and gradually including more and more words. Younger children, and those whose language development or play skills lag, can learn from playing with more mature partners. And yes—pretend play can enhance vocabulary as well as facility with literary language and storytelling techniques.

Of course, these benefits are not always realized. Sometimes the play becomes static and unimaginative as children play the same script over and over with little variation. Sometimes, a child or pair of children will dominate the play, forcing others to repeatedly play subservient roles or excluding the other children altogether. Sometimes play becomes wild, raucous, or destructive, or takes an imaginary course that excites some children but is disturbing to others. Too often, pretend play reveals and reinforces hurtful stereotypes that children pick up despite the best efforts of their parents and teachers. And, quite frequently, miscues and communication gaps cause creative play to founder, especially when the players don't know each other well, are just beginning to learn each other's language, or are simply typical 3-year-olds who need some support from a responsive partner to build their ideas.

These are the teachable moments—the times when adult involvement can make play more interesting and productive, support children as they align their ideas or work through conflicts and disagreements, clarify or extend concepts, and promote important values.

Coming in late to preschool one day, Kwan and his mother join Aniya at the art table, where Aniya is busy making a "cake" from some rather stiff clay.

"I'll make the cake, then I'll bake the cake, before I take the cake," Aniya chants to herself as she tries to shape the mound of clay. Kwan begins to bake a cake as well, pounding his clay with a potato masher. Kwan's mother speaks to him in Korean, then smoothly shifts to English.

"You're using a potato masher to make your cake. But the dough is too stiff. Would you like to try a mallet?" Kwan exchanges the potato masher for a mallet, and Aniya takes one as well.

"We're using the mallets to make cakes," she says, and Kwan flashes her a smile. Both children fall silent as they pound their clay. Kwan's mother jump-starts their conversation.

"What's the occasion?" she asks. "Is it someone's special day?"

"It's Katya's day," Aniya answers brightly, remembering that Katya had a birthday that week.

Techniques for Enhancing Pretend Play

- Provide interesting props and prop collections.

- Provide inspiration through books and storytelling.

- Help children make the props and costumes they need.

- Ask questions from the sidelines. "What's the occasion? Is it someone's special day?"

- Use rare words that fit the play context. "Do you need some *provisions* for your journey?"

- Add a new element that builds on the dramatic action or takes it in a new direction. "Should we get some ice cream to have with the cake?"

- Be flexible. If the children ignore or misinterpret your idea, adapt to their script. Remember that play doesn't need to be totally logical.

- Reverse roles. Take the part of a whiny baby; a distraught, confused, or naughty child; or a demanding customer, and let the children be the caretakers, teachers, disciplinarians, or service providers who must find creative ways to respond to you.

- Illustrate consequences. As you play your role, highlight the consequences of your own and your playmates' actions. Model appropriate ways to express and explain your feelings.

- Help children who are struggling learn and practice "scripts." For example, you might coach a child in how to play "store" or "doctor," enacting your role and modeling or prompting his.

- Compromise creatively. Find ways to include different ideas in a common game.

- Ask questions that support problem solving.

- Set limits when necessary. Remind children of safety rules and group norms such as an agreement among the children that "You can't say, 'You can't play'" (Paley, 1993).

"It's Katya's day," Kwan repeats. "We're making cakes for Katya."

"What kind of cake does Katya like?" Kwan's mother asks.

"Chocolate," Kwan answers.

"With lots of pink icing," Aniya adds.

"And candles," says Kwan. Aniya grabs a fistful of craft sticks and hands some to Kwan. "Put lots of candles on yours," she commands. Kwan's mother discreetly waves good-bye, leaving the children to their play.

THE LANGUAGE OF PLAY

Every weekday morning, Robert crosses the street with his father to go to his family child care program. Robert is rarely happy about saying good-bye to his father, no matter how many times they read "just one more story." His teacher has learned that it is best not to try to engage Robert in conversation for the first few minutes after his father leaves. Instead, she lets Robert play in a corner with his "muscle men," odd-looking plastic figures that Robert pretends are good guys and bad guys who fight each other. After a few minutes of mostly silent pretending, Robert puts down his toys and happily joins the group.

Although Robert's play is private, he conveys messages through his behavior: "I need some space, and I need to be in control. If I can't stay with my Dad at my own house, then at least let me decide when I'm ready to play." Fortunately for Robert, his teacher is a good "listener."

WISHFUL THINKING

At 3½, Haley discovered that accidentally making a mess and volunteering to clean it up was a good way to get positive parental attention. Haley's parents were not so pleased, however, when Haley deliberately knocked over her milk and eagerly offered to wipe up the spill. Her father explained that intentionally spilling milk was not acceptable. The next night at dinner, Haley slyly knocked over her milk when her father's back was turned. "It wasn't intentional, Daddy. I bumped it with my elbow," she explained in her sweetest voice.

"Your elbows need to learn to be careful," her father countered. "You tell them that milk is for drinking, not spilling. We'll clean up the spill when we finish eating."

Like most preschoolers, Haley craves her parents' attention and is eager for their approval. The milk-spilling game was fun when she got both. Though she spilled the milk on purpose, she wasn't trying to be naughty. Her cleverly phrased excuse expressed her wish to stay in her father's good graces. For the 3- or 4-year-old wishful thinker, saying something with conviction can almost make it so.

It didn't take Haley's parents long to figure out what she was up to, and they couldn't help but be charmed by her use of an impressive, newly learned word to justify her actions. At the same time, they needed to let Haley know that they were unwilling to play her game, and that there were better ways to get their attention at mealtime.

Recognizing the wishes for connection and approval that often lie behind a child's naughty behavior or creative excuses can help parents to be more empathetic. As they set limits that help children master their impulses, they can communicate their understanding of the children's wishes and find playful ways to redirect them into more appropriate activities.

Playful, imaginative, and even silly talk was very much a part of Haley and her father's relationship, so it didn't seem strange to either of them when he reminded her elbows to be careful. Parents with different cultural and family backgrounds, or more literal-minded outlooks or more literal-minded children, will find other ways to get the message across (e.g., "Because I love you, I can't let you behave this way, even though I understand that you want to.").

Whether or not they feel that playful redirection is an appropriate response to minor disciplinary infractions, parents and caregivers who enjoy verbal play can engage magical and wishful thinking to help children cope with imagined hurts and minor crises. The following scenarios illustrate effective techniques.

Fight Magic with Magic

Forbidden to play with toy guns, 4-year-old Gavin makes one with his fingers and "shoots" his 2½-year-old brother, Dwayne. "Pyew. Pyew. You're dead."

Dwayne runs to his mother and tearfully complains, "Mommy, Gavin pyewed me dead."

"Oh, dear," his mother responds, as she waves her hands over his body, "I'll have to use my bio-scanner to bring you back to life. Now, you remind Gavin that people are not for pyewing. And put on this bullet-proof suit, just in case he forgets again."

Make a Game of It

Running into the kitchen, 3-year-old Lisa falls and hurts her knee. There's no blood, but Lisa looks like she's about to cry. Thinking quickly, her father punches a number into his imaginary cell phone. "Hello, People Store," he says in an urgent voice, "We have an emergency. We need a new knee—stat—in a size three. Oh, the left one. Yes, thank you. Please bring that over right away." He then pretends to answer the door, "Oh, thank you for coming so quickly. Here's your money, People Store delivery person. This is just what we needed." Lisa laughs as her father "replaces" the hurt knee.

The next day, when Lisa's father stubs his toe, she orders him a new one from the People Store.

Send a Letter from a Magical Friend

"Mama," asks 3½-year-old Allie at bedtime, "when I wake up, will it be tomorrow?"

"Yes," her mother replies.

"Good," says Allie, "'cause tomorrow is Lightning McQueen's birthday, and we're going to Radiator Springs to celebrate."

"Honey, I told you that Radiator Springs isn't a real place," her mother says gently.

"But it is real, Mama. I SAW it in the video. And Lightning will be very upset if I miss his party."

Realizing that it is futile to argue with her magical thinker, Allie's mother replies simply. "Let's see what tomorrow brings."

The next morning, Allie finds an envelope beside her pillow. "Look, Mama," she says excitedly as she waves the envelope in her mother's face. "I got a letter! Do you think it's from Lightning McQueen? Maybe it's a party invitation."

Feigning surprise, Allie's mother reads the note. "Dear Allie. I was hoping you could come to my party. It's tomorrow at supper time. But there was a big snowstorm in Radiator Springs and all the roads are closed so no one can get here. So, I'm asking all my friends to celebrate my birthday at their own homes. Put some candles on a cake and sing "Happy Birthday" to me really, really, really loud. If all my friends sing really, really, really loud, I'm sure I'll be able to hear you. Love, Your friend, Lightning McQueen."

"I can sing loud," says Allie, clearly entranced. "Can we make a real cake for Lightning's birthday? With real candles to blow out?"

"Well," says her mother. "It is a special occasion. When I get home from work we'll make a cake together."

VERBAL CREATIVITY AND WORD PLAY

At 3½, Farah is a very verbal child who loves to play with words. One of her favorite games is "Baby Talk."

She starts it by assigning roles. "Mommy, you pretend to be the Mommy, and I'll pretend to be the baby."

Her mother obliges. "Okay, cutie baby, did you learn any new words today?"

Farah responds by saying something like "cah" as she points to a toy car, pretending that she's just learning to say the word and not yet saying it right. Of course, her baby self knows many more words than most 3-year-olds do.

Telling stories together is another favorite activity for Farah and her mother. Farah especially likes made-up stories that are built on real-life memories. Farah loves when her mother tells her favorite story: "Mommy and Farah were walking to day care, when Farah said, 'What's that noise?' Mommy said, 'That's a car warming up.' Then Farah said, 'Let's go inside the car,' but Mommy said . . ."

At this point in the story, Farah fills in the blank with a forceful imitation of her mother: "No way!"

Farah's mother continues: "After Farah said, 'I WANNA GO INSIDE the car,' Mommy said, 'Okay.' So we opened the door and played around with the radio and the lights and honked the horn, when all of a sudden the guy came outside and said, 'Hey! What are you doing inside my car? Get your own car!' And we said, 'We can't because. . .'"

Farah fills in, "Daddy took the car to work."

Farah's mother picks up the story again: "And the guy said, 'I don't care. Get out of my car!!'" Farah dissolves into giggles, then asks to hear the story again.

Young children's language is often unintentionally poetic. Lacking a word or phrase that conveys the meaning they intend, they make up one that is original and especially apt. A sea turtle is a "turtle bird," a taste of horseradish "bites my mouth," a splinter is a "skin tear," eating too many bananas can make you "consternated."

At other times, preschoolers deliberately play with sounds and words, as Farah did when she pretended to be a baby. Children who hear a lot of words used in interesting ways to create pleasing patterns as well as to convey meaning have rich fodder for verbal creativity. They can draw on the oral traditions of their communities; the songs they have learned at home, school, church, or the library; favorite books and movies; and overheard conversations that they didn't quite understand to come up with their own variations.

In *Ways with Words* (Heath, 1983), a classic study of children's learning of spoken and written language in three communities in the Piedmont area of North and South Carolina, Shirley Brice Heath captured how children in one African American working-class community learned to talk—and the many ways in which adults and older children modeled, prompted, and rewarded their inventive use of language.

The following poem was created by Lem, one of the children Heath observed, when he was just 2½. Lem had been playing near two older children when he heard a church bell in the distance. They stopped their play momentarily to listen to his poem.

Way
Far
Now
It a church bell
Ringin'
Dey singing'
　　　ringin'
You hear it?
I hear it
Far
Now
　　(Heath, 1983, p. 170)

As Heath points out, Lem's way of marking the beginning and ending of his narrative, his use of rhyme and repetition, and his involvement of the listener through a question ("You hear it?") are characteristic of his linguistic community. In Lem's world, as described by Heath, poetic language was part of everyday conversation. Children like Lem received a daily dose of poetry—not from children's books or preschool teachers, but simply from listening to the play songs, verbal sparring, instructive narratives, personal accounts, and Sunday sermons that they couldn't avoid overhearing in a community that put a premium on verbal creativity. Rhyme, alliteration, and spur-of-the-moment wordplay figured prominently in the games of older children. Performance was also important, especially for boys, who were rewarded for their ability to hold the floor and regale an audience.

As a preschooler, Lem was able to use his verbal skills to deflect his mother's scolding.

> On one occasion, Lillie Mae, exasperated with Lem for taking off his shoes, asked him what he had done with the shoes and suggested: "You want me ta tie you up, put you on de railroad track?" Lem hesitated a moment and responded:

> Railroad track
> Train all big 'n black,
> On dat track, on dat track, on dat track
> Ain't no way I can't get back
> Back from dat track
> Back from dat train
> Big 'n black, I be back (Heath, 1983, p. 110)

It is no accident that hand clapping rhymes, finger plays, and action rhymes are staples of early childhood curricula in communities around the world. For example, the following action rhyme is often used as part of a unit on animals, creepy crawlers, or reptiles and amphibians. It is accompanied by motions such as snapping the alligator's jaws, rolling hands, and swimming like a frog. Children can learn to sign the key words in American Sign Language as they say them in English.

> Once there was an alligator
> Sitting on a log.
> She looked in the water
> And she saw a little frog.

> In jumped the alligator
> Roll went the log.
> Splash went the water and
> Away swam the frog.

Action, hand, and finger rhymes are fun to act out with a partner or in a group, or to recite in chorus. The fun-to-listen-to poems of authors such as Nikki Giovanni, David McCord, Mary Ann Hoberman,

Alma Flor Ada, F. Isabel Campoy, and Eloise Greenfield can inspire children to create additional verses or construct poems of their own. Poems can also provide gateways to imaginary worlds that children can create and elaborate on—with the help of child or adult playmates. The power of a poem like "Island of Dreams" is enhanced when parents share their childhood memories of secret or special places and help children to visualize what the words depict.

Island of Dreams
Come away with me to my island home.
It's a place that's free, where a child can roam.
In a forest deep, over mountain streams
We will soar and leap as we chase our dreams.

We will wake each morn with a new day smile
When the roosters crow—in Calypso style.
We will rush outside and we'll greet the sun
While the dew-wet grass makes slip-sliding fun.

Later on we'll go for a donkey ride
To a secret place where the rainbows hide
And birds-of-paradise with their bright orange wings
Are the flowers that bloom by the bubbling springs.

Then we'll prance on up to our private pool
Where we'll dash and splash till we're nice and cool.
We will find some magical flying fish
Who will leap sky high and will grant our wish.

MORE IS CAUGHT THAN TAUGHT

"When you yell at me, Mommy," said not quite three-year old Amanda-Faye, "it really hurts my ears. You can do one of two things. You can tell me in a nice voice or not tell me at all. What is your decision?"

Although she had come to expect such sophisticated language from her verbally precocious daughter, Amanda-Faye's mother was dumbfounded by her daughter's words. "Here was my child telling me how it felt when I yelled at her and giving me a choice. I knew that what she was saying came from the things that were said to her. It was so empowering—to this little child, and to me!"

Amanda-Faye may be verbally precocious, but her story—recounted by her mother, Linda Irene Jiménez, an early childhood educator, in the book *In Our Own Way: How Anti-Bias Work Shapes Our Lives* (Alvarado et al., 1999, p. 32)—will be familiar to many parents of preschoolers. Three- and 4-year-olds are notorious imitators. In their pretend play as well as in their responses to questions and scoldings, they often show their parents and teachers exactly how they look and sound.

Learning through observation as well as experience, young children pick up subtle messages about how people should behave. They learn to use words in ways that empower them—or to keep their thoughts and feelings to themselves. As every parent eventually learns, examples speak louder than words. Or, as the title of a child care program improvement handbook produced by the Federation of Child Care Centers of Alabama (1998) reminds us: "More Is Caught than Taught."

Forbidden words are especially appealing to preschoolers, who soon learn that saying a word such as *poopy-caca* is a surefire way to get a laugh from their peers. Parents who forbid or discourage swearing by or in front of children are often amazed at how quickly their children copy the occasional swear word they overhear and how appropriately—and embarrassingly—they use it. One clever father—whose children had picked up more swear words than he was comfortable with—told his oldest "a secret": "The worst word in the whole wide world is *gank*. Whatever you do, don't say, 'Gank' in public." Soon, of course, *gank* had replaced the litany of inappropriate words that his 2- and 4-year-old sons had learned.

For 3-year-old Marcie, who had "caught" adult ways of speaking and could use them to her advantage, a "bad" word was any word she didn't want to hear. When her mother called, "Good morning! It's time to get dressed!" Marcie would respond forcefully. "No! That's a bad word. That's NOT okay!"

WHY? WHY? WHY?

Emmy (age 3):   "Papa, what's college? I mean, why is it
                called college?"
Grandfather: "I don't really know."
Emmy: "Why don't you know?

Curiosity is so characteristic of the preschool years that the National Academy of Sciences panel on preschool pedagogy titled their report *Eager to Learn* (National Research Council, Committee on Early Childhood Pedagogy, 2000). Young preschoolers are full of questions and often both adept and persistent in asking them:

- They want to know what people are doing and why, how things work, and why they have to do things they don't want to do or can't do what older people can. "What's that man doing? Why is he wearing a helmet? Can I have a turn? Why won't you let me?"

- They repeatedly ask what is going to happen and when and why it is taking so long for an anticipated event to occur. "Are we there yet?" "Will my birthday be tomorrow?"

Questions Preschoolers Ask

- "How much is 'some'?"
- "Is today a new day? Will tomorrow be a new day? Why are there so many days?"
- "Mommy, does the baby in your tummy have a little cup so he can catch the milk you drink and take a drink, too?"
- "I'm a boy. Did I used to be in Daddy's tummy?"
- "Does Darth Vader poop?"
- "Why do people act mean?"
- "Snow is frozen water, right? But you said ice is frozen water. So how can that be?"
- "If people stay at Day's Inn, where do they go at night?"
- "Daddy, are you frustrated?"
- "Where does the water go after it goes down the drain? Then where?"
- "Why are the faucet handles cold when the part where the water comes out is hot?"
- "Why do people have skin?"
- "What is electricity?"
- "Why does the moon have different shapes?"
- "How come I can see the moon when it's not even night?"
- "What do baby frogs eat? Why do they have tails? Why are they called 'tadpoles'?"
- "Is it hard for fish to breath under water? Why don't they drown?"
- "Why do people die?"

- They notice things that adults overlook and ask questions that reveal their logical but literal interpretations of what they see and hear. "Grandma, why are you talking to my tummy? It doesn't have ears."

- They pick up discrepancies between words and deeds or between one explanation and another and demand to know why the world doesn't work the way they think it should. "Why does Grandpa put sugar in his coffee? Doesn't he know that sugar is unhealthy?"

- They are curious about the meanings of words that are new to them and of idioms that use ordinary words in new ways. "What does it mean to be caught in the rain?"

Like Emmy, they can at times be so eager to learn that they can't wait for the answer to one question before asking another.

SEEING PATTERNS AND MAKING CONNECTIONS

Three-year-old Rocio proudly shows Pilar, her home visitor, the world map that her uncle gave her. "Here's Florida, where we live. And here's El Salvador. That's where I come from."

"That's right," Pilar confirms. "And here is Colombia. That's where I lived when I was a little girl."

On the next visit, Rocio has the map ready. "Here's Florida, here's El Salvador, and here's Colombia."

"You're right," Pilar replies, obviously impressed.

"And I learned a new country," says Rocio. "This is Canada."

"Right again!" Pilar compliments. "Would you like to know where Mexico is?"

The next few visits each begin with a "world tour." Rocio points to countries she knows, and Pilar teaches her a new one. Sometimes, Pilar brings a library book about one of the countries on the map. One day, when Pilar points out Kenya after they read *Bringing the Rain to Kapiti Plain* (Aardema, 1981), Rocio asks if they can take a trip there.

"It's very far away," Pilar explains. "It would take a long time to get there, even on an airplane."

"Is it as far as Disney World?" asks Rocio.

For Rocio, the world map was special because her uncle gave it to her and because it came with a story about her family's past. As she shared it with her home visitor, it became a bond between them as well, a weekly ritual that allowed Rocio to show off her knowledge and her heritage while the home visitor broadened Rocio's horizons.

Obviously a quick and eager learner, Rocio was nevertheless a typical 3-year-old in her concepts of space and time. She understood that some places were nearby and some were far away, but she was just beginning to realize that those that were further away took longer to get to. Her understanding of how distances related to each other was still grounded in her experience. She could not grasp the vast distances that her map represented, nor did she realize that a place such as Disney World—a 3-hour drive from her house that had felt interminably long—was closer to her than far away El Salvador or much farther away Kenya.

Children learn these concepts gradually, through conversation, direct experience, and analogy. Adults support this learning with words and visuals that help children locate themselves in space and time.

- "Disney World is in Orlando, which is in Florida. We live in Florida, too, but it takes us a long time to get to Disney World because we live in Miami—down here—and Orlando is way up here."

- "Florida is in the United States, and the United States, Canada, and Mexico are all in North America. Kenya is in Africa, which is on the other side of the Atlantic Ocean. When we go to the beach, we swim in the Atlantic Ocean, but we can't see across to the other side because it is so big."

- "First we'll wash our hands and then we can cook dinner. We have to hurry, because Mommy will be home in half an hour and I bet she's going to be hungry."

- "Let's see how fast we can clean up your toys. 1, 2, 3. . . 29, 30, 31. Thirty-one seconds! I think that is a new record. Remember, yesterday we had to count all the way up to 55?"

- "Today is Tuesday. Do you know what tomorrow will be? Monday, Tuesday . . . That's right, Wednesday. Grandma is coming on Thursday, the day after Wednesday."

- "Let's check the schedule. After story time we'll have activities and snack and then we can go out on the playground."

- "Amanda's birthday is going to be soon, when it's still winter. Your birthday is in the summertime."

At 3½, Brett, the youngest of three children, had participated in many such conversations at the family dinner table. His father, a math teacher, was always finding ways to get his children thinking about sizes, amounts, and distances, and to help them see patterns and make connections. A lot of the problems he posed were way over Brett's head, but Brett enjoyed trying to keep up with his siblings, and they were patient with his attempts. One day, Brett's father asked, "What if we could drill a hole all the way to the center of the Earth. It would be really, really deep; deeper than the deepest part of the ocean, even deeper than Mt. Everest is tall. How could we measure how deep it would be?"

Brett's older sister answered first, "We could get a really long, long rope and put a weight on the end of it and drop it down to the bottom and then pull it up and measure it."

"Maybe," his brother added, "we could get a really tiny helicopter that can fly really fast, and see how long it takes to go down to the bottom and come back up."

Then Brett piped up with an answer that impressed them all: "We could drop a stone into the hole and count—1, 2, 3. . . until it reached the bottom."

Many "educational" toys for young children—and many of the games adults play with them—help children put items and events into categories and sequences and to recognize and create patterns. We give them measuring cups or Russian matryoshka dolls and ask them to nest them from largest to smallest. We let them play with shape sorters and stacking toys, and we help them recognize the different shapes of street signs and windows. We give them beads to string and encourage them to alternate colors or make more complex repeating patterns. We give them blocks, tangram pieces, or shape cut-outs to arrange into two-dimensional patterns, and we help them use mirrors to explore symmetry. We give them puzzles, pegboards, lotto games, and sorting trays and ask them to put matching or complementary pieces together or to fit missing pieces in place.

As director of the Washington-Beech Preschool, a city-supported school located in a tenant-run housing development in Boston, Ellen Wolpert felt that it was essential to provide the children with a lot of concept-building and pattern-highlighting activities. She was equally concerned, however, about fostering the children's language development and building their emotional resilience. She wanted the children to feel good about themselves and their families and to learn joyfully from and with each other, across boundaries of race, gender, social class, ethnicity, ability, sexual orientation, and language. She felt that it was especially vital to build the preschoolers' capacity to resist the negative stereotypes of themselves and others they would surely encounter in the world outside their school (Wolpert, 2005).

Wolpert devised an ingenious way to do all of these things at once. In addition to the standard pattern-making toys that had children match, sort, order, and arrange by simple attributes such as shape and color, Wolpert created her own games and puzzles. But instead of using simple shapes, pegs, or pictures of animals and common objects, Wolpert used pictures of people. From books, calendars, magazines, literature from nonprofit organizations, and other sources, she and her colleagues collected images of children and adults doing ordinary activities—eating, sleeping, fixing hair, working, playing, reading, celebrating, and joining together to improve their communities. The pictures were deliberately chosen to contradict stereotypes of who can do what, who can be friends or family, and whose lives and what work are important. Because the people in the pictures came from diverse communities in Boston and other cities in the Unites States, as well as from countries around the world, the individuals and groups had many things in common and also many salient differences.

Wolpert pasted the pictures onto cards, laminated them, and used them to create two- and four-piece puzzles and matching, sorting, and sequencing games. She taught the children to play these games by stating aloud how the pictures were alike and different. "This picture shows two boys eating, and this one shows two girls eating. But the boys are standing up and eating with their fingers and the girls are sitting at a table and using chopsticks." As the children created their own matches, sorts, and patterns, they used rich and increasingly complex language to talk about how various cards were alike or different and belonged or fit together. Because these games were embedded in a well-thought-out curriculum, with many opportunities for children to learn about their own community and the wider world through books, field trips, pretend play, and conversation, they fostered self-esteem and appreciation of diversity along with intellectual gains.

WHAT DID YOU LEARN IN SCHOOL TODAY?

For many children in the United States, 3 is a watershed age—for some, it is the first time they go to "school" rather than staying at home with a parent or family member; attending occasional playgroups; or being cared for by a family child care provider, neighbor, or nanny. Four-year-olds are even more likely to be in center-based Head Start, prekindergarten, preschool, or other child care programs.

These programs vary in approach and quality, and parents who have a choice look for one where both they and their child will be comfortable. At the same time, they want to be assured that the program meets professional standards—such as accreditation by the National Association for the Education of Young Children (NAEYC) or the National Family Child Care Association (NAFCC)—and that it will be effective in supporting their child's intellectual, social-emotional, and language development.

In 2007, researchers at High/Scope Educational Research Foundation, a Michigan-based organization known for its high-quality preschool programs, curricula, and teacher training and its careful evaluations of children's learning over time, published the results of a 10-nation study of preschool teaching practices and their relationship to intellectual growth over time. (Montie, Xiang, & Schweinhart, 2007). The researchers observed classrooms with 4-year-olds in 10 countries (Finland, Greece, Hong Kong, Indonesia, Ireland, Italy, Poland, Spain, Thailand, and the United States) and tested the children using instruments and descriptive categories that had been carefully developed to be equivalent across language and culture. They retested the children at age 7 on the language and cognitive tasks. Their results showed clearly that some aspects of effective or "developmentally appropriate" practice transcend culture, language, and setting.

The researchers found strong associations between children's scores on their tests at age 7 and their preschool experiences. Cognitive performance at age 7 was linked to

- Less time spent in whole-group activities at age 4 (leaving more time for small-group activities and self-chosen pursuits)

- Having a greater number and variety of things to play with at age 4 Language performance at age 7 was linked to

- More activities that children chose for themselves at age 4 and relatively fewer preacademic lessons and large-group social activities

- Preschool teachers who had completed more years of full-time education, including college

- *More* interaction with teachers—but only in countries where the 4-year-olds spent most of their time working or playing individually or in small groups and engaging in self-chosen activities

- *Less* interaction with teachers in those countries where adult-centered teaching and other whole-group activities predominated

In other words, this transnational study underscores the importance of active exploration for young children's concept learning and the importance of active speaking for their language learning. A program that encourages children to experiment, to think and talk about new ideas, to approach situations with an open mind, and to engage in a range of self-chosen activities will support the children's development. On the other hand, programs that approach early childhood education in an overly didactic way—teaching concepts and skills mainly through adult talk and rote child response—provide less support for intellectual and language development.

Still, it is tempting to teach young children by talking *at* them—giving them instructions, long explanations, and academic lessons. They pick up information so quickly that it's hard not to think of them as "little sponges," ready to sop up whatever adults have to teach. Indeed, when 4-year-olds play "school" or pretend to be teachers, they often lecture their students—even if they have only been in child-centered, play-based classroom and home settings themselves.

Similarly, it can be fun to quiz children on what they've learned. "What color is the elephant?" "How many legs does a spider have?" Most children are eager to show off their knowledge to proud parents and teachers, and many love to shout out answers in a group setting. But the most powerful conversations, the ones that build conceptual as well as factual knowledge, push beyond pat answers. They build on children's spoken and unspoken questions and concerns and engage them in challenging problem solving and reflective talk.

SOLVING PROBLEMS

The preschool classroom is abuzz with conversation. The teacher has explained the problem. The snack for the day is carrots, but a baby is coming to visit. The children immediately see the problem: Carrots are too crunchy for babies, who don't have teeth and could choke on a hard carrot even if they could take a bite. They put their heads together to figure out how to turn carrots into baby food, decide on a course of action, and then try it out to see what happens.

Dr. Lucia French of the University of Rochester showed a film of preschoolers' deliberations on making baby food from carrots at a workshop on mathematical and scientific development in early childhood sponsored by the National Academy of Sciences (Beatty, 2005) to illustrate a remarkably effective program she had developed called *Science Start!* The baby food project wasn't part of the prepared curriculum, but the children were able to apply the *Science Start!* strategies they had learned. Their teacher had received thorough training in ways to promote scientific reasoning and discourse. Each day, she presented the children with engaging science-based content or an intriguing practical problem, and the children practiced "a simple cycle of scientific reasoning—reflect and ask, plan and predict, act and observe, report and reflect" (French, 2004, p. 138). With science at the center of a comprehensive curriculum, children not only asked questions but also planned activities to find the answers. They listened to storybooks and consulted books for information. With their teacher's help, they recorded observations in charts, graphs, and dictated reports.

In some of the *Science Start!* classrooms, the lessons continued at home. Periodically, the children brought home "Zip Kits," plastic bags containing simple household materials and directions for using them to investigate phenomena such as floating and sinking, color mixing, and magnetism. Parents were instructed to listen carefully to their children's questions, hypotheses, observations, and conclusions, and to record some of these so that the teachers could understand what the children were thinking. At the same time, of course, the parents learned to appreciate their children's higher order thinking and language abilities, and to ask them questions that supported and enhanced their problem solving and extended their factual knowledge and conceptual understanding.

Not surprisingly, children in *Science Start!* classrooms are highly engaged by the inquiry process and work together effectively to solve the problems and extend their knowledge of the high-interest content. *Science Start!* is not just a science program, however; it turns out to be such an effective way to build vocabulary and promote literacy that it has been adopted in more than 40 preschool and Head Start classrooms and serves as a central evidence-based component of several federally funded Early Reading First projects.

Science Start! provides especially rich and engaging material for children to talk about and gives teachers and parents powerful tools for engaging them in information-rich, brain-building conversations. But adults don't have to be science experts or specially trained teachers to support children's natural scientific curiosity and engage them in problem-solving discourse. To help promote children's scientific and problem-solving skills, adults can do the following:

- Present an intriguing object, process, or problem, or start with a child's discovery or question.

- Ask questions to get children started. "What do you see, hear, and feel?" "What could we do with this?" "How do you think it might work?" "How could we find out?" "What do you think would happen if . . .?"

- Model problem-solving. Think aloud, and share your own questions, hypotheses, and problem-solving approach. Try out some of the children's ideas.

- Encourage children to share observations and ask more questions.

- Use and encourage precise words. "When you look at your *reflection* in a spoon, how does it appear?" "What happens when you turn the spoon over, so it's *convex* like a hill instead of *concave* like a bowl?" "When you turn the spoon *sideways*, how does it *distort* the image?" "Can you make your nose look *longer*?"

- Help children talk about what they did and what they found out.

TWENTY FUN THINGS TO DO WITH PRESCHOOLERS

1. *Play I Spy:* Give the child a fairly detailed description of an object without naming it, and see if she can guess what you see. "I spy something yellow that's long and skinny and has a sharp point." When the child takes a turn, encourage her to give you a lot of clues to help you guess what she is spying.

2. *Look at the world through lenses:* Have the child look through "rose-colored glasses" (made with colored gels or cellophane and a simple cardboard frame), a magnifying glass, a cardboard tube, a camera, or binoculars. Ask him to describe or tell a story about what he sees.

3. *Find out what's under the familiar ground of the neighborhood:* Turn over rocks, dig holes, study sidewalk cracks, peer into a storm drain, and trace the roots of trees and bushes. Scoop up a handful of soil and strain it through a sieve. Watch squirrels, birds, chipmunks, ants, and earthworms. Take a subway ride. Talk with the workers who repair water, gas, and sewer pipes. Pull up a weed and investigate its roots. Encourage the child to represent her discoveries by telling stories, drawing pictures that show what's under the ground and what's on top, or building a terrarium.

4. *Pretend to be animals:* Read books such as *Pretend You're a Cat* (Marzollo & Pinkney, 1997), *Sea Elf* (Ryder & Rothman, 1993),

Chipmunk Song (Ryder & Cherry, 1992), or *Lizard in the Sun* (Ryder & Rothman, 1994) that invite you to pretend to be animals or to imitate their movements. As you try moving like different animals, talk about what you are doing and feeling. Use the Internet and children's books together to learn more about the child's favorite animals and how they behave and communicate.

5. *Experiment with balance:* Try building tall towers, long bridges, and seesaws from blocks and other materials. Ask the child what happens when he puts something heavy on the very top of a tower or on one end of a bridge or seesaw. What happens when he moves a block toward the center of a span or orients it a different way? Look at real bridges, seesaws, scales, towers, mobiles, and sculptures, and talk about what makes them balanced or tippy.

6. *Turn a bookshelf into miniature play space:* With the child's help, set up a doll house, garage, farm, space station, or undersea world, with a different room or area on each shelf. Arrange small toys and dolls to create the setting, and encourage the child to move them around as she plays out pretend stories. You can even place a photograph, child's drawing, or book toward the back to set the scene. Once you get her started, the child may have many ideas of things to add to her pretend world.

7. *Role play:* Take on the roles of favorite storybook characters as you engage in everyday activities. Or create your own cast of imaginary or puppet characters with distinct perspectives. For example, Cookie Monster might want to eat everything in sight; Goldilocks might forget her manners and need to be reminded. Encourage the child to talk with your imaginary and puppet friends, just as you talk with his.

8. *Make a mural:* Engage a group of children in creating a wall-sized picture of a real or imaginary place, event, or storybook scene. An easy way to begin is to map out large areas of sky, land, and perhaps water or buildings, using colored construction paper. Different contributors can then draw or find pictures of people, animals, or objects that belong in the different areas, cut them out, and paste them on the mural.

9. *Take a magic carpet ride:* Sit with a child or a small group on a rug, couch, or platform and pretend that you are flying off on a magical adventure. Solicit their ideas on where you might visit, and then begin a story detailing your adventure. Describe the wonderful sights below, and ask questions that convey your excitement

and invite participation. "Look—there's a circus parade. Can you see the elephants?"

10. *Introduce photography:* Take digital photographs of the child at work or play, focusing on sequences such as building a block city or making a traditional holiday dish. Or give the child a chance to take pictures of the things that interest him on a bus trip or a walk around the neighborhood. Enlist his help in selecting pictures to print, discussing what happened first, next, and so forth; arranging a display; and telling the story to family, friends, and visitors. Zoom in on details, and make games in which the child matches an enlarged detail with a photo that shows its context. Talk with the child about the clues he used to find a match.

11. *Make wordless "talk books":* Talk books tell a story through drawings, magazine cut-outs, or photographs. Encourage children to exchange talk books and to tell their own stories to go with the pictures. Talk books can be especially valuable for children who are learning to speak a second language and for parents who are not comfortable reading aloud or who have difficulty getting children's books in their home language (Eggers-Piérola, 2005).

12. *Eat foods from around the world:* Let children handle, smell, and taste foods such as coconut, dates, kiwi, passion fruit, sugar cane, pineapple, pawpaw, plantain, ackee, cherimoya, star fruit, papaya, carob, tomatillos, and clementines, as well as strongly flavored prepared foods such as curry, chutney, dulce de leche, plum sauce, and chili. Talk about the colors, tastes, and textures, as well as where the foods come from.

13. *Make interesting molding materials:* Help the child make "oobleck" (begin with equal parts cornstarch and water, adjust the mixture so that it pours like liquid but feels solid when pressed), "silly putty" (1 tbsp white glue, 1 tbsp liquid starch), or soapsuds clay (3/4 cup Ivory Snow, 1 tbsp warm water, beaten with electric or hand mixer and add a drop or two of food coloring). After mixing the ingredients, encourage the child to knead, pull, stretch, squish, roll, pinch, poke, sculpt, and bounce the materials she has created. Talk about how these materials feel and what happens when the child pulls sharply or slowly. Ask her if she can figure out how to make oobleck squeak or snap, draw pictures in soapsuds clay, or make silly putty bounce and roll. Experiment with different proportions, and talk about how the resultant materials behave.

14. *Cook together:* Help the child choose and combine ingredients for fruit salads, healthy sandwiches, omelets, and pasta dishes. Encourage him to make up appropriate names for his creations. Make snacks and lunches special by involving the child and his friends in decorating individual portions or platters using raisins, cereal pieces, slices of cheese, fruits or vegetables, herbs such as chives or parsley, and sauces to create pictures and designs. Read books about food such as *Gathering the Sun* (Ada, 2001), and talk about where different foods come from, how they are grown, and the people who grow and harvest them.

15. *Practice the ABC song, rhymes, and counting:* These are easy to practice during spare moments, such as while waiting for a bus or stoplight, during bath time or dressing, or after the last bedtime story. See how many times you and the child can sing the ABC song or recite a favorite rhyme before the subway comes or the child gets her socks and shoes on. When the child has learned to count to 20, try counting together to 100, then practice counting by 2s, 5s, or 10s.

16. *Explore rainbows:* Make rainbows with prisms or water spray; find them in soap films, pictures, and the sky. Experiment with the direction of the light—see if the child can "catch" a rainbow on her body. Teach the child songs such as "I Can Sing a Rainbow," "Des Colores," or "Somewhere Over the Rainbow." Help him make a rainbow paint set by putting a dollop of white glue into each cell of an egg carton, adding a drop of one or more colors of food coloring to each, and mixing with cotton swab "paint brushes." Or, put several dollops of shaving cream or whipped cream on a table or mat and tint each with a different food coloring. Several children can work together to mix colors, figure out how to make a particular shade, or make a rainbow picture. For a special treat, place a drop or two of food coloring in each section of a filled ice cube tray before freezing. Add some colored ice cubes to whipped cream or shaving cream and watch the colors change as they melt. As children mix, paint, and experiment, talk with them about all the colors in their rainbows and what they did to create each one.

17. *Make maps:* Help the child make maps of real and imaginary places. Begin by exploring an area or talking with her about an imaginary space. What are the important places or landmarks? Which are near each other, and which are farther away? What paths go from one to another? Ask the child to represent her ideas visually by drawing a map freehand, by cutting out pictures and arranging them on a large piece of paper and then

connecting them with "roads," or by using different colors or shapes to represent landmarks and then creating a key that identifies what's what. Working alone or with friends, the child may enjoy creating treasure maps; plans for obstacle courses or block constructions; or maps of rooms, a neighborhood, or favorite storybook places.

18. *Turn junk into treasure:* Read books such as *The Wonderful Towers of Watts* (Zelver & Lessac, 2005) or *The Tin Forest* (Ward & Anderson, 2006). Help the child make a family or classroom recycling center, collecting things such as bottle tops, small boxes, buttons, foil, cardboard tubes, Styrofoam trays, egg cartons, yogurt containers, parts to broken toys and gadgets, and other beautiful or potentially useful "junk." As you help the child sort his junk into baskets or bins, talk about what things go together and how you might use them to create sculptures; inventions; or play worlds such as a city, sports arena, magic garden, dinosaur land, or moonscape.

19. *Explore different artistic techniques:* Read picture books illustrated by collagists such as Ezra Jack Keats, Leo Lionni, and Eric Carle or by quilters such as Faith Ringgold. Look at prints by artists such as Henri Matisse, Romare Bearden, or Marc Chagall. Talk about the techniques the artists used in their works. Help the child use water colors, paste, paper and cloth scraps, ribbon, foil, string, stamps, greeting cards, box tops, and labels to make her own talk book, story quilt, mural, or picture book.

20. *Make a personal museum:* Help the child collect rocks, shells, interesting seed pods, toy dinosaurs, buttons, postcards, stamps, pictures related to a theme, or other small treasures and arrange them in pleasing displays in shoe boxes, small jars, jewelry boxes, drawers, or egg cartons. Some children may want to identify and label their treasures with the help of guidebooks or Internet sites. Others may wish to create patterns, group like things together, or make pictures or dioramas. Encourage the child to expand his museum over time and to give tours to visitors.

BOOK LEARNING

Visiting with his grandparents in Chicago, 3-year-old Jackson was entranced by the sights and sounds of a big city. He especially liked seeing vehicles he had only read about—taxis, police cars, buses, and elevated trains. When a fire engine whizzed by with its lights flashing and siren blaring, Jackson could barely contain his excitement. "There must be a cat stuck in a tree," he said. "The firefighters are hurrying to get it down." Jackson's parents recognized the influence of one of his favorite books.

In her classic poem, "There is No Frigate Like a Book," Emily Dickinson likened books to boats that could carry their readers to distant lands. For Dickinson, nothing could match the power of well-written words to engage the imagination, carry the reader on a transformative voyage of discovery, and thereby nourish "the human soul."

> "The poetry and prose of the best children's books enter our minds when we are young and sing back to us all our lives."
>
> —Vivian Gussin Paley, *The Boy Who Would Be a Helicopter* (1991, p. 44)

The books adults share with young children may not be as deep as those that moved the 19th-century poet, but they have equally profound power.

For 3- and 4-year-olds, the words in their books matter but the words they exchange with adults as they enjoy books together are even more important. The power of reading with children is captured in the report *Learning to Read and Write: Developmentally Appropriate Practices for Young Children, A Joint Position of the International Reading Association and the National Association for the Education of Young Children* (1998). The following paragraph summarizes the relevant research.

The single most important activity for building these understandings and skills essential for reading success appears to be *reading aloud to children* (Wells, 1985; Bus, Van Ijzendoorn, & Pellegrini, 1995). High-quality book reading occurs when children feel emotionally secure (Bus & van Ijzendoorn, 1995; Bus et al. 1997) and are active participants in reading (Whitehurst et al. 1994). Asking predictive and analytic questions in small-group settings appears to affect children's vocabulary and comprehension of stories (Karweit & Wasik, 1996). Children may talk about the pictures, retell the story, discuss their favorite actions, and request multiple rereadings. It is the talk that surrounds the storybook reading that gives it power, helping children to bridge what is in the story and their own lives (Dickinson & Smith, 1994; Snow et al. 1995). Snow (1991) has described these types of conversations as "decontextualized language" in which teachers may induce higher level thinking by moving experiences in stories from what the children may see in front of them to what they can imagine.

It is the talk that surrounds the storybook reading that gives it power, and different kinds of books foster different kinds of talk. Stories of people, or of animal characters who behave like people, invite comparisons with children's own experiences and questions about why the characters are acting in particular ways; what they may be feeling or thinking and why; and what the consequences of their thoughts, feelings, and choices might be. Whether or not these books are written as cautionary tales or moral fables, they can provide life lessons.

> At a staff meeting, a home visitor talked about her work with a family that had been worrying her. The mother was very young, but, through many supportive visits, she and her son had come to enjoy reading and playing together, and the child was beginning to use age-appropriate language. Pregnant with a second child, however, the mother had become increasingly distant, and her son's behavior was spiraling out of control. When the mother asked if her son's grandmother could take her place for the home visit activities, the home visitor worried that she might be considering abandoning her son physically as well as emotionally.
>
> With some persistence and support from her supervisor and colleagues, the home visitor was able to reengage the mother, along with the grandmother. She brought in a carefully chosen book, *Are You My Mother?* (Eastman, 1960), to share with the family. As his mother read the story, the little boy became increasingly engaged—laughing, imitating the animal sounds, and anticipating some of the words. At the end—as the baby bird and his real mother were reunited—the mother saw the question in her son's eyes. "I am your mother," she repeated pointedly, "and you are my best little boy." Mother and son hugged each other, and continued to cuddle and play as the home visitor gently excused herself. At the next visit, the boy and his mother were eager participants.

Nonfiction books (and fictionalized science or social studies books such as *The Magic School Bus* series or realistic stories of children in other countries) also invite conversation—but of a different kind. They are sources of information and often of field-specific vocabulary, and thus prompt factual questions and explanations, often leading to extended conversations and the search for more information from books, the Internet, or family members and friends with relevant expertise. Predictable texts—with obvious patterns and repeated lines—prompt shared readings, with the child chiming in or even taking the lead once the pattern is obvious or the book familiar. Similarly, books with searchable illustrations (e.g., the *Where's Waldo?* series and many shape, hidden picture, and "what's wrong with this picture?"

The Books Preschoolers Like Best ...

- Include a range of fiction and nonfiction picture books, ABC books, poetry, humor, and even some wordless books and chapter books

- Have beautiful illustrations with a distinct artistic style that fits the theme of the book

- Feature children who look like them or share their cultural backgrounds, family structures, interests, personalities, or names. For children of color, those with obvious disabilities or challenges, and others who may be growing up in a world where "people like us" are too seldom visible or too often stereotyped in mainstream culture, the realistic images and affirmation of identity that books can provide are essential, even (and perhaps especially) for children as young as 3.

- Are often part of a series featuring a character or set of characters

- Are fun to read aloud and to listen to

- Often feature literary language with rhyme; rhythm; repetition; alliteration; or unusual sentence structure, cadence, and phrasing

- Often have plots that build, piquing children's curiosity about what will happen next

- Use human or animal characters who share their feelings and challenges

- Often tell reassuring stories about characters who struggle with sibling rivalry, conflicts with friends, feelings of smallness, guilt, or inadequacy, or feelings of being left out or different

- Allow them to try on different adult roles

- Explain common phenomena

- Draw on folk traditions

- Capture the language of their community

- Reinforce positive feelings about their background

- Help them understand and appreciate people whose cultures are different from theirs

- Sometimes are "above their heads" but help them answer their questions or pursue a special interest

- Fuel dramatic and creative play with interesting facts, scenarios to reenact and vary, characters to emulate, or things to make and do

books) and labeled pictures prompt attention to visual detail and supported problem solving. An ABC book—or any book with clear print—can prompt letter and word identification games.

Bilingual books (with words in two languages) or translations of familiar books, well-known songs, or nursery rhymes can prompt discussions of different ways of saying and showing the same thing. Similarly, children often enjoy reading different versions of familiar tales and creating their own.

Whether at home, in a child care setting, or through a public library, every preschooler should have frequent access to a balanced book collection, including

- Books about children like themselves—and children who are different

- Books that engage their emotions and model positive behavior and clever solutions to problems

- Books with patterns that invite participation in reading

- Books they can act out

- Books that relate to what they're studying in school and expand their horizons

- Books related to their individual special interests and questions

- Books for picture and print detectives, including ABC books

- Books in their home languages

- Books with accompanying audio recordings or songs, such as those created by author Alma Flor Ada and musician Suni Paz

- Books they have created themselves or that have been created with or for them by parents or teachers

Reading aloud frequently from a diverse collection of books that invite conversation may be the single most important thing that adults can do to build preschoolers' language.

GOING DEEPER

"I wish I could ride an escalator," said Toby, after reading the book *Corduroy* (Freeman, 2007) with his grandmother and their home visitor. "You can!" both adults said together, as they realized simultaneously that Toby had never had that experience. "I've been meaning to take him to the mall," his grandmother explained, "but it's two buses and I haven't had the time." The home visitor had another idea: "There are escalators in some of the subway stations. Why don't we go ride one for our next home visit?"

Children learn a lot from books and the pictures they contain, as well as from book-inspired conversation. But real understanding often requires real-world experience. Adults can provide these experiences and help children make the connections.

In an interview for a television special, physicist Richard Feynman explained how his father had taught him to think when he was a very young child:

> Even when I was a small boy [my father] used to sit me on his lap and read to me from the *Encyclopedia Britannica,* and we would read, say, about dinosaurs and maybe it would be talking about . . . the tyrannosaurus rex, and it would say something like, "This thing is twenty-five feet high and the head is six feet across,". . . he'd stop and say, "Let's see what that means. That would mean that if he stood in our front yard he would be high enough to put his head through the window but not quite because the head is a little bit too wide and it would break the window". . . Everything we'd read would be translated as best we could into some reality and so I learned to do that—everything that I read I try to figure out what it really means. (Feynman, 2001, p. 3)

At the Lucy School near Baltimore, Maryland, adults often facilitate these more thorough understandings *before* they read the books. One technique is through drama and problem solving. For example, before introducing the book *The Giant Jam Sandwich* (Lord & Burroway, 1987), the teachers led the class through an imagination and problem-solving exercise. Following the book's basic storyline, the children pretended to be hungry wasps flying into a town and then took on the roles of townspeople who didn't like getting stung. Only after the townspeople had invented and acted out several ideas for getting rid of the troublesome wasps did the teachers lead them to the book's fanciful solution—a giant jam sandwich.

The Pyramid Model, an approach pioneered in the Netherlands by Jef van Kuyk (2003), uses a four-step process to build children's background for a carefully selected story and to support in-depth investigation of a set of related concepts:

1. *Orientation:* Sensory activities and opportunities to "mess around" with things that will figure prominently in the story

2. *Demonstration:* Teacher-presented lessons and storybook reading and discussion

3. *Broadening*—Questions, analogies, opportunities for reenactment and retelling, reading of related books, and other activities that extend the story themes and concepts

4. *Deepening:* Questions and problem-solving challenges that help children understand the concepts on a deeper level

For example, a unit on water featured the book *Tikki Tikki Tembo* (Mosel & Lent, 1968), a Chinese folktale about a boy who fell into a well. Before reading the book, the children experimented with buckets, water, and pulleys and tried walking on bricks around a tree "well" as fast as they could without falling in. The teacher read them the story on several occasions, talking with them about the events the words described and encouraging them to look closely at the pictures. Over the course of the multiweek unit, she introduced a variety of activities to broaden and deepen their understanding. These included

- Asking questions such as "How do you think Tikki Tikki Tembo felt when he was in the well? What could he have done to keep himself calm?"

- Encouraging children to retell and play out the story, using puppets or taking on roles

- Helping children to vote for their favorite characters, make a graph of their responses, and then talk about why some characters were popular while one wasn't chosen at all

- Challenging children to create their own water-holding wells in the sandbox, using perforated plastic pipe and stones

FUNDS OF KNOWLEDGE

Another way to push beyond pat understandings is to tap the "funds of knowledge" of the important people in children's lives so that, over time, children can participate in a variety of experiences and family conversations that explore the layers of meaning represented by words and stories. Often, this involves creating books that capture personal and family experiences and introduce young children to jobs, traditional crafts, and everyday skills in which their parents or grandparents have special expertise (Ada, 1988; González, Moll, & Amanti, 2005).

> The display of children's books looked like an art exhibit. Each book was carefully crafted. Some featured beautiful photography; others were adorned with ribbons and glitter; several sported collage or crayon illustrations; one was cut in the shape of a baseball glove. Some were bilingual, others written only in Spanish. But this display was not set up in a museum, and the books were not created by professional artists or authors. Rather, they had been created by Head Start parents, with or for children they loved.

The teachers who facilitated this book-making project were participants in an Urban College language and literacy course, Classroom Connections, developed by Costanza Eggers-Piérola, author of *Connections and Commitments: Reflecting Latino Values in Early Childhood Programs* (2005), for the Education Development Center (EDC). An article in EDC's December 2007 online newsletter described the ways in which the teachers built on their own, the children's, and the parents' funds of knowledge:

> Using bilingual text, family photos, printouts from the Internet, and drawings, the artists have showcased their diversity through colorful displays that blend contributions from teachers, young children, and families. . . . .
> Back in their own classrooms, teachers work closely with students and their families, using what they know about the children's home life as inspiration for lessons. For example, one teacher noted that many of the children in her classroom are familiar with the hairdressing profession, and so developed a curriculum unit around the bilingual children's book, *Hairs/Pelitos,* by Sandra Cisneros. Related activities may include having a hairdresser visit the class, going to a neighborhood salon, or creating a salon in the classroom. In this way, a rich vocabulary and activities emerged from the children's own interests and experiences.
> Some activities—such as the creation of the books and calendars— can involve parents as well. "The families created books about what they experienced coming to this country. Some knew very little English and

worked with the educators to generate words that were important to the family. For instance, one family wrote 'realize' and its Spanish equivalent 'realizarse' and had a message to their child about being proud of their Salvadoran heritage. Seeing something like this impacts the way children see and feel about their families," says Eggers-Piérola.

MAKING MEMORIES

What can individuals remember from early childhood? How far back do memories go? Researchers exploring childhood recollections have learned that both the timing and content of our earliest memories are influenced by cultural and individual patterns of talking about events.

In the Māori culture of New Zealand, for example, individual and family histories play important roles, and the past is a frequent topic of conversation. In a cross-cultural study of New Zealand adults, psychologist Harlene Hayne (MacDonald, Uesiliana, & Hayne, 2000) found that Māori respondents, on average, traced their earliest memories back to 32 months, not even 3 years old. In contrast, the average for her Caucasian respondents was 42 months, whereas those of Asian descent averaged 57 months. A similar contrast in age of earliest recollection between Asians and Caucasians has been found in studies conducted with American and Korean college students (Mullen, 1994; Mullen & Yi, 1995).

One possible explanation for these differences in recollection is that individual history is a less important conversation topic in "collectivist" or "interdependent" cultures that emphasize mutual support and group success than in those that put a higher premium on individual achievement. Indeed, in an unpublished study of adults in rural India, whose culture she characterized as highly interdependent, memory researcher Michele Leichtman (cited in Winerman, 2005) found that only 12% of those interviewed recalled a specific childhood event, in contrast to 69% of her American interviewees. An Israeli study found that adults who had been raised in a kibbutz collective community reported later earliest memories than those who had been brought up primarily by their parents, whether or not they had lived in a kibbutz setting (Harpaz-Rotem & Hirst, 2005).

Another explanation for these cross-cultural findings may lie in differences in the ways in which adults talk with children about events in the recent past. In a study conducted in the United States, young children whose parents had encouraged them to retell the story of a recent event remembered more details than did children who had not engaged in these conversations when asked about the event a few weeks later. The children's memories were especially rich when their

Language-Building Family Rituals

- Eating meals together while sharing news of the day, planning upcoming events, having a conversation about the food, and so forth. Some families start daily or weekly mealtime rituals when their children are quite young, such as taking turns saying grace, sharing the "best" and "worst" thing that happened, telling jokes, or involving the children in setting a fancy table.

- Saying prayers together each night

- Reading or telling bedtime stories, sometimes including stories about the child's own adventures or the parent's childhood experiences

- Giving books as presents on birthdays and other occasions

- Involving children in holiday preparations, or in chores that everyone does together, such as gardening, washing the car, or putting away groceries

- Having a kid's night to cook, in which young children get to help choose and prepare the meal

- Having weekly family movie nights (Visit the web site http://www.teachwithmovies.org for suggested films and accompanying Guides to Talking and Playing for Growth.)

- Participating in Sunday or Shabbat dinners for which the extended family gathers

- Having special days with just one parent and one child, scheduled in advance, with the child helping to plan the day. (This need not be a whole day to feel special, and the plans need not be elaborate. The child might choose the breakfast menu, you might go on a simple outing to the library or other favorite destination, and then you might play a favorite game or make something together. What makes the adventure memorable is your undivided attention.)

parents had helped them to elaborate their stories by including more and more information (Leichtman, Pillemer, Wang, Koreishib, & Han, 2000). Similarly, children in related studies remembered more—and developed stronger language and literacy skills—when their mothers used a more elaborative reminiscing style, frequently talking with their preschoolers about past events and asking open-ended questions that encouraged the children to tell detailed stories about daily life (Fivush, Haden, & Reese, 2006; Pillemer, 2000).

No matter how far back our memories extend, the events we recall most vividly tend to be "firsts" and celebrations, traumas and triumphs, and moments captured in frequently displayed photographs and oft-repeated stories. But our fondest childhood memories are often of the daily and weekly rituals through which families build children's language and their funds of knowledge.

JUST US KIDS

Blessing and her friend Noah were happily building castles with wooden blocks until Noah snatched the arch from Blessing's pile. "Give that back," Blessing ordered. "I was using it."

"I need it for my doorway," Noah countered. "It's mine."

Hearing their bickering, their teacher decided to seize the teachable moment to help them develop some negotiating skills. "Is there a way to solve this problem so you can both be happy?" she asked, taking the block and holding it behind her back.

"I had it first," Blessing asserted. "It's mine, and I was using it."

"I was using it first," said Noah. "For my doorway."

"Well, I wasn't here, so I don't know who was using it first. What can we do that will make you both happy?"

"We could share," said Blessing.

"I don't want to share," Noah griped.

Blessing had another idea. "We could take turns."

"Okay," said Noah, "but I get the first turn."

Blessing was tired of arguing. "Okay, you can go first."

"That's very kind of you, Blessing," said the teacher. "Will that make you happy, Noah?"

"Yes," said Noah, reaching for the block.

His teacher kept the block behind her back. "But remember, I asked how we could solve the problem so you would both be happy. Noah, can you think of a way to make Blessing happy?"

"I could say, 'Thank you, Blessing,'" Noah responded.

Blessing agreed, "That would make me happy." Noah thanked her, took the block from the teacher, and proudly completed his doorway.

When you're 3 or 4, getting along with other kids can be a major challenge. You all want the interesting toys, and none of you have a lot of patience. Furthermore, when you really want something or are bent on completing a project, it's hard to see another person's point of view. But, when adults step in too quickly or too frequently to solve the inevitable conflicts, or when, having gotten involved, they impose a solution or accept a one-sided solution, they deprive children of important opportunities to use their words to solve problems.

In spite of their sometimes frequent conflicts, most preschoolers want to have friends. Language is the basic currency of their social relationships, and play partners who will follow their directions or support and expand their stories are especially valued. Friends or siblings who play together frequently often create an ongoing story that grows more elaborate over time.

Watch, wait, and wonder—then find a way to join the play. It works for parents and teachers who want to build children's language, but it also works for preschoolers who just want to be part of the gang. Many socially successful 3-year-olds intuitively understand this wisdom. They will hang out at the edge of a group, playing quietly, until they sense an opening. They will then offer a prop or suggestion, extend an idea, or volunteer assistance in a way that advances the group's agenda.

Other preschoolers are natural leaders. They stride confidently up to a peer or group, introduce themselves, and set the play agenda. If an initial overture is rebuffed, they know how to come back.

Mandy and Gavin had been visiting the twins, Allie and Amy. At the end of the visit, the children exchanged polite good-byes. But Allie, who had played only with Mandy, refused to say good-bye to Mandy's brother.

"Why did you say good-bye to Mandy and not to Gavin, Allie?" her mother asked when their guests had left.

"I don't like boys," said Allie, rather fiercely.

Allie's mother decided that this was a good time to teach courtesy.

"What if Gavin said good-bye to your sister but not to you? Would you feel sad?"

"Maybe," said Allie. "Maybe not."

"I think Princess Jasmine might feel sad if Cinderella said good-bye to Sleeping Beauty and not to her," Allie's mother continued.

"Yeah, Bert might feel sad if Big Bird said good-bye to him and not to Ernie," added Amy, not wanting to be left out of the conversation.

"And Uncle Jerry would feel sad if we said good-bye to Aunt Karen and not to him," Allie continued, not to be outdone.

Although the point had been made, the girls continued to come up with more and more examples.

Children whose parents model and encourage courtesy and friendliness are likely to pick up these traits. Children who are temperamentally shy benefit from encouragement to interact with peers and intentional adult support (Kagan, 1999), as do those who may be left out of social groups because they are younger; less adept with words; different in their interests, abilities, preferred language, or appearance; or too ready to use physical force rather than words when conflicts arise.

Three- and 4-year-olds learn language from adults, but they also learn a lot from their peers. Adults can set the stage and tone for these language-building conversations and ensure their benefits for all children.

Preschool Pick-Up Lines

- "Hi. I'm _____."
- "Do you want to be my friend?"
- "Here's a flag for your sand castle."
- "Let's play _____."
- "Can I play, too?"
- "We both have curly hair."
- "I like your shirt."
- "Want some of this lemonade juice I made?"

Facilitating Language-Building Conversations Among Children

- Set up environments that encourage peer talk. Such places might include a sandbox or block corner where children can build together or connect their constructions, intimate spaces such as forts and lofts, an open space with large items that groups of children can use to create forts and obstacle courses, a table or corner where a joint construction can be left up for several weeks and added to and played in over time, or a stage or puppet stage that invites children to plan and put on a show.

- Bring in interesting items that will spark questions and conversations. These might include unusual gadgets, artifacts reflecting your own and the children's cultural backgrounds, or souvenirs from family trips.

- Invite guests who can share stories and answer children's questions. These might include parents and grandparents, community elders, adults whose jobs relate to areas children have asked about or are investigating, and professional artists, musicians, authors, and storytellers.

- Encourage cooperative activities such as putting together a floor puzzle or playing a computer game that requires joint decision making.

- Encourage children to speak in their home language as well as English. If you can, model for them how you use their home language and then translate for those who do not understand.

- Partner children with others who speak their language.

- Give a nonverbal or quiet child a job or role that makes it easy for more talkative children to include him in their play.

- Coach children who need help or teach them "pick-up lines."

- Use pretend play and storytelling to help children understand and navigate the social world.

Great Ways to Feel Big and Powerful (when you are only 3 or 4)

- Help with a "grown-up" job.

- Take care of someone or make someone feel better.

- Master a self-chosen challenge, such as completing a puzzle or shooting a basket.

- Be part of a group or team.

- Stand up for yourself or for someone who is being treated unfairly.

- Be the hero of your own story.

I THINK I CAN

"You're not the boss of me," 3-year-old Emily insisted when her sister told her to set the table, "I'm the boss of myself."

Three- and 4-year-olds like Emily want desperately to be "big." A girl may try on her mother's clothes, makeup, and jewelry—especially the real stuff that is supposed to be off limits. A boy may imitate his father's walk or try to use his tools. Both girls and boys enact the roles of superheroes, and they sometimes pick on younger or more vulnerable children, especially if they have been picked on or bossed around. Like adults, children are most likely to be aggressive when they feel vulnerable. They may lash out if another child threatens their social position by calling them a name or playing with their best friend or by stealing their parent's attention. Unlike adults, however, they are still learning to separate action from intention, and they may interpret an accidental bump as a deliberate act of aggression that requires retaliation or adult punishment.

Like the hero of Steven Kellogg's classic picture book *Much Bigger than Martin* (1992), 3- and 4-year-olds have their own ideas about how to be "big." In Kellogg's story, the narrator is tired of being pushed around by his big brother Martin, always having to take the smaller piece of cake and play the less desirable role in Martin's games. He tries different solutions, eating apples because he has heard they "make you grow" and watering himself like a plant, before finding one that works.

Martin's little brother's solution is a literal one—he makes himself a pair of stilts. But of course, the problem of feeling small is an ongoing one for young children, which is why they love stories of small heroes. Watty Piper's *The Little Engine That Could* (1978) has taught generations of young children to take on challenging big people tasks and persist until they succeed by chanting "I think I can."

> "Wow! This classroom is gorgeous," the preschool director told her staff one Monday morning before the children arrived. "Did you do all this yourselves?" The teachers beamed. In preparation for their unit on polar animals, they had transformed the classroom into a winter wonderland. Paper snowflakes hung from the ceiling; winter scenes adorned the walls. The reading corner held an intriguing collection of books about polar regions, hibernating animals, tracks in the snow, and winter fun. One shelf unit had been turned into a set of dioramas, with photographs taped to the back and toy animals arranged in front. The water table had been turned into an Arctic seascape, with rubber polar bears, walruses, and seals perched on foam blocks and whales swimming amid shaving cream icebergs. "There's so much here for the children to investigate and talk about," the director continued, "and I'm sure they'll have fun learning about animals in winter. But I think that you are working too hard."
>
> As the teachers' expressions changed from pride to surprise, the director explained. "You've done all the planning. I wonder what would happen if you let the children help. The room might not look as beautiful as it does now, but it would be theirs! I'm sure their good ideas would spark a lot of conversation and give you even more opportunities to explore their questions and expand their vocabularies."

"You are working too hard." Busy parents are constantly relearning that lesson. A 3-year-old's "help" isn't always helpful, especially if her parents are in a hurry. But 3- and 4-year-olds love being part of adult activities. Often, when adults solicit their ideas, they come up with ways in which they really can help. Meaningful contributions build skill and self-esteem-and give them stories to tell.

From Language to Literacy

(4–6+ Years)

"Once upon a time there were two polar bears, a brother and a sister, who lived in a frozen land. Every morning, they set out to hunt for their breakfast. One day, the little sister couldn't find any food. She walked a long, long way, searching for something to eat. . . "

Four-year-olds Kenny and Sara listen raptly as their classmate Maisha reads this story to them, running her finger under the text and making sure they can see the pictures as she turns the pages. They have no idea that the words their classmate is "reading" are not the ones written on the pages. When an adult approaches, Maisha falls silent and holds the book against her chest; as soon as the adult walks away, she resumes her "reading."

A generation ago, reading was widely thought of as something children had to be ready to learn. Although some parents read to their children regularly, gave them alphabet blocks to play with, or taught them to write their names, no one expected children to do much reading before kindergarten or first grade. Teachers and parents alike assumed that learning to read required proper instruction, and that most preschool-age children lacked the requisite patience, hand–eye coordination, and ability to grasp key concepts to profit from reading lessons. Children who learned to read without formal schooling were considered to have unusual abilities.

Today, early educators recognize how much a child like Maisha has already learned about reading. She knows how books work and can turn pages in order. Although she can tell her own story from the pictures, she knows that the real story—the words that the reader is supposed to say—is carried by the print. Furthermore, she knows that the print is read from left to right, top to bottom, and she has a rough idea of how much talking the print on each page represents. She also knows a lot about how a story of a particular type is supposed to sound. Her rich vocabulary and facility with storybook phrasing enable her to weave what she knows, sees, and imagines into a story that her classmates believe is really in the book.

Like most 4-year-olds who have been to school or whose families work with them at home, Maisha is an accomplished "emergent reader." The skills she is building as she listens to storybooks; engages in rich language-building conversations; and plays at reading, writing, and storytelling provide critical foundations for the next phases of literacy acquisition. So, too, do the explicit and informal lessons she receives in rhyme, alliteration, letter recognition, storytelling, and vocabulary from her family, community, and teachers.

Emergent readers often spend a lot of time practicing reading-like behaviors. They turn pages, repeat familiar words, fill in parts of the story, and may even point to some of the words as they "read" them. Some memorize favorite books and recite them aloud or correct an adult who misreads a word or tries to skip part of the story. They may even recognize particular words and be able to point them out, run a finger along under the text as they say each word, or find the word *ball* because they know it starts with a *b*. They may be quite good at finding words that rhyme or that start with the same sound. But the real breakthrough—the point at which a child begins to read independently or conventionally—occurs when she realizes that letters represent the sounds she hears in words, and when she brings together her knowledge of letters and print with her knowledge of sounds in words.

A child like Maisha is highly motivated to master this next step. Reading is a valued activity in her social group, as well as something she enjoys. And, although her spellbinding storytelling can fool her peers into thinking she can read "for real," she knows that there is more to reading than what she can currently do.

THE READING PROCESS

Unlike talking, reading does not come naturally. Humans have only been reading for a few thousand years, and even today, many of us can't do it. Only about 200 of the world's 6,000 or so languages have a written form. And although many children surprise their parents and teachers by learning to read with little or no deliberate teaching, most require explicit instruction.

Spoken language comes first. With a rich repertoire of words and phrases, children can retell stories they have heard and craft new ones of their own. They know many ways to say the same thing and can choose words for their sounds and associations as well as for their meanings. They understand—intuitively—how parts of words fit together, and they can make new words and nonsense words by playing around with word parts.

Reading takes spoken language to a new level. Words that are written down rather than spoken in conversation lack the immediate, shared context that makes their meaning and significance clear. A writer can't respond to a reader, as a speaker does to a listener, answering questions or correcting misperceptions and misconceptions. A reader must hold sequences of words and sentences in mind; imagine what the writer is describing; and empathize, analyze, and "read between the lines" without being able to hear the intonation, ask what was meant, or respond to the quizzical look that suggests that an interpretation was off track. A writer, therefore, is likely to use language that is richer, more precise, and more evocative than that of ordinary speech, with longer and more complex sentences, more adjectives and adverbs, and a sprinkling of apt but arcane words that might seem pretentious in everyday conversation. The first challenge for the reader, though, is to figure out what spoken words the written words represent.

In many writing systems, the symbols on the page stand for ideas, whole words, or syllables. In alphabetic systems, however, symbols represent phonemes—the individual sounds that make up words. The reader of an alphabetic language needs to grasp the alphabetic principle—that letters and letter combinations represent the sounds that are put together to make the words. Knowing the sounds that letters "make" and how to blend these sounds into words, the reader can "crack the code" and sound out words.

> When toddlers are stretching their language capacities,
> putting together their native language expertise in ways that
> will promote their future success at reading, learning a second
> language cannot take the place of learning with one's own
> first language. Pre-schoolers' experiences with their own
> language allow, for example, phonemic sensitivity to develop;
> the child can then experience the alphabetic insight and get
> the idea needed for learning to read. (National Research
> Council, 1998, p. 157–158)

In an orthographically regular language such as Spanish or German, the correspondence between alphabetic symbols and phonemes is straightforward. For the most part, each letter represents a particular sound and each sound is represented by just one letter. Languages like French and English, however, present a greater challenge, especially for beginning readers. In English, for example, frequently used sounds, such as the long *a* in *way,* are represented in multiple ways, as in the words *whey, weigh, wait, gate,* and *great.* Several letters (*c, g, s,* and all of the vowels) can represent multiple sounds, as can frequently used letter combinations such as *th, ti, ea, oo, ie,* and *gh.* Furthermore, the sound associated with a single vowel such as *a* often, but not always, depends on the letter(s) that follows it, as in *at, ate, ah, car,* and *care.* Some of the letters in words such as *sign, nighttime,* and *lamb* are not pronounced at all; these silent letters may or may not affect how other letters in the word are pronounced.

The more words children know in a language, and the more they know about how these words are used and what they mean in various contexts, the easier it is for the children to pick up the patterns of symbol–sound correspondence that govern regular and irregular spellings. With practice, these associations become so automatic that experienced readers barely notice them.

OUTSIDE-*IN* AND INSIDE-*OUT*

In a classic article, Grover Whitehurst and Christopher Lonigan (1998) described the reading process. In order to figure out what the words on a page say and what they mean, the reader works from the outside in and from the inside out. Clues from outside of the printed word prime the reader's guesses as to what the word might be, and then enable the reader to check whether her guess about the word makes sense. These context clues allow the reader to interpret the meaning of an individual word as well as the meaning of the passage that contains it. Clues from inside of the word are also vital. They enable the reader to map the written letters onto the sounds they represent, blend these sounds together into a word, and associate a spoken word with the written one. Fluent readers move seamlessly, rapidly, and automatically back and forth between inside-*out* and outside-*in* analysis, usually without awareness.

When beginning readers approach unfamiliar text, their focus is on decoding. As they work to apply their inside-out knowledge of symbol–sound correspondence, they support their hunches with everything they know about the content of what they are reading—using pictures, context, their expectations of what word might fit in a sentence, and the logic of the story as clues. As these processes become more and more automatic through repeated practice, children become fluent readers.

Everything that makes young children want to read and write and helps them to do so in their own emergent ways—and everything that promotes attention, familiarity, practice, and play—makes a difference to children's mastery of early decoding skills. The more children learn about words and stories, books and other uses of print, and letters and sounds, the easier it will be for them to learn to read. And the more they try to read and write with real words and letters, the more they will learn about reading and writing, letters and sounds, and how the alphabetic principle works.

Experienced readers process text rapidly and automatically. Over time, their brains develop specialized circuits that can make lightning-speed connections, leaving them time to focus not just on the meaning of individual words but also on the cadence of a sentence, the feelings evoked through the choice and arrangement of details, and whether or not they agree with the author's central message.

STEPS TO READING

Building a brain is like building a house. When you build a house, you have to start at the bottom. First you put in the foundation; then the structural frame; then the plumbing, heating, and electrical systems; and finally the finishing details. If the foundation is weak or the frame lopsided, the house will never be right. It's easier—and a lot less expensive—to get the basics right the first time than to go back and redo them (National Research Council and Institute of Medicine, 2000).

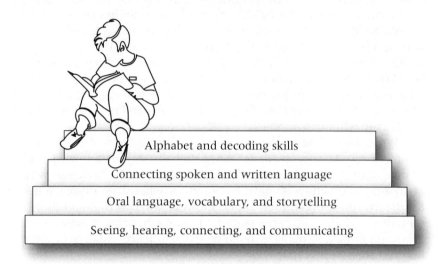

Alphabet and decoding skills

Connecting spoken and written language

Oral language, vocabulary, and storytelling

Seeing, hearing, connecting, and communicating

Figure 6.1. The steps to reading are built on early experiences that build connections in the brain.

We now know that learning to read is a process of brain building and brain training. Early experiences build the connections in the areas of the brain that deal with seeing and hearing, social connection and communication, basic information processing, and then language (see Figure 6.1). As children learn to recognize letters, associate them with sounds, and blend sounds into words, specialized neural circuits are built. With repeated use, these circuits become capable of such rapid processing that word recognition becomes automatic and reading becomes fluent. Now the reader has time to think not only about what the text says but also about what the author is trying to convey (Wolf, 2007).

Learning to read starts in infancy, as babies establish relationships with caring adults, explore their environment with their bodies and senses and learn to make sense of and connect to what they see and hear. Their early experiences of relating, learning, and back-and-forth communication build the foundation for all that follows.

Oral language is the next step, and this is where too many of our children get tripped up. They learn enough words for everyday communication but not enough for discussing subjects beyond the realm of shared experience. With limited vocabularies and limited opportunities to use their words in all kinds of straightforward, playful, and information-seeking ways, they don't learn enough words—or enough about how words work—by the time they enter school to make the next step an easy one.

Experts estimate that a novice reader needs to know 5,000–6,000 words in a language in order to learn to read in that language (Chall, Jacobs, & Baldwin, 1990; Moats, 2001). The average child in the United States knows more than 6,000 words in his primary language by kindergarten or first grade (Biemiller & Slonim, 2001); children with enriched language backgrounds are likely to know more than twice that number and thus to have an ongoing edge (Hart & Risley, 1995). But too many of our children are not getting early language experiences that are rich enough to provide a strong base for reading, especially if they are growing up in resource-poor circumstances. Many of these children will enter school with only half of the vocabulary they need for reading, even though their language use may be quite appropriate in their families and communities (Bowman, 2007).

The third step includes two parts that are increasingly fitted together. In order to read an alphabetic language, children first need to be able to hear the separate sounds that make up words, or to connect spoken and written language. They also need to be able to blend sounds together into words. These abilities are often referred to as *phonemic awareness*. At the same time, children need to develop some rudimentary ideas about how their language is written, often called "concepts of print." They come to recognize, for example, that the writing goes from left to right, that spaces indicate breaks between words, and that words are written with letters. Knowing the names of many of these letters prepares children to take the next step. Even in languages with complex spelling rules, such as English, many of the letter names are similar to the phonemes that they usually represent.

Children who have good phonemic awareness and can name a majority of the letters can begin to work out the alphabetic principle. Once they get this idea—that the letters represent the phonemes that are combined into words—they can begin to figure out how to translate letters on a page into a spoken word. Interestingly, children who reach this point in their home language can use this awareness as they learn to read their second one, even when the alphabet is different.

The fourth step—learning specific alphabet and decoding skills— is a big part of the kindergarten and first-grade curriculum, at least in the United States, where 5- and 6-year-olds are expected to learn how to read simple stories written with short, regularly spelled words. For many children with strong foundational skills, this step is so natural that they barely notice they have taken it. Once they grasp the alphabetic principle, they suddenly realize they can read! The letters flow together as words, and the words tell a story. The child is launched on a lifelong adventure, and will never look back.

Most children, though, need a helping hand in order to step into independent reading. Instruction and practice with phonics help them to hone their phonemic awareness by attending to individual sounds and to link these sounds with letters and letter combinations. With instruction and practice in writing, they become increasingly proficient at recognizing and forming letters and using these letters to represent the sounds that they hear. In writing what they hear with invented spelling—often using a letter to stand for the whole syllable that its name sounds like and leaving out silent letters and less salient sounds—children internalize the alphabetic principle.

Familiar, highly patterned texts with simple stories, illustrative pictures, and a lot of words that they can sound out enable beginning readers to bring together enough inside-*out* and outside-*in* cues to get most of the words with sufficient ease and speed to link them into meaningful sentences. When they stumble as they attempt to read aloud, an adult can help them over the bump so that they don't lose the gist of the story. Their spelling will become more regular and consistent over time as they go back and forth between reading and writing.

The stair-step metaphor is useful for illustrating how each skill builds on prior ones and supports those that come later. But it also can be misleading. Children continue to explore with their bodies and all of their senses and to hone their nonverbal communication skills, even when they can talk. Language learning doesn't stop when children's vocabularies reach 6,000 words or when they develop phonemic awareness and sophisticated concepts of print. Rather, children continue to increase their vocabularies as they learn to read. Once they become adept at basic decoding, reading is likely to be the major source of their vocabulary growth (Stanovitch, 1986).

WORD POWER: THE LANGUAGE FOUNDATION

Children who enter kindergarten with rich vocabularies are primed for success. They have a wealth of background knowledge about the physical, natural, and social world. They can use their words to ask pointed questions, reason their way through problems, express strong emotions appropriately, and make friends. They can also use their words creatively and can appreciate word play and verbal humor. They can understand and follow multistep directions, and they are on track to becoming successful readers. Their varied vocabularies and general facility with language hold a wealth of knowledge of how words are formed and put together into sentences that help them crack the code as beginning readers. More important, the wealth of knowledge that these words represent enables them to understand and enjoy more sophisticated texts and to learn new words more rapidly from context. Their initial literacy advantages compound as their education progresses (Snow et al., 2007).

In pre-K and kindergarten programs and in their neighborhoods, 4- and 5-year-olds are likely to encounter all sorts of new words and new uses of familiar words. From books, they learn about faraway places, long-ago times, and things that are too small to see or that exist only in collective imagination. They may learn words such as *transmission, wrench,* and *mortar* from watching people repair cars, homes, or sidewalks. Older children may teach them popular songs, jump rope and hand clapping rhymes, jokes, riddles, and put-downs and rejoinders that introduce new vocabulary and new uses of familiar words while also playing with initial and rhyming sounds.

No matter how much language children are learning outside of their homes, they still need language-building parent involvement. For a child, that comes, as it has since babyhood, from casual conversations and private games; from sharing and talking about books; from family rituals and gatherings that bring people together; and from singing and storytelling, questions and answers, shared humor, and deliberate teaching. It may also come from joint storytelling and pretend play and from the discussions of plans, tools, tasks, and techniques that young children engage in with older family members as they work on projects together.

Some children will continue to engage in pretend play with their parents well into middle childhood, talking to and for dolls and imaginary friends or asking their parents to take on roles as they act out stories and scenarios. Others will increasingly move their pretend play out of the home or behind closed doors, giving their parents glimpses into their imaginary worlds but denying full access (Segal & Bardige, 2000). Parents, too, differ both in the extent to which they encourage their children's continued pretending and in their eagerness to join as partners.

As pretend play declines as a parent–child interaction pattern, other kinds of language-building conversations take its place. More grounded in the real world and with increasing curiosity about and understanding of how the world works, by 5 or 6 children can be a real help in the family. As they learn how to help with everyday and seasonal chores, home improvement projects, and preparations for special

Tips for Talking with 4-, 5-, and 6-Year-Olds

• Talk about the child's favorite subjects. Let him be the expert and teach you what she knows.

• Give the child time to tell her story without interruption. If she loses the thread or confuses you, ask about why a key event occurred or what happened next.

• Ask questions that help the child focus on specific events or details, or that challenge him to clarify or elaborate.

• Resist the urge to quiz or interrogate. Ask questions whose answers you really want to know.

• Wonder and speculate together.

• Use interesting, specific, descriptive words, in contexts that make their meaning clear.

• Talk about words. When you introduce a word that is new to the child, talk about other words that sound similar to it or have similar—or opposite—meanings.

• Share your own interests and experiences with the child. Teach her the specialized vocabulary of your craft, job, or hobby.

• Be playful. Use humor—including simple puns, standard forms for jokes and riddles, and obviously ridiculous suggestions.

• Pose some interesting problems that challenge the child's thinking.

• Ask about the child's favorite books. Talk about your favorites, as well.

• Help the child articulate his feelings. When you suspect that he may be feeling angry, jealous, frustrated, confused, distressed, guilty, or anxious, talk about times when you have shared these feelings, or choose an appropriate storybook and talk about how the characters felt and how they coped with the challenges they faced. Share just enough information to get him talking—asking questions, describing his own and others' feelings, or suggesting an alternative course of action for himself or for a storybook character.

- Key into the child's questions, including those that she may have difficulty putting into words or may ask indirectly by asserting facts and theories that she isn't sure are true. When you don't know the answers or have only limited expertise, talk about how you can learn more together.

- Don't give up on the dolls, toys, and imaginary friends that still matter to the child. If you continue to treat his imaginary companions as worthy conversation partners, he will know that you value his imaginary world and will continue to share it with you.

- Help the child reflect on her own learning. What does she want to know? How have her skills improved over time and what has she learned? How did she figure out a problem or come to a decision? What can you do to help her as she seeks to master a challenge?

- KEEP TALKING—AND LISTENING—A LOT!

events, they learn the tools, techniques, specialized vocabulary, and funny stories of their family's skills, interests, and hobbies.

Even when their parents protect them from watching potentially disturbing news on television, children are likely to pick up information about what is happening in the world and to want to participate in adult conversations about local and world events. They may share a parent's interest in sports teams or public figures, or they may eagerly follow the career of a personal hero whom they would like to emulate. Increasingly, they will develop interests and expertise of their own—with their own words, factoids, and stories to share.

HARD QUESTIONS

As children spend more time with peers and older children at school and in their neighborhoods, they pick up a wealth of information, trivia, and occasional misinformation. They learn from overheard conversations, television, and each other as well as from explicitly educational experiences. They also spend a fair amount of time thinking—pondering the implications of what they have read or heard; trying to apply their knowledge to a real-world challenge, such as fixing a broken toy or getting a classmate to stop calling them names; and puzzling over abstract ideas, seeming contradictions, and things that just don't make sense to their concrete minds. Their questions often reveal their eagerness to learn about other places, people, and times and their curiosity about what lies beyond the known world of their experience and their picture books.

- "How come polar bears only live at the North Pole and penguins only live at the South Pole?"

- "Can we celebrate Chanukah and Christmas and Kwanzaa, too? Why not?"

- "Does God get hungry?"

- "Do pets have their own heaven, or do they go to people heaven?"

- "What came before the Big Bang?"

- "What's the biggest number?"

- "Where was I before I was in Mommy's tummy?"

- "Do people on the other side of the world walk upside down? Why don't they fall off?"

- "What does that sign say?"

- "Did you know that a blue whale is the biggest animal there is, even bigger than an elephant?"

- "My teacher said that Christopher Columbus discovered America. How can you discover a place where people already live?"

TELL ME A STORY

"Children don't learn language from watching TV," the parent educator explained in Spanish and English to the assembled Head Start parents, "although they may learn some choice words and phrases that way. To really learn a language, they need a person to talk to. They need back-and-forth interaction and meaningful conversation."

The parents weren't so sure. They knew that their 4- and 5-year-olds were learning more than just isolated words from the television shows they watched together because their children talked about lessons they learned from the shows and incorporated the shows' characters into their play.

The parent educator clarified. "Children younger than 3 are just learning their first language or languages, and TV is no substitute for a real person who can figure out what they are trying to say and help them put it into words. Older children can learn quite a bit from well-chosen TV shows that engage their interest and challenge their thinking. But of course, they learn a lot more when they can talk about what they are learning and reenact the stories in play."

"Should I watch TV with my son in Spanish or English?" asked a mother who was just learning English herself. Before the parent educator could explain the pros and cons of each choice (children learn new concepts more easily in their home language first, and this is especially true of concepts related to reading; watching and listening to a familiar or easy-to-follow story in a new language can help a child practice that language), the mother answered her own question. "When we watch in Spanish, he just sits there and takes it in. But when we watch in English, he translates for me. So I think English is better for him, too."

The parent educator agreed. "It's your conversation that's important. When he translates and answers the questions that you ask when you don't quite understand or know how to say something, you both are learning the English words. But I hope you'll also take the opportunity to talk in Spanish about TV shows and storybooks you both enjoy and to continue teaching him his first language. Being bilingual has many advantages."

Like children's books and real-life experiences, television and videos can be a source of stories that children can enjoy, retell, replay, and extend. Indeed, popular children's shows are a favorite play theme for 4-year-olds and kindergartners. Just as adults discuss the latest episodes of popular sitcoms with friends and co-workers, children love to come together to reenact—and extend—the stories they all know from television.

Whether inspired by storybooks, television shows, videos, real-life events, or imaginary events and characters, children not only ask for and tell stories but also retell and reenact them over and over. A good story improves with each retelling, as the teller adds or changes details, skips parts that seem to bore the audience, adjusts the timing to heighten suspense or get a laugh, draws explicit or implicit analogies to a listener's experience or behavior, and finds just the right words to make a description evocative or a line memorable and fun to repeat. At age 4 or 5, children can vary familiar stories and tell quite elaborate real-life and imaginary stories without adult help, using various kinds of props and prompts, including

- Dolls, action figures, puppets, and toys

- Picture cut-outs or images that can be arranged and rearranged on a flannel board, magnet board, or computer

- Albums, scrapbooks, and photo displays

- Costumes, props, and occasionally scenery—with friends to act out the different parts

- Blank or partially filled-in books to which they add their own pictures and dictated words

- "Totem poles" (made by gluing pictures to a cardboard cylinder) that remind them of the key characters or sequence of events

- Stages for performances that they put on for family and friends

- Audience feedback, participation, and questions

TALKING ABOUT WORDS

The Head Start class had been discussing the differences between plants and animals. "Animals move, breathe, and eat." The teacher explained. "Oh, then I'm an animal," one boy proudly concluded. As the teacher complimented his good thinking, a classmate blurted out indignantly, "My mama says, 'Don't never let anybody call you a animal. You're a boy.'"

Of course, both children were correct. An "animal" can be any vertebrate or invertebrate, or the word's use can be restricted to nonhuman beasts and humans who behave "like animals." Many 4- and 5-year-olds are delighted to discover that the same word can have two or more meanings and that this can be a source of word fun. Of course, most children have been using many words in more than one way since toddlerhood. If they speak or have heard more than one language, they already know that there are different ways to say the same thing and may even realize that a word such as the English *see* means something very different than the Spanish *si*. They may have been puzzled by a name that blatantly mismatches its owner, such as a place to sleep called "Day's Inn" or a dark-skinned man named "Mr. White." But their awareness of double entendre and their ability to manipulate it is new. Now they can get a simple knock, knock joke and even learn to tell it:

Knock, Knock
Who's there?
Boo.

Boo who?
Boo-hoo-hoo. Now we're both crying.

With a little help, they can enjoy the humor of riddles and jokes that rely on puns and of books with characters like Amelia Bedelia in the Amelia Bedelia books (e.g., Parish, 1992), who make silly mistakes because they confuse homonyms such as *steak* and *stake*.

The following African American children's game was captured in a Mister Rogers video that is part of the Family Communications (2005) *From Lullabies to Literacy* program. As children recite the lines, they touch the parts of their own or their partners' bodies that the puns name.

Hey, *Chest*-er
Eye see you're *back* from the *arm*-y.
It's been y-*ears* and y-*ears,*
But *eye* still *nose* ya.

The more children play with both the sounds and meanings of words—and the more that they talk about words as words with the important adults in their lives—the better prepared they will be for the challenges of interpretation that they will encounter as they learn to read and write. The following poem plays with various meanings of some "simple" words: *run, home,* and *race*. As they share the poem with children, encourage parents and other caregivers to talk with them about the different meanings these words have in different lines. They might also talk about what *spot, support,* and *speech* mean in the poem and other meanings or uses that children know for these words.

Home Run Poem
Today I hit a home run
And then went running home,
Because my nose was running
And I had to write a poem.

I ran along the river
That runs along our street.
I ran into my best friend
At the spot we usually meet.

"I'm running for class president,"
He said, "Please vote for me."
And so I promised to support
My friend's candidacy.

I said, "I'll help you win that race,
If you will race me home.
I'll help you write your campaign speech,
But first, we'll write my poem."

PIECES OF THE PUZZLE: CONNECTING SPOKEN AND WRITTEN LANGUAGE

At her Fun Times Family Child Care, Joan Matsalia makes song boxes for all of the children, even the babies. She gives each child a recipe box in which to keep a collection of index cards that represent their favorite songs. She writes the name of a song on the front of a card and illustrates it with a simple cartoon. On the back, she pastes a mailing label on which she has printed the words to the first verse. Children can request songs from their boxes at nap time or circle time, when they are having their diapers changed or waiting to be picked up, or to sing on a field trip. They can take a card home to teach a song to their family, or they can bring home some blank cards so their family can add some new songs.

"The kids love the idea of pulling out a song from their very own box when it is their turn to choose," Joan explains, as she conducts a literacy workshop for her colleagues. "Over time, it helps them to make the connection between hearing the words of a song and seeing them in writing. They come to understand that words are the things that tell us what to say or sing when we read."

Young children hear and use spoken language throughout their days, everywhere they go. They also see written language everywhere—on their clothing and toys, on street signs and billboards, on packaged foods and picture books, even on television. But in order to connect spoken and written language, they need to realize that written words are different from pictures. They are not just symbols for things, but symbols for the words that are used to name and talk about the things.

If you ask most 3-year-olds to say a long word, they are apt to give you a word like *snake* or *yardstick* rather than one like *elephant* or *encyclopedia*. Similarly, if you ask which word is longer, *turtle* or *eel*, a child may confidently assert that *eel* is the longer word. If pressed for an explanation, he may tell you that eels are much longer than turtles or that turtles are round but eels are long. A long word, in many

3-year-olds' minds, is a word that describes something that looks long or that takes long to read, do, or say. They don't yet realize that a word can exist apart from the thing or action it names or describes, and that words can have their own characteristics.

To really "get" this idea, children need to learn a lot of words and to begin to think about words as words. They need to be able to pull a word out of its conversation context and to focus on its meaning and sound. It also helps to have many "up close and personal" experiences that draw their attention to print, and eventually to the features of print that represent the features of words.

LEARNING ABOUT PRINT

Annie is not even 3, but she can already read her name! It's right there on the box of her favorite kind of macaroni—Annie's! She helps her dad find it on the supermarket shelves, and she gets the box for her mom when it's time to make dinner. Every day at child care, Annie cooks macaroni in the play kitchen, using an empty box of her favorite kind.

Even toddlers can learn to recognize environmental print—the signs, logos, and symbols that are common in their environment and are frequent topics of conversation. They pull out favorite books for the umpteenth reading, reach for their favorite cereals as they pass them in a shopping cart, and get excited when they see the familiar sign for their favorite fast food restaurant. They aren't actually reading, of course, but are tuning in to the whole picture of font, size, color, graphic art, and letters. Like Annie, they focus especially on the written words that have personal meaning.

Children learn more and more about the content of their favorite stories through repeated readings and accompanying conversations that reinforce words and concepts, make new connections, and deepen understanding, as well as through their own involvement in retelling or reenacting the story. In a similar way, they learn more and more about how words are written through

- Repeated exposure and examination

- Conversations that draw their attention to print, highlight key features, make new connections, and deepen understanding, and

- Their own attempts to write in various ways for various purposes

Books are just one of the many sources that young children can use to gain familiarity with print. Early educators talk about "print-rich environments." These are homes, classrooms, and communities that not only display print in many forms (and often in several languages, alphabets, and nonalphabetic writing systems) but that also draw children's attention to the print and help them make meaningful connections between written and spoken language.

The following four vignettes illustrate a variety of print-rich environments.

When her father comes to pick her up from Head Start, 4-year-old Trinity shows him the block city that she built with her friends, Amber and Lilit. Laid out on a carpet that looks like a city map, there are buildings made from blocks, cardboard tubes, and empty yogurt containers. Toy vehicles labeled "ambulance," and "fire engine" wait at "stop" and "yield" signs on the carpet's roads, and a collection of rubber animals stand quietly in a block pen labeled "zoo." "Here is the church, and here is the steeple. Here is the train, and here is the zoo," says Trinity.

Her father is impressed. "I'd like to live in that town," he says. "I could just get on the train and go to the zoo whenever I wanted to. You and your friends are great builders!"

"We can read, too!" announces Trinity, much to her father's surprise. "This sign says 'stop' and this says 'fire truck' and this," she exclaims, pointing to the sign she asked her teacher to write, "says, 'Don't knock down!'"

"Can I have a really big piece of paper?" asks 4-year-old Steven. "Me and Matt are playing basketball with the clothes hamper and we need to make a scoreboard."

Walking into José and Kristen's home, the first thing you notice is that everything is beautifully arranged. Although they have two children, ages 10 and 4, there is almost no clutter. A small statue of Buddha, the focal point of the living room, is surrounded by carefully presented offerings of child-gathered seeds, leaves, and flower petals and a child's drawing with a caption of wiggly lines and letter-like forms. A similar drawing is posted on the refrigerator door. A beautiful book of world art lies open on the coffee table. In the girls' room, a low shelf holds a few children's books; higher ones hold adult and young adult books and religious texts. A basket of crayons and markers and a box of scrap paper and greeting cards sit on a low table, placed near the neat school desk with its calendar, file drawers, school notebooks, journal, and dictionary. It is clear that reading, writing, and aesthetics are important to everyone in this family, and that even the 4-year-old's work is valued.

———————————

Like many pre-K classrooms, the one at the Martin Luther King School has words all over the walls. The calendar and schedule, names on the children's cubbies, class list at the entrance, job chart, and parent bulletin board are typical of early childhood programs. But this room has clearly been transformed by the children and their teachers. A large box in one corner is labeled "hibernation cave." A piece of chart paper taped to the wall lists some intriguing facts: "Bears can get cavities from eating too much honey." "Bears can go all winter without any food." The usual house corner sports some unusual signs: "Medicine Refrigerator," "Vet's Office," "Recovery Room—Do Not Disturb."

Print-rich environments take many forms, but those that are most effective have some common features:

- *Print is salient for children—it doesn't just blend into the background.*

    —Print is posted at the children's eye level or is imprinted on books, toys, storage bins, and other objects that children can handle.

    —Print is relatively large, is in a clear font, and is artfully displayed.

- *Print conveys meaningful messages and serves useful purposes.*

    —Lists, notes, schedules, and labels help children and adults organize time and materials.

    —Signs give helpful directions or information: "Welcome," "Closed," "Shhhhh—my baby is sleeping."

    —Specific labels such as "La Bodega de Briana," "Medicine Refrigerator," "Our Science Museum," and "Fluffy the Rabbit" personalize the space and support children's activities.

- *Children can see that reading and writing are valued grown-up activities.*

    —Adult reading materials, such as books, magazines, catalogs, recipes, directions, mail, and newspapers, are visible and frequently used while children are present.

    —Adults let children see (and sometimes even help with) their grown-up writing activities, such as making lists, exchanging mail, ordering supplies, taking notes, recording measurements, doing schoolwork, and keeping records.

- *Print and associated materials inspire children to read and write, emergently, with help, or independently.*

  —Books and other reading materials for children are accessible and attractively displayed in multiple activity centers.

  —Intentionally arranged materials—such as a prescription pad and pen in the doctor's kit; an order form clipped to a school supplies catalog; a set of blueprints in the block corner; or an office with a keyboard, a play phone, and a stack of bills—inspire children to incorporate emergent or beginning reading and writing into their pretend play.

  —Writing materials and supports such as letters or words they can copy make it easy for children to make the things they need for their play and projects—such as tickets, menus, product labels and prices, travel logs, scorecards, maps, secret codes, signs, mail, and awards.

- *Children's spoken words and early writing attempts are proudly saved and shared.*

  —Wall displays and albums, portfolios, or scrapbooks showcase children's interests, productions, and activities—providing opportunities to reminisce together and to talk about the process of creation as well as the final product.

  —Labels, captions, signatures, and quotes enhance children's art work and other products.

Of course, even the most beautifully crafted, artfully displayed, and clearly valued print doesn't have much meaning without someone to interpret it (See Figure 6.2). Emergent readers need adults to share print with them and to talk with them about its meaning and use. They need to be cued in as to what various features of print stand for so that they can identify words, letters, sentences, and punctuation.

Adults can draw children's attention to print and highlight its features as they point out signs and labels and explain what they say and how they are useful. For example, while looking for apple juice in the supermarket, an adult might point out the signs that indicate the fruit juice aisle, as well as the "apple juice" label on the bottle. They might show children the *a* at the beginning of *apple,* or point out the words on a label that indicate that a product is real or pure fruit juice.

Similarly, adults can draw children's attention to the print as they share books. Usually, the most natural time to do this is before

निश्चय ही एक रचना जो अत्यंत सलीके से लिखी गई हो,
अति सुंदर तरीके से तराशी गई हो और कलात्मक तरीके से
प्रदर्शित की गई हो, निरर्थक हो जाती है जब तक
कोई उसकी उचित व्याख्या करने वाला ना हो।

بالطبع ان اجمل ماصنع ببراعةٌ ، و نمعر ضه بغ كاء وفن ، و ما يبنم بالقيمة الئهينة الو افـصةٌ و
الخذ يرة بالا حنرام ، لا يساوي شيئاً بدون ان يفسر ه و بترجمه شخعر ما .

Figure 6.2. Can you find the letters and words in this beautiful calligraphy?

reading the story. A parent or teacher can ask a child to find a particular book and then ask her what clues she used—or give her some
clues to support her search. He can then point out the title, author,
and illustrator on the cover. He might mention that the author's
name starts with the same letter as the child's or a friend's name,
show her how the author's name appears within the book, or ask her
to repeat the title as he points to each of its words. While reading the
story, the adult might run his finger under the text (or help the child
to do so) or point out key words such as a character's name or a
repeated refrain.

Once children begin to show an interest in how print works, parents and teachers can engage them as "print detectives"—finding
labeled objects or words and letters in their books and in environmental print. Most children will be especially interested in finding "their"
letters—either their initials or all of letters in their first names.

- After reading a short page of a familiar story, see if the child can
  locate a key word, such as the name of the main character or the
  beginning of a refrain.

- Read a story with a strong pattern. After the child has learned to
  retell the story, have him create his own versions with similar patterns. Help him make his own books, using word and picture stickers, dictation, and drawings.

- Show the child how letters make words, for example, by helping her
  find some of the letters she needs to write her name with magnetic
  letters, blocks, or rubber stamps.

As children increasingly approximate real reading and writing in their play, they will reveal their increasing knowledge of how print works. They may look at the print or follow it with a finger or pointer as a story is read, going from front to back, top to bottom, right to left. They may ask, "What does that say?" about environmental print or words on book covers and pages, or insist on exact reading of the text when the reader skips words or pages (e.g., "That's not what it says. Read it the right way.") Their writing will progress from squiggly lines to letter-like forms to the use of random and then increasingly accurate letters. Even at the squiggle stage, they may leave spaces to indicate words and sentences, or place a signature in an appropriate spot. Some children enjoy making their own books and reading them back, using scribbles or letter-like forms to represent writing or asking an adult to write their words.

As print detectives, children may be able to point to a repeated chorus or rhyming word as they chime in when the reader pauses, identify words (in print) that begin with the same sound, or find a word that begins with the same letter as a friend's name and make an appropriate guess as to what it says. Eventually, they may attempt to represent the sounds they hear as they write with invented spelling.

Five-year-old Kori, who was learning to read in kindergarten, made up a song with her 2-year-old brother as they bounced along on a jeep ride. Later, their mother incorporated the words into a poem that the children could read, using word art to highlight some of the correspondences between spoken words and their print representations

Bump, jump, jiggly jump.

Bump -ety, jump -ety, bump, bump.

Bump, jump, over the hump

Bump -ety, jump -ety, jump.

(Excerpted and adapted from *Poems to Learn to Read* By, Bardige & Segal, 2005, p. 59.)

Kori's poem—or at least her mother's rendition—had many features that helped to support Kori's transition from emergent to beginning reading. First, most of the words were Kori's own, and she could sing them back from memory. There were lots of words beginning with the letter *j*—and these were easy for Kori to identify because she had two cousins—Jennifer and Joshua—whose names began with that letter. The word *art* helped Kori with *jump*, *jiggly*, and *over the hump*, and also amused her. Finally, the poem gave Kori's mother a chance to show her how letters are put together to make words. They practiced reading "j-ump, jump," and then Kori's mother helped her pick out the rhyming words "b-ump" (*bump*) and "h-ump" (*hump*).

TUNING INTO SOUNDS—AND BUILDING PHONEMIC AWARENESS

For people who speak, read, and write a language fluently, separating words into component sounds and blending sounds to make words are automatic processes. But for young children—and for anyone trying to learn a language whose sound system is unfamiliar—these are skills that require learning and practice. The conscious awareness of how sounds make up words that is key to decoding an alphabetically written language emerges over time and is heightened both by play with sounds and by focused attention to print.

Poems and nursery rhymes are not the only sources of sound play that preschoolers experience. Sound play is embedded in some of the best prose picture books for children, including those with strong patterns that are often used as texts for beginning readers. Children's authors who draw on African American traditions, including Julius Lester and Ashley Bryan, often embed snippets of poetry into their prose stories. Familiar characters such as Mickey Mouse, Rudolph the Red-Nosed Reindeer, G.I. Joe, Ronald McDonald, Humpty Dumpty, and Dora the Explorer have alliterative or rhyming names. Even the affectionate nicknames and not-so-nice taunting names that children call each other often involve taking words apart and playing with their sounds. Most 4- and 5-year-olds enjoy word play—as long as it remains playful—totally unaware that it primes their brains for the phonemic awareness that will enable them to read.

Dressed in his Batman cape and his grandfather's big black hat, Mose regales his family with the magic tricks that he and his father have been practicing. "Bippity-boppity-boo," Mose cries, as he makes a coin disappear. Then—"Alacazam-alacabam"—he brings it back again. With another wave of his wand and a "Hi-ho-Houdini," he pulls a long purple scarf out of his sleeve. He tips his hat to the audience to show that it's empty, swoops it behind his back (where his father surreptitiously places a stuffed rabbit inside), then tells the audience to watch carefully as he stuffs the scarf inside. As he slowly pulls out the scarf, he carefully enunciates all of the syllables of his most impressive magic word: "Supercalifragilisticexpialidocious." "Voila!" Mose pulls the rabbit out of the hat and proudly takes a bow.

Children who know a lot of nursery rhymes, have good verbal memories, and are quick to supply a strongly cued missing rhyme when a reader pauses to encourage the audience to fill in the blank have a leg up on reading (Adams, 1990; National Research Council, 1998). Indeed, these kinds of skills are so critical for cracking the code that children who don't pick them up at home, in their preschool child care settings, or by playing with older children in the neighborhood need explicit instruction.

This instruction need not be boring; in fact, it works best when it is light-handed, frequent, and fun. In a classic and often-quoted article for *Reading Teacher,* Hallie Kay Yopp (1992) summarized the professional consensus about "phonemic awareness activities:"

- Keep a sense of playfulness and fun; avoid drill and rote memorization.

- Use group settings that encourage interaction among children.

- Encourage children's curiosity about language and their experimentation with it.

- Allow for and be prepared for individual differences.

- Make sure the tone of the activity is not evaluative but rather fun and informal.

Tongue twisters are fun for adults and children alike and often play on the initial sounds of words. The following collection includes tongue twisters in English and other languages. Try saying each slowly and precisely, then rattling it off as fast as you can. Can you say them all three times quickly?

- Peter Piper picked a peck of pickled peppers.

- Rubber baby buggy bumpers.

- She sells seashells by the seashore.

- A skunk sat on a stump and thunk the stump stunk, but the stump thunk the skunk stunk.

- Is this your sister's sixth zither, sir?

- Tres tristes tigres tragaban trigo en un trigal. (Spanish: Three sad tigers were swallowing wheat in a wheat field.)

- Palakang Kabkab, kumakalabukab, kaka-kalabukab pa lamang, kumakalabukab na naman. (Tagalog or Filipino: A Kabkab Frog, croaking, it was just croaking, now it's croaking again.)

- Mbuzi hali nazi kwa vile hawezi kupanda ngazi ndipo azifikie nazi. (Swahili: A goat cannot eat coconut because it cannot climb up a ladder to reach the coconuts up in the coconut tree.)

The progressive tongue twister "Una Mosca Parada en la Pared" (A Fly Standing on the Wall) is traditional throughout Latin America:

Una Mosca Parada en la Pared
Una mosca parada en la pared, en la pared, en la pared.
Ana masca parada an la parad, an la parad, an la parad.
Ena mesca perede en le pered, en le pered, en le pered.
Ini misci piridi in li pirid, in li pirid, in li pirid.
Ono mosco porodo on lo porod, on lo porod, on lo porod.
Unu muscu purudu un lu purud, un lu purud, un lu purud.

"The Apples and Bananas Song" familiar in the United States follows a similar pattern:

The Apples and Bananas Song
I like to eat, eat, eat, eat
I like to eat, apples and bananas
I like to eat, eat, eat, eat
I like to eat, apples and bananas

I like to ate, ate, ate, ate
I like to ate, ay-ples and bay-nay-nays
I like to ate, ate, ate, ate
I like to ate, ay-ples and bay-nay-nays

I like to eat, eat, eat, eat
I like to eat, eep-ples and bee-nee-nees
I like to eat, eat, eat, eat
I like to eat, eep-ples and bee-nee-nees

I like to ite, ite, ite, ite
I like to ite, i-pels and bi-ni-nis
I like to ite, ite, ite, ite
I like to ite, i-pels and bi-ni-nis

I like to oat, oat, oat, oat
I like to oat, o-pals and bo-no-nose
I like to oat, oat, oat, oat
I like to oat, o-pals and bo-no-nose

I like to oot, oot, oot, oot
I like to oot, oop-ples and boo-noo-noos
I like to oot, oot, oot, oot
I like to oot, oop-ples and boo-noo-noos

Now we are through, through, through, through
Now we are through with A E I O U

The following rhyme game presents children with several clues to help them find the rhyming word that completes a couplet. Parents, teachers, or older children can make up rhyming clues, and can adjust the difficulty of the clues to help a child succeed. The missing words might refer to objects in sight, or be related to a theme. While playing the game with young children, it is important to emphasize the word to be rhymed. Here, as an example, is a set of rhymes that give clues to articles of clothing:

It goes on my head—how about *that*?
It starts with a "huh." It's called a _____.

I'll take this off if the weather gets *better*.
Now it's keeping me warm. It's a _____.

My mama says I'm full of *beans*.
Especially when I wear blue _____.

When I fell in the puddle, I didn't get *hurt*.
But I splashed some mud on my long-sleeved _____.

I can tiptoe softly over *rocks*
When I don't wear shoes but just wear _____.

For second-language learners and speakers of dialects in which word endings tend to be dropped, choose rhymes that highlight sounds that may be more difficult for them to distinguish. At the same time, be sure to listen for words that rhyme in a child's dialect but may not rhyme in yours. For example, *twist* rhymes with *this* in a jump rope rhyme that is popular in many African American communities (Meier, 2008).

Teddy bear, teddy bear
Do the *twist.*
Teddy bear, teddy bear
Do like *this.*

Dr. Jean Ciborowski Fahey, who had seen too many children with poor phonemic awareness struggling to read in first grade, developed a simple set of games that parents can play with 3- to 5-year-olds. She also created a short video, *Raising Readers* (Fahey, 2007), to show parents how much fun the games can be. For example, the Listening Game begins with an adult asking the child to repeat a word. "Say, 'baseball.'" The child replies, "Baseball," and the adult continues, "Now say it again, but don't say, 'base.'" The child replies, "Ball." The child in the video has no trouble separating the parts of compound words, but he clearly thinks the game is fun. In fact, he quickly learns to drop either the first or last part of the compound and to suggest new words to play with. "Say, 'Donald Duck,'" he challenges his dad. "Now say it again, but don't say, 'Donald.'"

The next step in this game is more challenging. "Say, 'beard.' Now say it again, but don't say, 'buh.'" "Say, 'stone.' Say it again, but don't say, 'own.'"

A second game involves making special books in ways that highlight the sounds that make up words. Parents and children are urged to save labels from household products, cut them out, and then make a simple book by folding several sheets of paper together, stapling along the fold, and pasting one label onto each left-hand page. The children then write something about each product in their own way, using the sounds they hear. For example, in *Raising Readers*, Shakisha writes "I LCK KSU" opposite the label from a package of cashew nuts, and reads it back to her mother as "I like cashews." Her mother then writes the words in her way as Shakisha watches, explaining, "This is your writing. This is mine." They can now read the page together. As parents and children share the book over time or add new pages, parents can sharpen their children's awareness of sounds that they may not have tuned into by playing the Listening Game.

Dr. Fahey's listening and book-making games focus on taking words apart. Other games can focus on the complementary skill of blending. One oft-used technique is to ask a child to say sounds such as /c/ /a/ /t/ faster and faster until they blur together. For some children, the blending is obvious, and they say "cat" on the second or third try. Others need a more graphic demonstration, with the sounds accompanying colliding letters in a television or computer program, or a group of children each singing a sound—drawing it out dramatically like a member of a barbershop quartet and then leaning into the next child: "mmm"—bump—"aaaaa"—bump—"nnnn." The trio gets faster and faster until "mmm-aaaaa-nnnn" becomes "man."

WRITING IT DOWN

Shannon, at 4, was not too interested in naming letters or learning to write. She loved picture books, though, especially nonfiction science books and poems and stories about the natural world. One spring day, her family child care group took a field trip to a nearby wildlife refuge. The children had hunted for salamanders, caterpillars, centipedes, and insects, and they documented their sightings by coloring in squares on simple tally charts. Shannon was fascinated with the numbers—4 legs on salamanders, 6 on insects, 100 on a centipede, 3 body sections for insects (not counting legs and wings). When they returned from the trip, Shannon begged for crayons and paper. Very carefully, she drew an insect, with a head, thorax, abdomen, two eyes, two antennae, and six legs. Next to it, she drew a picture of herself. "Can you help me label my drawing?" she asked her teacher. As she had many times before, the teacher prepared to write what Shannon dictated. But this time, Shannon wanted to write the label herself. "Just write *insect* on a piece of paper so I can copy it," she said. With great effort and concentration, Shannon succeeded at her self-chosen task.

Many Reasons to Write

A writing-rich environment gives children many reasons to write. As they watch adults and older children, little ones see that writing is an important form of communication. They see that people write down things they want to remember or tell other people and that these messages can be saved, displayed, or sent to be read later.

Children love to get mail, and classroom mailboxes, bulletin boards, home note folders, and other message centers can give them many opportunities to exchange writings, drawings, notes, invitations, cards, and letters with classmates, teachers, and parents. Teachers can encourage their use in many ways:

- Giving children recycled greeting cards and envelopes to write on

- Providing stick-on labels with classmates' names

- Creating wall displays that show the process of students' work and encourage them to retell the story of a field trip or investigation or creation

- Encouraging parents to write notes to their children and children to write back

- Talking with children about all of the ways that they can share what they are doing with families and friends

One of the first things that most children learn to write with real letters and proper spelling is their own name. Many learn to recognize their classmates' written names as well or to identify the letter or sound that each name starts with. Some preschoolers can even write best friends' names or select them from a pile and copy the letters. Indeed, many preschool teachers and family child care providers make a point of teaching children who want to learn how to write their names—by hand, on a computer, or with stamps or letter blocks—and arrange materials and activities to help children learn each others' names as well. Popular techniques include

- Posting a class list and labeling children's cubbies, drawings, and portfolios with their names

- Creating nametags—often decorated by children themselves or created with their photographs—that can be used for many purposes

- Providing a letter wall with hooks, where children can hang up their nametags and then get them to put on a job chart or activity center schedule

- Associating a piece of fabric with each child's name—using the fabric on a pillow or seat cushion, the cubby (along with the name), and classroom charts (along with the name)

- Talking about letters—especially initial ones—while helping children sign their art work

- Talking about whose names start with the same sounds (e.g., Fifi, Phoebe, and Frank) or letters, or whose names sound similar (e.g., Kate, Katie, Kayla, and Katlyn).

Such techniques enable 2-, 3-, and 4-year-olds to learn to recognize their own and each others' names, and help many 4-, 5-, and 6-year-olds learn to write them. Names are important as well as familiar, and being able to write his name or address a note to a classmate can give a child a special sense of power.

Each morning, the tribal Early Head Start teacher gathers the
2-year-olds in a circle. She holds up a name and asks who it belongs
to. All of the children help to identify the owner, who steps forward
to be honored. As each child takes his turn, the teacher helps him to
lead the group in answering a question or imitating a special
gesture. After formally thanking him for his contribution, she holds
up the next name. This ritual helps each child to see herself as a
valued member of the group. It also gives visiting parents a chance
to see how smart their children are. At 2, they can already
recognize their own and each others' names and can answer the
teacher's questions or follow her directions in their Native American
language and in English!

Preschool writing can go well beyond writing names and labeling
drawings, or even making books, lists, greeting cards, and props for
pretend play. Adults also write tally marks, numbers, and other symbols and arrange their writing on charts, graphs, and PowerPoint slides
as they keep track of information or present it to others. When parents
and teachers encourage their investigations and give them appropriate
writing tools and materials, even quite young children can do the
same. They can paste stickers on papers and calendars, complete simple graphs by coloring in squares, put nametags on their possessions,
and arrange pictures to tell a story.

Writing Every Day

In a writing-rich environment, everybody writes every day. When teachers
make plans, write messages to parents, fill out forms, create labels and
wall displays, and capture children's words in print, they show children what they are doing and invite their imitation or participation.
When children want to play store or doctor or bean bag basketball or
take an imaginary journey, they can get help from adults to make the
signs, order forms, scoreboards, and maps that they need. When the
class pet or mascot visits a child's home for the weekend, she takes
along a set of child-dictated care instructions and a journal so that the
host family can read about her previous adventures and add their own
entry. When children plant seeds; watch the weather; conduct exper-
iments; or build a collection, display, or museum, they use measuring
tools, charts, diagrams, and lab notes—just like scientists—to keep
track of their observations. When the class takes a trip or hosts a special visitor, they all share in the planning, list-making, scrap-booking,
and thank-you note writing. The library keeps growing as children add

books, captioned photo albums, tape-recorded songs and stories, recipes and projects, and portfolios of their work that they can revisit and can share with others.

Although many preschool classrooms have writing centers, far fewer have teachers who actively and frequently support children's early writing efforts (Dickinson & Sprague, 2001). Yet this is one of the most powerful ways to help children make the connections between spoken and written language that enable them to grasp and use the alphabetic principle. In the Home School Study of Language Development (Dickinson & Tabors, 2001), the presence and active use of a writing center was a key factor distinguishing Head Start programs whose graduates did well in primary grades from those whose graduates were less successful. The most successful teachers intentionally incorporated some letter/sound correspondence activities while encouraging emergent reading and writing.

NOW I REALLY KNOW MY ABCS

Researchers have found that children who know their letters when they enter school are quite likely to become good readers. Indeed,

> [a]mong the readiness skills that are traditionally evaluated, the one that appears to be the strongest predictor on its own is letter identification. . . . Just measuring how many letters a kindergartner is able to name when shown letters in a random order appears to be nearly as successful at predicting future reading, as is an entire readiness test. (National Research Council, 1998, p. 113)

This finding, which has been confirmed in a number of studies (Hammil & McNutt, 1980; National Research Council, 1998; Scanlon & Vellutino, 1996), is one of the reasons why Head Start and other programs test preschoolers on letter identification and emphasize the ABCs. But just because letter naming correlates with early reading success doesn't mean that it is the sole essential ingredient. Obviously, being able to recognize and name letters helps children to understand reading, writing, and spelling instruction. At the same time, it may be a proxy for associated processing skills that play an even more critical role in decoding text and linking it with meaning. In one study, for example, recognizing numbers correlated even more highly with early reading success than did recognizing letters (Scanlon & Vellutino, 1996). Children who have had lots of experience with print-rich and writing-rich environments and associated play talk are likely to be good at recognizing numbers and letters and at deriving meaning from text.

For most children, learning the ABCs is a developmental process with identifiable steps that gradually integrate with growing concepts of print and phonemic awareness.

- Knowing the song and/or knowing the names of some letters that are handled as individual blocks, puzzle pieces, magnetic letters, or toys

- Recognizing letters in context—for example, being able to say the letters in one's own name

- Recognizing letters as distinct from drawings or numbers

- Recognizing individual letters

- Being able to name letters quickly when they are presented in a random order

- Writing letters

- Associating letters (and letter combinations) with particular sounds and vice versa

- Using letter knowledge in reading and writing

Children learn the names of letters in the same way that they learn names of objects, actions, and attributes—through repeated encounters in meaningful contexts and many opportunities to use the words. The "letter of the week" ritual, though ubiquitous in preschools, is probably less effective than providing children with ABC blocks, puzzles, stamps, stickers, or plastic letters and giving them many opportunities to ask for the letters they want as they arrange them to make their names or other important words.

Another effective method for children who enjoy them is sharing ABC books, such as *Las Letras Hablan* (Cruz-Contarini & Suarez, 2001) or *Dr. Seuss's ABC* (1960). ABC books can be chosen or created to reflect children's special interests, such as dinosaurs, toys, cars and trucks, sea life, tools, creepy crawlers, household items, children's home countries or words from their languages, or other places to visit. The following poem, for example, could be turned into a simple ABC book by writing a line or two onto each page of a homemade book and illustrating them with children's drawings and/or animal pictures cut from nature magazines or downloaded from the Internet.

An Alphabet of Animals
Alligator, aardvark
Buffalo, baboon
Caterpillar climbing
Constructing a cocoon.

Dog and duck and damsel fly
Elephant, egret.
Five flamingos flying
Gorilla getting wet.

Horse, hyena, hippo
Iguana in a zoo.
Jaguar in the jungle
Koala, kangaroo.

Lambs and llamas leaping
Mud mound-making mole
Nautilus, narwhale
Otter
Penguins at the pole.

Quetzal
Robin, rhino
Salamander, sole.
Turtle, tortoise, terrapin
Urial
Vulture, vole.

Walrus in the water
ibe**X**, ory**X**
Yaks.
Zebu and zippy zebra
With stripes upon their backs.

The animals in our world
Are as different as they can get.
And while I learn about them,
I learn the alphabet.

Like other ABC books—both purchased and homemade— "An Alphabet of Animals" can draw children's attention to print and to correspondences between written and spoken words. Parents and teachers can use some of the following techniques to enhance letter learning without taking away from the fun of sharing the book:

- Point to letters as you say their names; let children take over this job on subsequent readings.

- Encourage children to memorize the words, including the letter names if they are part of the poem or story, and to say them with you.

- Have children sing the ABC song, then slow it down and point to each highlighted letter as they say it, scanning down the page or turning pages of the book.

- Make a puzzle by copying pages, pasting the copies onto tagboard or cardboard, and cutting them into several pieces. You can make puzzles that involve matching a letter with appropriate pictures or words, assembling a letter from parts and other cues, or matching upper case letters with their lower case counterparts.

- Engage children in making their own ABC books on the same theme by finding or drawing pictures for each letter.

- Make letter cards by pasting pictures from the book onto cardboard squares and adding the appropriate letter. Let children use the letter cards to spell out their names and other favorite words.

- Focus on a few letters. Find upper and lower case examples, words that start with the letter, or objects and people whose names start with or contain the letter. See if children can name the letters out of context.

- Turn to random pages in the book and see if children can name the letters.

- Talk about the shapes of different letters. Compare and contrast similarly shaped letters such as *c* and *o*; *b, p,* and *d*; and *m, n, w,* and *v.*

- With a homemade book or puzzle, give children stickers of lower case letters to put on appropriate pages that feature their upper case counterparts.

- Find an ABC book in another language or even one written with a different alphabet. Talk with children about what is the same and different about the way letters and words are written in the two languages.

TWENTY (MORE) FUN WAYS TO BUILD LITERACY

1. *Make regular trips to your local school or public library:* Enlist the librarian's help in finding books related to the child's special interests or current questions, any special emotional or family concerns (e.g., moving, a death in the family, a parent's job loss, or being teased), or favorite authors and genres.

2. *Make a habit of telling (picture) books by their covers:* Before you open a book, point out the title, author, and illustrator as you and the

child read the names, or see if the child can recognize the author, illustrator, or main character of a book that is part of a favorite series. When you introduce a new book, help the child find clues that might indicate whether the book is fiction or nonfiction, humor, or how-to. See if he can guess what the story might be about or where it might take place.

3. *Post the words to your favorite songs and poems on chart paper for choral reading.* You can use rebuses (pictures that stand for words) to shorten or accompany the text. Read the words together, with a child or adult pointing to each word as it is read.

4. *Put on a play or puppet show based on a favorite folk tale or story.* An easy way to minimize rehearsals is to have an adult narrator who tells the story and cues the characters. Keep the props, costumes, and scenery simple, but be sure to make tickets and programs, and to use signs like "The Forest," "Gingerbread House," "Applause, Please," and "The End" as needed.

5. *Share jokes and riddles that play with words:* Tell the child a joke such as "What do you do if your puppy can't come into the store with you? Leave him in the *barking* lot." Check out joke and riddle books from the library, and help the child make her own collection of favorites, complete with her own illustrations.

6. *Play storytelling and memory games:* There are many storytelling and memory games that are good to play with individuals or groups of children. Examples include:

   a. "I Packed My Bag and In It I Put . . . ": Have the children sit in a circle and name items one child at a time. The first child says something he put in his bag, and each subsequent child repeats all previously named items and adds a new one. The children can choose random items, items needed for a particular journey, or one item that begins with each letter of the alphabet.

   b. "Fortunately, Unfortunately": Begin a fanciful adventure story in which the main character encounters a series of cliffhanger challenges. "I was walking along the street when a giant meatball almost fell on my head. Fortunately . . . ." The next person then adds to the story, and, as the next threat looms, says, "unfortunately . . . " and lets the next person continue by adding more to the story.

   c. "Tall Tales": Begin by reading stories with the children that rely on imagination and exaggeration, such as *And to Think*

That I Saw It on Mulberry Street (Seuss, 1989) or *Tar Beach* (Ringgold, 1996). Then, take turns telling your own tall tales. Start with a simple story, such as "Today on the playground we found a frog." Take turns adding to the story to make it more and more fantastic.

d.   "Story Bag": Place several interesting small objects—such as a hair ornament, a piece of string, a child's toy or action figure, and a key—in a bag. Have the children draw out the objects one at a time and use them as part of an individual or group story.

7.   *Decode directions together:* Whether reading a recipe, learning a new game, assembling a toy or piece of furniture, or making a repair, enlist the child's help in following the directions. She can help you collect the needed parts or materials and arrange them in order, and she can keep track of steps in the process. Even if she can't read the directions, she may be able to recognize the pictures and some of the words.

8.   *Make "Me" Books:* Help the child make a "me" book, in which he shares vital information and off-beat facts about himself. For example, the child can include his name and those of other family members; favorite activities, clothes, and colors; important milestones such as losing a tooth or learning to ride a bike; and odd bits of information such as how many light switches are in his house or apartment or how many fire hydrants he passes on the way to school.

9.   *Compare name lengths:* Help children clap out their names and those of their friends, pets, and family members, one clap to each syllable. Whose names have only one clap? Two? Three? Does anyone's have four or more? Then try writing the names on graph paper or homemade grids, one letter to each square, to see how many letters are in each name. Children may be intrigued to discover that a one-clap name like "Blake" has the same number of letters as a three-clap name like "Anara."

10.   *Pay attention to letters on signs and license plates:* Encourage the child to look for letters as you take a walk, drive, or bus ride, or find them on product labels as you unpack groceries. See if he can find all of the letters in his name or all of the letters of the alphabet, one at a time. For example, you might find an *a* in *Staples*, a *b* on a license plate, and then a *c* on a sign that says, "No Parking Here to Corner."

11. *Look for words in words:* For example, show the child the word *top* in *stop*, the word *can* in *candy*, the word *pot* in *potato*, and the word *mall* in *small*. Engage her as a "print detective" to find other examples.

12. *Make a word maker:* Cut two strips of paper, approximately ½ inch wide and 4 inches long. On the first strip, write the initial consonants (onsets) *b, m, p, r,* and *t* in a vertical column, leaving a space on each end for pulling. On the second strip, write the syllable endings (rimes) *an, at, ake, et,* and *ug.* Cut two pairs of parallel slits in an index card, spaced so that you can thread a strip through each pair to show one onset and one rime at a time. As the child pulls the strips through the slots, he will be able to make many real words and a few nonsense words. Let the child help you make new strips with other letters or letter combinations that he would like to try.

13. *Make word and sentence puzzles from familiar text:* Write some words, phrases, or sentences from a favorite book or song on index cards, then cut each card like a puzzle—with the cut between syllables, or between onset and rime (e.g., Good–night, moon. Goodnight light and the r–ed balloon.)

14. *Plan an Unbirthday Party:* The term *unbirthday* was coined by Lewis Carol in *Through the Looking Glass* and popularized in the song, "A Very Merry Unbirthday," in the Disney film *Alice in Wonderland.* Ask the child what she thinks an unbirthday is, and what she would like to do at an unbirthday party. Let her help make invitations and place cards, choose the menu, and write a shopping list. At the party, you might have each child decorate her own plate and cup and write her name on it. Children can then work together to decorate an unbirthday cake or a tray of brownies. For presents and favors, each child can bring a homemade book or card to exchange or make story puppets by copying pages of favorite books, cutting out pictures of characters, and gluing each to a craft stick.

15. *Give homemade books or favorite books as special presents:* You can give such gifts to children and also help them to give books to their friends. Each gift should include a personal note about why the book is special to the donor or why it was chosen or created for the recipient. To make the gift even more special, include a recording of the donor(s) reading the story.

16. *Plan a real or imaginary trip or outing:* Enlist the child's help in planning a real or imaginary trip or outing that the whole fami-

ly would enjoy. It can be as short as a trip to a nearby park, zoo, or pick-your-own farm or as long as a cross-country bus tour. Collect travel or tourist brochures, or find information in the newspaper or on the Internet. Decide together where you would like to visit, and use maps to figure out how to get there and how long it will take. Older children can help to plan a budget as well as mapping out the route and acting as navigators.

17. *Make your own board games:* Begin by asking the child to choose a theme: a trip to an amusement park, a stroll through an enchanted forest, a deep sea dive or submarine voyage, a space flight or time machine journey, a train ride through a place she's been reading about, or the travails of a storybook character. Sketch out a path and divide it into squares. Label the start and finish. The child can then illustrate the rest of the board and label several of the squares as theme-related places. You can also write directions, such as "Go ahead 2," "Go back 1,""Take a card," or "Take a short cut to Big Rock Candy Mountain" on some of the individual squares. Make a deck of index cards with theme-related directions, such as "Take a ride on the roller coaster" or "You got lost in the forest. Miss one turn." Players can use a die, spinner, or a flipped penny (e.g., heads = advance one square; tails = advance two squares) to move around the board.

18. *Go on a scavenger hunt:* You can do this at home, in the neighborhood, or at a place you are visiting. Give each child or team a list of things to find, for example, an animal's home, a red car, a square inside a rectangle, something purple, a good hiding place, something that holds water, the letter *a*. Go over the list to make sure that each child or team can read all of the items. (You can use picture or color clues to help beginning readers.) As they see items on the list, children can check them off. When all items have been found, they can report back and share their discoveries.

19. *Play word games:* Some traditional favorites that 4- to 8-year-olds enjoy include

   a. "Twenty Questions": The first player thinks of an object and gives a clue to its identity (e.g., "I'm thinking of something you can play with.") Other players take turns asking questions until they guess correctly. Novice players often throw out guesses immediately (e.g., "Is it a dollhouse?"); with experience, children learn to ask questions that narrow down the possibilities (e.g., "Is it in this room?" "Is it bigger than a basketball?")

b.   "Categories": Have the children sit in a circle. Begin by establishing a rhythm of two claps followed by two knee slaps. Keep the pattern going, with everyone joining in. Once the rhythm is established, suggest a category (e.g., furniture) from which the children can pick certain objects (e.g., tables, desks). Speaking only on the claps, name the category and give an example (e.g., "Categories . . . names of . . . furniture . . . such as . . . tables"). Play then passes around the circle, with each person naming an object in the category. Try to get all the way around the circle.

c.   "Geography": This game can be played with geographic locations or with other words for younger children. The first person names a place (e.g., New York). The next person then names a place that starts with the last letter of the place just named (e.g., Kansas), and so forth.

d.   "Hangman": Think of a word or sentence. Draw one blank for each letter, leaving spaces between any words, and then write out the alphabet. Have the child try to guess your word or sentence by guessing one letter at a time. For each correct guess, write the letter in the appropriate blank (or blanks if the letter appears more than once). For each incorrect guess, cross out that letter in the alphabet. See if the child can guess the word in 10 or fewer tries. (This is often easier for beginners if you use a short sentence with many familiar words, such as "I went to the store today.")

e.   "Anagrams": Write a phrase or sentence, such as a child's whole name, "I love words," or "Happy Birthday." See how many words the child can make using some of the letters from the phrase or sentence (e.g., from "I love words" you can make the words *red, door, river, woods,* and many other words that beginning readers can spell).

20.   *Set aside special times for reading and conversation:* Read to the child at bedtime, or let her take a turn reading a familiar passage. Vary the bedtime ritual to include an opportunity for the child to ask an interesting question or for the family to play a word game together. Begin family meal times with a chance for everyone to share a funny story, the best and worst events of their days, or something they learned. Take 15 minutes after

dinner for a family read aloud, sing along, or sustained silent reading time.

CRACKING THE CODE

The last of the steps from emergent to beginning reading is often referred to as "cracking the code." With all that children have learned about stories, print, words, sounds, and letters, they still need to associate specific letters with specific sounds, in the context of meaningful text. It's not enough for children to be able to figure out what a word says—they have to be able to decode the word and apprehend its meaning quickly and easily enough to turn their attention to the meaning of the sentence and of the larger story. In order to read fluently, children have to master some specific word recognition and word analysis skills—and to practice them until they become automatic.

For some children, these skills are learned through years of play, emergent reading, and conversation. For most, they need to be taught explicitly and practiced repeatedly and with focus. Either way, code-cracking skills and strategies are grounded in the oral language that written language represents. When the language foundation is solid and continues to grow through play talk, questioning, and reading together, it provides a firm basis for learning to read and for reading to learn.

Although his language and emergent reading skills were strong, Ned struggled with reading in kindergarten and received special tutoring at the beginning of first grade. Like many children with previously undiagnosed auditory or visual processing or memory difficulties, he could learn individual words and letters, but he couldn't bring all of the clues together quickly enough so that what he read made sense. Fortunately, his school had a Reading Recovery (http://www.readingrecovery.org) tutoring program, and his mother was able to work with him on most evenings.

By the end of first grade, Ned had learned to read. He devoured books for beginning readers and soon moved on to simple chapter books. Although he couldn't read all the words, he became a devotee of the sports page, and he rarely left for school in the morning without reading the headlines and checking the box scores.

The next spring, as his mom was clearing out the closets, she came upon a box of Ned's early primers. Ned pulled them from the give-away pile. "Remember these, Mom? We used to read them

together. Here's *Mac and Tab* (Primary Phonics Storybooks, 2001),
and look, *Sheep in a Jeep* (Shaw & Apple, 2005)! I loved reading
those books with you!" For Ned, the memories of struggle had
faded. His mother's patient attention, the joy they both felt over his
small successes, and the rhythms of the texts they had read over
and over again were the memories that endured.

THE WHOLE STORY

For a long time, educators debated between "whole language" and
"phonics" methods of teaching reading. Whole language advocates
emphasized high interest text, with a wealth of contextual clues that
would enable children to read along with their emergent skills even if
they couldn't decode each word on their own. Phonics advocates
emphasized carefully sequenced instruction in letter–sound correspondences, combined with a lot of practice with beginning and ending sounds. They advocated primers filled with simple, regularly
spelled words, such as "The cat sat on the mat," which would provide
children with opportunities to apply their growing phonemic awareness and alphabet knowledge.

For most children, the best strategy is not one method or the other,
but rather a combination of both. Effective whole language teachers
have always integrated phonics strategies as they built on children's
outside-*in* knowledge, and effective phonics teachers have always provided many opportunities for children to apply their inside-*out* knowledge in reading and writing interesting texts as well as phonetically
controlled primers. Effective teachers in both camps have combined
targeted instruction with support and coaching and have fostered both
a love of reading and the skills needed to read independently.

Reading researcher Marilyn Jager Adams (1990) was one of the
first to synthesize the research. Her work informed the National
Academy of Sciences research report, *Preventing Reading Difficulties in
Young Children* (National Research Council, 1998) and its companion
book for teachers, *Starting Out Right* (Committee on the Prevention of
Reading Difficulties in Young Children, National Research Council,
1998). What had been called the "reading wars" were effectively
ended for professionals by this synthesis, which is reflected in the joint
statement of NAEYC and the International Reading Association,
*Learning to Read and Write: Developmentally Appropriate Practices for Young
Children* (1998) and in the book by the same name (Neuman, Copple,
& Bredekamp, 2000) that elaborates on the principles and provides
examples for teachers.

The PBS show *Between the Lions* (http://pbskids.org/lions) uses sophisticated, research-informed strategies to help children make the transition from emergent to independent reading. The show takes a whole-part-whole approach, starting with a meaningful "whole," or context, guiding children's exploration of "parts" (details of words, sounds, letters, and other print and story features) within that context, and then giving children opportunities to apply their knowledge of parts as they again work with the whole or with a new, related story. Parents and teachers can incorporate a similar whole-part-whole approach into everyday book-sharing and writing activities, by using some or all of the following steps:

1. Set a context: a story, song, poem, or project.

2. Talk about the whole to engage and build background knowledge: What is happening? What will happen? What can be inferred? What might you learn or find out? Elicit children's thinking and model yours.

3. Zoom in on the parts. Talk about key words and their meanings.

4. Zoom in tighter, to focus on word parts, sounds, and letters. Help the child to listen closely and pay close attention to the print.

5. Go back to the whole. Encourage the child to participate in reading and rereading so that she can use her letter and word knowledge in context. Create related opportunities for the child to use her knowledge in meaningful writing as well, such as creating a new ending for a story or making signs for a pretend play project.

6. Broaden the context and deepen the understanding. Make connections to the child's experiences and invite critical conversation. Extend the learning with related books, investigations, and writing and storytelling activities.

The whole-part-whole model is also a good image for the trajectory of reading instruction. In preschool, the focus is mostly on the whole, as emergent readers develop vocabulary, conceptual knowledge, and basic understandings of how words, sounds, print, and stories work. Still, children spend some time focused on the parts, manipulating individual letters and sounds and exploring their relationships.

In their kindergarten and first-grade classes, children are likely to encounter specific reading and spelling instruction and simplified texts that provide practice with the letters and sounds they are learning. Most likely, they will begin with frequently used initial consonants, or onsets, such as /b/, /d/, /f/, /m/, /r/, /s/, and /t/ and common syllable endings, or rimes, such as /-an/, /-at/, /-ee/, /-end/, /-op/, and /-ing/. Soon, they will be able to read many words made by combining these onsets and rimes in different ways, along with some basic sight words such as *I, the, do,* and *said.* As they practice with worksheets, computer programs, and simplified primers, they will also be reading books, songs, poems, lists, labels, and other writings filled with words that don't fit these elementary patterns.

Once children crack the code, usually by the end of first grade but often as early as 4 or 5, they don't need much phonics instruction. They can turn their attention to the whole as they read for information and for pleasure. Still, they spend some time on focused word study and spelling activities, deepening their knowledge of how the parts work so that they can tackle more challenging wholes.

I CAN READ!

Whether they are reading simplified texts or more naturally written narratives, when children are first learning to apply the alphabetic principle and decode words on their own, it is important to provide support so that they can read fast enough to get the meaning of what they are reading, enjoy the process, and build confidence.

Some supports for beginning readers are provided by the text itself:

• Predictable, patterned text, with rhyme or other repeated elements

• Regular spelling and controlled vocabulary

• Use of a limited set of common words

• Relatively simple sentence structure

• Picture clues, rebuses, and word art

• Organization of lists into categories

As a child attempts to read, an adult can provide other supports as well:

• Letting the child read stories that she is very familiar with and may know by heart

• Reading aloud together

• Reading in chorus with other children so that every child can feel successful as well as supported as they share the fun of group performance

The Books that Beginning Readers Like Best...

- Include both books that are read aloud to them and books that make it easy for them to do some or all of the reading themselves

- Are well written; sentences have natural cadence or fun-to-say rhythm and are likely to be of varied length, rather than all being short and choppy

- May use controlled vocabulary, alliteration and rhyme, and an abundance of short, regularly spelled words, but these are woven into a playful poem or interesting narrative

- Often have predictable text that gives multiple clues (e.g., pictures, rhymes, strong story patterns) about what may be coming next

- Don't have too many words on a page—unless an adult is reading the book to the child

- Contain humor that is based on word play, ridiculous mistakes, wild exaggeration, or characters with predictable habits and fun-to-say names

- Often contain invented words such as "heffalump," "Circus McGirkus," and "grinchy"

- Deepen children's knowledge of their heritage and of the traditions and values of their communities

- Often feature children or childlike characters who outwit adults

- Teach children words, factoids, clever sayings, games, and strategies that they can use to impress or entertain their friends

- Often feature children or eccentric adults who use knowledge and clever thinking to solve mysteries

- Often feature children or childlike animals who behave as they do and are challenged by tricky social problems such as teasing or bullying, feeling left out, or having difficulty mastering a skill that other children master easily

---

- Have a distinctive voice or style, and may use ethnic or regional dialect

- Are often quite sophisticated, reflecting individual tastes and interests or family traditions, favorite books, and shared hobbies

- Address or answer children's questions and spark new ones

- Reading part of a highly patterned text with strong emphasis and expression, and then letting the child read another part that follows a similar pattern

- Highlighting key vocabulary words before you begin reading

- Helping the child break words into syllables and smaller parts

- Supplying the word when a child gets stuck so he doesn't lose the flow of the sentence, then going back to analyze these difficult words later

- Talking about the meaning of the story

At Curriculum Night, a first-grade teacher talked with a group of parents about how they helped their children to practice reading at home. "I cover up the pictures so he really has to focus on the words," one parent volunteered. "I know that if he's just guessing he's not really reading."

"You're right," the teacher responded. "And there's a lot of research on your side. Good readers focus on the letters in the words and the sounds they represent; they don't just guess. But what you see as guessing can also be an important part of the process for a beginning reader. Decoding the words isn't enough—you still have to think about the context to know what they mean. And unless you get the meaning, you're not really reading." She then wrote on the blackboard: "The notes were sour because the seams were split" (Bramsford & Johnson, 1973). She asked the parents to read it aloud. "It's a simple, first-grade sentence, and you all decoded it very well. But what does it mean?" she asked. No one had a clue. The teacher then held up a picture of a musician in traditional Scottish clan regalia trying to play a torn bagpipe. The parents laughed as they got her point.

Many books are written especially for beginning readers. Dr. Seuss's Beginner Books are still some of the best—combining word play, controlled vocabulary, and picture clues. Others, such as *Mrs. Wishy-Washy* (Cowley, 1999) and *King Bidgood's in the Bathtub* (Wood & Wood, 2005) use very predictable text. The Usborne Phonics Readers, such as *Frog on a Log* (Cox & Cartright, 2006) give children practice blending onsets and rimes. For children learning to read in Spanish, Alma Flor Ada and F. Isabel Campoy have produced a large collection of ABC, rhyme, and counting books and other easy readers.

Of course, beginning readers also need a lot of beautiful, high-interest, well-written, informative, multicultural fiction, poetry, and nonfiction books to listen to and enjoy. Just because a child can read on her own should not mean that the adults in her life stop reading aloud with her.

KEEPING THE CONVERSATION GOING

Mother 1: "I'm thinking of home-schooling Jacob again next year. He's already learned to read, and I've really enjoyed teaching him. I'm not convinced the public schools can do a better job than I can, at least not in first and second grade."

Mother 2: "My kids have had great experiences in the public schools, from pre-kindergarten on. But we've always home-schooled them as well. We still do, even with all the homework and outside activities they have in middle school. We've never stopped reading, investigating, and thinking things through together. They get a lot out of school, but I think they've learned even more at home."

Henry Louis Gates, Jr., Director of the W.E.B. Du Bois Institute for African and African American Research at Harvard University, expressed a similar endorsement of intentional home-schooling, but with a vision that includes the extended family and the neighborhood.

> My fascination with black language stems from my father's enjoyment of absolute control over its manipulation. My father has mastered black language rituals, certainly; he also has the ability to analyze them, to tell you what he is doing, why, and how. He is a very self-conscious language user. He is not atypical. It is amazing how much black people, in ritual settings such as barbershops and pool halls, street corners and family reunions, talk about talking. Why do they do this? I think they

do it to pass these rituals along from one generation to the next. (Gates, 1989, p. xi)

The value of play talk doesn't end when children enter school or when they learn to read. In the best of circumstances, teachers continue to engage children's curiosity with a rich curriculum that builds— and builds on—the questions, learning strategies, interests, and linguistic strengths that each child brings. At the same time, families take every opportunity to keep the conversation going. At formal and informal gatherings, in intimate and public settings, at regular events like mealtimes and during unexpected down times, children soak up language and make their voices heard in thought-provoking, playful, and personal conversations. As they interact with family and extended family members and with other caring adults, they hear and engage in "talk about talking," as well as talk about reading, writing, and media presentations. Children thrive when all the people in their lives tune in to their questions; appreciate and nurture their imaginations; and make a point of teaching them language and life lessons, folk traditions and academics, aesthetic and moral values, and the skills of work and play.

Building Language– Supporting Communities

Once upon a time, neighborhoods were full of young children—and adults who talked with them. Front porches, backyards, stoops, playgrounds, and plazas drew people together and provided frequent opportunities for young children to hear and participate in conversation. Shopkeepers, neighbors, and community helpers knew the young children in their community and were likely to engage them in conversation. Extended families often lived near each other, and everybody played with babies. Such communities provided children with rich funds of knowledge and many chances to listen and talk. A 10-year study of Chicago neighborhoods found that children living in neighborhoods with high levels of concentrated disadvantage exhibited fewer mental health problems when adults could rely on each other to look out for each other's children (Xue, Leventhal, Brooks-Gunn, & Earls, 2005).

Today, we acknowledge that "It takes a village to raise a child." We also know that it takes concerted effort and public commitment to create and sustain a healthy village. But the payback is enormous. Child development experts teach us that the early years provide a critical foundation for lifelong health and development, and that robust language, built through the "serve and return" interaction of talking with babies, is a vital part of this foundation (National Scientific Council on the Developing Child, 2007). Economists have told us that public investment in the institutions, programs, and systems that support the healthy development of all young children in a community has a high rate of return, and that there are few investments that a community can make that are likely to bring better societal benefits or larger long-term monetary savings (Heckman, 2005; Rolnick & Grunewald, 2003).

Communities and states throughout the nation are taking these messages to heart and finding creative ways to build, rebuild, and sustain the healthy villages that support children in their early language-learning years (ZERO TO THREE Policy Center, 2007 and 2008).

THE CHALLENGE

The "villages" of yesterday are gone. Most parents of young children are in the work force at least part time. The majority of U.S. children spend some time in nonparental care beginning in babyhood. Many spend long hours away from their parents, often with multiple caregivers or in several different settings. (NICHD Early Child Care Research Network, 2005)

In 1991, with funding from the National Institute of Child Health and Human Development, a group of leading early childhood researchers set out to investigate the child care experiences of American children and the impact of those experiences on the children's development. They recruited 1,364 families with children born that year, and they followed the children from infancy into childhood. When the children were 6 months old, the researchers observed them in their primary child care settings and rated the quality of caregiving they were receiving from the parents, relatives, center-based caregivers, or family child care providers who were taking care of them. The observational scale they used emphasized language-supportive behaviors such as sharing a laugh or smile, responding to children's vocalizations and nondistress (as well as distress) signals, offering praise or encouragement, telling a story, singing, asking questions, and reading to a child. The researchers judged that 70%-80% of the children were receiving care that was "moderately or highly positive."

When the children were 15 months old, however, the likelihood of "positive caregiving" being highly or somewhat characteristic for any particular child had dropped to just more than 50%. At 24 months, positive caregiving was observed to be somewhat or highly characteristic for only about 42% of the children. Indeed, when the researchers extrapolated from the children whose care they had observed to the general population, they concluded that positive caregiving was "somewhat" or "highly characteristic" for less than 40% of American children between 1 and 3 years old (NICHD Early Child Care Research Network, 2005).

Other large-scale studies of child care have used more global measures of quality, looking at health and safety, furnishings and equipment, supports and opportunities for active play and motor development, learning activities, and relationships among adults as well as caregiver–child interactions and supports for language and reasoning. The findings from these studies were even bleaker. Whether researchers looked at center-based care; licensed family child care; or care by relatives, friends, and neighbors, less than one third of the settings provided toddlers with consistently good care (Galinsky, Howes, & Kontos, 1995; Gamel-McCormick & Amsden, 2005; Howes et al., 1998; Marshall et al., 2004; Whitebook et al., 1995).

These findings, however, shouldn't come as a surprise. Caring for toddlers in a group setting is demanding work, requiring training and skill, as well as flexibility and enthusiasm. Caregivers can't do it day in and day out if there are too many children or if the setting is over-stimulating, unsafe, or boring. When appropriate supports are avail able, caregivers are able to maintain a language-rich environment—attuned to the needs of each child and the group as a whole—and children thrive. But the cost of such care is far more than most parents can pay, and few communities have been able to build an adequate supply of high-quality settings and provide the ongoing supports needed to maintain quality. State supports for early education and care have focused largely on 4- and 5-year-olds. The federal Head Start program serves 3-year-olds as well, but it reached only about 327,000 3-year-olds in fiscal year 2007 (ACF, Head Start Bureau, 2006), fewer than half of the children whose below or near-poverty-level family incomes made them eligible for its services. The federal Early Head Start program for children under 3 served just 2.5% of those eligible in 2006 (Center for Law and Social Policy, 2008), and has expanded only slightly.

At the critical age for language learning, public investments in children's education are lower than they will be at any time during childhood (Bardige, 2005). And the caregivers and teachers on the frontlines, who are doing their best to provide safe, loving, growth-promoting care, are not doing enough talking.

The challenge is daunting across the economic spectrum, but particularly so in communities facing poverty, segregation, high or rising crime and public disorder, an influx of refugees from war or other traumas, or a rapid change in the demographics and needs of their young families. At times, neighborhoods that are poor in economic resources can be rich in supports for robust language development. They can be places where tight-knit linguistic communities become supportive extended families, or where neighbors speaking multiple languages learn English together while their children learn each other's languages, as well. Too often, though, children growing up in such neighborhoods face stresses that can compromise their development: poor nutrition and health care, neighborhood and sometimes family violence, environmental toxins, a dearth of basic resources such as safe places for young children to play or sources of high-quality children's books, and a climate of fear that keeps families isolated and children indoors. Too often, as well, the children enter schools where their language or dialect is not understood or valued, where the strengths they bring are unnoticed, where their teachers struggle to keep up with the myriad demands of too many children with too many deep and divergent needs, or where the curriculum has been impoverished in an ironic effort to leave no child behind.

SUPPORTING PARENTS AND CAREGIVERS

A mother and father brought their two sons, ages 2 and 4, to a family restaurant for dinner. As they took their seats at their table, the waitress handed each boy a paper placemat and a box of crayons. Both boys began to draw, talking quietly to each other. But their parents had come prepared. The mother pulled a portable DVD player out of her tote bag, and the father helped her put headphones on the boys and started the movie. Except for the business talk of ordering dinner, the parents and children were silent for the rest of the meal.

Two preschool teachers who were eating in the same restaurant witnessed this incident. The teachers could see that the boys were well cared for and well behaved, yet they worried about the language experiences these children were missing. They worried, too, that the incident they observed was more typical than anomalous; that families across the economic spectrum were increasingly plugging in, zoning out, and missing out on critical conversation time. They worried that the calls and campaigns of child development professionals for a "media free childhood," "unplugged play (Conner, 2007)," and "family meals" (Weinstein, 2005) were not reaching a wide-enough audience with sufficient power to change behavior. They knew that one quiet dinner—or even one overly violent movie or television show—would not harm a well-loved and well-developing young child, but, like Nancy Carlsson-Paige (2008) and other researchers, they worried about the patterns they were seeing in their community.

"Education begins at home." "You are your child's first and most important teacher." "All parents need and deserve support and up-to-date parenting information." "Every family has strengths." "Professionals may know child development, but parents are the experts on their own children." "One of our community's biggest assets is the love that our parents have for their children." These are the mantras of a diverse and growing movement to support families during their children's early years and to build on their ability to support each other.

Family support efforts take many forms: pediatric visits that include attention to the parents' needs and anticipatory guidance about upcoming developmental challenges; family fun nights and parent-involvement activities at child care programs, home visits and support groups for teen parents; "one-stop shopping" sites, where families can get help with child care subsidies and referrals, housing, health care, and other social services; parent-run co-ops and family centers; baby-and-me classes and playgroups; parenting courses and workshops; two-generation literacy programs; and programs that bring a parenting education curriculum or set of parent–child activities to families in their homes, workplaces, or neighborhoods.

Supporting early language development through play, reading, and conversation is the centerpiece of some of these programs; in others, it is but one part of a comprehensive approach. Similarly, some of these programs regularly bring families together for parent–child activities that are likely to provide rich language-learning opportunities; others work with each family in isolation or with parents and children separately. Increasingly, though, such programs are forging collaborative relationships so that together they can offer each family an appropriate mix of community connections and services.

AVANCE (http://www.avance.org), a parent education and support organization, has been serving low-income Latino families for 3 decades, first in Texas and then in New Mexico and California as well. The program began as an education program for mothers and babies, with parenting education and GED classes, toy-making workshops, and child care and parent–child activity sessions. These offerings remain the heart of its program, but AVANCE sites have grown with their clientele to include Head Start and after-school programs, community service and mutual support activities, college scholarships for both baby and parent alumnae, and a career ladder for former clients who become AVANCE employees. Over time, AVANCE has built supportive communities whose children graduate high school and go on to succeed in higher education at rates that are similar to those of children in communities facing far fewer economic and educational challenges.

Family support programs that rely on a home visiting strategy have begun to recognize that many of the children most in need of their services are not in their own homes for significant chunks of their days. Many of these programs are now bringing family support, language-building activities, child development information, screenings for developmental delays and sensory impairments, and information about community resources to children's grandparents, family child care providers, or other caregivers, as well as to their parents (Hamm, Gault, & Jones-DeWeever, 2005).

As successful programs have been replicated across the nation and have proven their effectiveness in short- and long-term evaluations, they have found new partners, both among providers offering complementary services or reaching different groups and among private and public funders seeking to make a difference in their communities.

In Seattle, Washington, outreach efforts have focused on helping low-income and immigrant families prepare their children for school success. The Business Partnership for Early Learning, a synergistic program that includes Parent-Child Home Program home visits and Play & Learn groups for parents and children, sponsors the outreach efforts that are "filling the preparedness gap" between young children from low-income families and their higher income counterparts. By the end of its second year, this demonstration project had already exceeded its planners' expectations. Parents were showing marked increases in language-promoting behaviors: engaging their children in frequent conversations, tuning in to their verbal messages, giving clear verbal directions, and using more words of approval. Children were enjoying books; engaging in more creative and inventive play; and using their words to ask for help, describe pictures in their books, and express pride in their accomplishments. They showed improved ability to concentrate, share, tolerate delays, and understand and complete developmentally appropriate activities. The City of Seattle funded an additional project site, and the planners continue to raise funds for program expansion (Business Partnership for Early Learning, 2007).

TAPPING CULTURAL STRENGTHS

Cohesive communities in which adults and older children collectively support young children's language—drawing on cultural traditions passed down through games, songs, stories, church services, family rituals, and ordinary talk—can be crucibles for rich language learning. In her book, *Black Communications and Learning to Read,* Terry Meier described the linguistic strengths African American children gain from growing up in such environments:

1. A sense of identity and self-efficacy strongly linked to one's ability to use language well

2. A disposition toward argumentation/conflict talk as a stimulating and intellectually engaging activity

3. Skill in, and a liking for, oral performance

4. The ability to think quickly on one's feet and to engage effectively in verbal debate

5. A strong tendency to take context into account in figuring out the meaning of a word, statement, or extended piece of discourse

6. A highly developed sensitivity to audience in communicative interactions

7. The ability to discern multiple possibilities of meaning in discourse and to "read between the lines" of what is literally being said

8. Sensitivity to verbal nuance and experience in interpreting metaphorical/figurative language

9. Experience in rhyming as well as in the use of other kinds of poetic language, including, for example, well-turned phrases and plays on words

10. Skill with in-the-moment verbal improvisations

11. Extensive experience in the collaborative construction of narratives and stories; and

12. Skill in the construction of imaginative stories that frequently
     fictionalize the self (and/or other familiar people) and that often
     include dramatic dialogue (2008, p. 99)

Despite the strengths of their linguistic and cultural heritage, children from predominantly African American neighborhoods often
struggle to learn to read and continue to fall behind on standardized
school tests. And yet, as Meier and others (Brooks and Scott, 1985;
Hammond, Hoover, & McPhail, 2005; Heath, 1983) have demonstrated, when first- and second-grade teachers tap into children's cultural
strengths and engage their problem-solving skills, children who had
been historically disadvantaged in school can soar.

In Latino cultures, *family* is not only an interdependent group but
a core value.

> For many Latinos, life revolves around the tightly knit, loving bonds of
> *la familia.* By tradition and design, grandparents, aunts and uncles,
> cousins, and friends of all ages are a constant presence in the family
> nucleus and assume responsibility for one another's well-being. Typical
> in Latino cultures in the U.S. and in Spanish-speaking countries, the
> value placed on *la familia* as the heart and soul of life ensures that each
> member is nurtured and supported by a strong network of kin related by
> blood and by affection. (Eggers-Piérola, 2005, p. 15)

When the National Latino Children's Institute set out to create a
tool that would help Latino families support their children's language
and learning, they tapped into this cultural strength. The institute presents lessons for parents as advice and family stories from a wise aunt—
Consejos de mi Tia. These *consejos* are embedded in a multimedia kit that
includes a community coordinator's handbook, recipes for family fun,
and a "tell me a story" poster. They blend child development research
with traditional and community-based wisdom, and they focus square-
ly on building the relationships and interactions that support robust
language development in the language-learning years. This community and family education effort is titled words for the future:

> *Words for the Future—Creando el futuro—*uses culturally appropriate mate-
> rials and strategies to gently guide parents through the process of learning
> how to best provide their children with the experiences they need. . . .
>
> Using research findings on how children learn and on multiple lan-
> guage acquisition, and recommendations from the community, the fol-
> lowing messages were developed for *Words for the Future:*

- The early years are critical years in a child's development.

- The parents are the child's first and most important teachers.

- Everything a child experiences teaches him something.

- Learning happens everywhere.

- Children learn better when they feel secure and connected. The family is the anchor in their life. Communication among family members is crucial.

- Use family culture and celebrations for learning traditions.

- Everyone has a role to play in children's development, including extended family and the community.

- The best time to learn languages is when you are young. Learning two languages is an asset.

- Words are so powerful that they can be the key to understanding the world, but they can also destroy.

- Listen to and watch your baby. Your baby will tell you what she needs and wants.

- Children who listen to adults reading will grow up to become readers themselves.

- You can find words in lots of places, including songs, poetry and stories.

- Latino children need to see themselves in books and stories.

- The health and well-being of children can enhance or crush their capacity to learn. (National Latino Children's Institute, n.d.)

The institute shares these messages in parenting workshops and community gatherings throughout the United States.

ENSURING LANGUAGE-RICH ENVIRONMENTS IN THE EARLY YEARS

The widening vocabulary gaps that Hart and Risley (1995) documented among children in poor, working class, and professional families were evident at 18 months. Other researchers have documented a 2-year lag in the vocabulary needed by 2nd-grade readers (Biemiller & Slonim, 2001) and a correlation between kindergarten vocabulary level and 10th-grade reading comprehension (Snow et al., 2007). At least half of the achievement gap is attributable to differential early childhood experiences (Brooks-Gunn & Markman, 2005; Jencks & Phillips, 1998).

> High-quality early childhood education programs have great
> potential for preventing later school failure, particularly if
> they place a strong emphasis on language development. For
> this reason, early childhood teachers need thorough
> knowledge about language and how to help children
> develop language and literacy skills.
>
> —Lucy Wong Fillmore and Catherine Snow (2008).

In every state, significant efforts have begun to improve the over-all quality of child care available to children in their first 5 years. No state, however, has yet succeeded in building a system that ensures all children an early education of high-enough quality to prime them for school success.

In Allegheny County, Pennsylvania, a consortium of private funders, the Allegheny Early Childhood Initiative coalition, tried to approach this goal. They aimed to create a network of high-quality centers to serve 80% of the low-income 2- to 5-year-olds in their community. They committed to a 5-year investment of philanthropic dollars sufficient to fill the gap between what the state would pay for subsidized child care and the real cost of a quality education in hopes of seeding a system that could be sustained with public funding.

The initial effort was both a resounding success and a heart-breaking failure. Children gained a year and a half in cognitive development for each year they were in the program. Kindergarten and first grade retention and special education referral rates were cut from above 20% to virtually zero in receiving elementary schools (Bagnato, 2002). But the ambitious initiative was doomed by high start-up and administrative costs and some unforeseen shifts in the policy climate. Public funds were not forthcoming, so the planners significantly scaled back the effort in its fourth and fifth years, leaving just a small group of high-quality programs in place (Gill, Dembosky, & Caulkins, 2002).

By 2008, the picture looked brighter. The dreamers who made up the Allegheny Early Childhood Initiative coalition did not give up easily. They continued to work with statewide groups advocating for universal state-funded prekindergarten programs (Pennsylvania was one of the few states without any state pre-K program); quality improvements in all early education and care settings; and a coordinated system of programs, policies, and services for young children and their families. A new governor made early childhood education a centerpiece of his administration. Pennsylvania implemented Keystone STARS, a continuous quality improvement system for early care and education and school-age programs, and found funds to launch a new, high-quality program, PA Pre-K Counts, that could expand to serve all 3- and 4-year-olds. The Pittsburgh area, like other communities in Pennsylvania, now has new—and improved—programs to prime its children for school success.

BUILDING A NETWORK OF SUPPORTS

For toddlers in Centereach, Long Island, the public library is the place to be. It's always welcoming to young children and their families and teachers, but it is especially fun on Saturdays, during the Parent/Child Workshop sessions. During these sessions, the big community room is set up like toddler heaven, with Duplo bricks, climbing toys, books, a pretend kitchen, and lots of other cool stuff for toddlers to explore. At circle time, children can act out movement songs or listen to stories as they sit on a parent's lap.

While the children are playing and learning and making new friends, their parents are doing the same. They're also getting information about health, nutrition, learning, or development from a pediatric dentist, nutritionist, speech therapist, or other community professionals who helped set up the workshop. These professionals engage parents in informal conversation and answer any questions they may have. To keep the fun going, families can sign up for home visits from the Parent-Child Home Program, which reaches out to low-income and immigrant families and brings toys, books, and language-building family fun activities to their homes throughout the 2-year span when their children are learning to speak their first language(s).

The program developed at the Middle County Library in Centereach has become a model (Deerr, Feinberg, Gordon, & Schull, 2006) for a national network of Family Place Libraries committed to supporting young children and their families. According to The Core Components of a Family Place Library (http://www.familyplacelibraries .org), each Family Place Library provides

- Collections of books, toys, music and multimedia materials for babies, toddlers, parents and service providers

- A specially designed, welcoming space within the children's area for families with young children

- The Parent/Child Workshop, a 5-week program that involves toddlers and their parents and caregivers, features local professionals who serve as resources for parents, emphasizes the role of parents as the first teachers of their children, facilitates early intervention, and teaches strategies for healthy child development and early literacy

- Coalition-building with community agencies that serve families and young children to connect parents to community resources and develop programs and services tailored to meet local needs

- Outreach to new and non-traditional library users, especially parents and very young children (beginning at birth)

- Developmentally appropriate programming for very young children and their parents

- Library staff trained in family support, child development, parent education and best practices (Family Place Libraries, n.d.)

Like other family support programs, Family Place Libraries serve child care providers as well as parents. They have become a particularly effective way of reaching out to "family, friend, and neighbor" caregivers who are not operating licensed centers or family child care homes, though they may be receiving public child care subsidy funds. Because so many children—including many from low-income families—are being served in such arrangements, state policy makers have begun to look for ways to assure that these children are having early experiences that will promote their later school success. States at the forefront of early childhood system-building efforts are looking at Family Place Libraries as an effective and scalable program model. The Build Initiative, a multistate partnership that helps states construct a coordinated system of programs, policies, and services for young children and their families, featured the Centereach program at its July 2007 meeting and posted information about the Family Place Libraries model on its learning community site (http://www.buildinitiative.org).

COMMUNITY SCHOOL READINESS WIRING

On March 12, 2008, the Mayor of Boston officially launched a 10-year initiative titled *Thrive in Five* (Thrive in Five, 2008). The prior planning phase took 1 year of work by an Action Planning Team that included parents, early childhood health and development experts, service providers, funders, and representatives from the state agencies that serve young children and their families. The team performed a detailed analysis of the needs and characteristics of young children's families, the resources available in their neighborhoods and how they were being used, and the demographic trends that would be likely to play an important role in the next decade. The team galvanized the participation of leading institutions—hospitals, museums, universities, corporations, and community-based agencies—and garnered input and support from leaders and parents in diverse community sectors. It pulled together existing initiatives and piloted others.

Boston's ambitious plan addressed four areas: families, educators, systems, and the city as a whole, with benchmarks and tools for assessing progress in each, and regular reports to the community and its stakeholders.

- *Families* would receive information that would help them play the role of their child's first teacher. This information would come not only through their child's child care and health care providers and from typical information sources, such as libraries, museums, radio and television, and the Internet. It would also be sent over "community school readiness wiring"—through brochures, posters, people, and events located at the places they were likely to frequent, such as workplaces, grocery stores, hair salons, and playgrounds.

- *Educators* would receive support to upgrade their facilities and knowledge and to achieve accreditation through NAEYC (for centers) and the National Association for Family Child Care (for family child care homes), with the goal of 100% accreditation by the end of the 10-year initiative.

- *Systems* of care would link pediatrics, early intervention, family support and mental health services, child care providers, and child welfare and social services agencies to provide every newborn with a welcome visit; every baby and young child with periodic health and development screenings; and every child or family in need of assistance with prompt, appropriate, effective services.

- *The city* would commit public resources and administrative leadership to ensure the success of Thrive in Five; align its departments to support the plan; strengthen linkages with housing, transportation, public safety, and other vital supports for families; and launch a citywide campaign to help the general public understand the importance of the early years and the specific roles played by people, organizations, and sectors in supporting school readiness.

The term *community school readiness wiring* aptly describes not only the plan for communicating with families and learning from them about what works best with their children but also the entire Thrive in Five vision of an interconnected city that shares a commitment to ensure that all of its children have the early experiences that prepare them to thrive. One of the central messages to be transmitted over the community school readiness wiring is the importance of talking with babies and young children. One example of how to do this was described in an article that appeared on the front page of *The Boston Globe* titled, "With Babies, Words for Wisdom: City Urges Parents to Nourish Young Minds with Talk:"

> Literacy coaches have begun fanning out among housing developments in the city, urging parents of infants and toddlers to embrace the unnatural role of a sportscaster. They should narrate a play-by-play of their actions, the coaches say, while bathing and dressing their little ones, riding the bus with them, and running errands—even if the babies respond with nothing more than a blink, smile, or coo. (Jan, 2008)

In sports-crazed "Red Sox Nation," that message is likely to resonate with young parents of every culture.

FOR CHILDREN WHO NEED MORE

Harold Cox was right: we need to get habits of talking with babies and understanding of their importance "into the drinking water." But, as he also realized, that will not be enough. In every community, we also need to ask his questions about the barriers that prevent engaged, enriching conversation and how they can be removed. If young children and their parents are spending too much of their time in situations that are not conducive to brain-building interaction or where baby talk is inappropriate, then we need to work together to make public spaces family friendly and to increase what former federal Child Care Bureau director Joan Lombardi (2003) calls "Time to Care." If cultural norms and beliefs are keeping some babies, parents, and caregivers too quiet, then we need to open cross-cultural conversations among adults and learn together how best to support healthy development in a bilingual, bicultural context.

We need to screen all children for sensory impairments, handicapping conditions, and developmental delays and provide prompt, evidence-based intervention as early as possible so that it can be maximally effective. And when isolation, depression, or overwhelming stress prevents loving families and caregivers from being fully available to young children, we need to invest in the targeted interventions and follow-up supports that can prevent or repair the damage.

In Juneau and surrounding communities in southeastern Alaska, Partnerships for Children, a collaboration among 15 organizations serving children and families has spread "a blanket of wellness" over the young children. The effort began in 2002, in response to reports from child care providers that increasing numbers of young children were exhibiting challenging behaviors and signs of emotional stress at increasing levels of severity. A large percentage of programs had felt compelled to expel at least one child in the previous year. In a pilot project serving more than 1,000 children and more than 200 staff members, young children were regularly screened for social-emotional concerns, with multiple agencies using a common tool. Licensed behavioral/mental health specialists consulted with the staff of child care and home-visiting programs to help them implement effective strategies for supporting children whose social and emotional needs presented challenges to their families, caregivers, or teachers.

In addition, Partnerships for Children is working to create "a seamless web" that gives all families with children younger than 8 years access to community services that support their children's health, growth, and development. To this end, Partnerships for Children has developed a resource guide and map of programs for families and has reached out to employers to promote family friendly workplace policies.

In New York City's Harlem Children's Zone—as in urban and rural communities in Texas, Florida, New Mexico, and Illinois that implement Dr. Brazelton's Touchpoints Approach (http://www.touchpoints. org)—paradigms have shifted. Children who would have once been born with the label "at risk" are now born "at promise." Parents with low levels of formal education attend "baby college" and are seen as the experts on their own children. Professionals who had worked in health care, child care, or family support "silos" now routinely collaborate, and their efforts are informed by the wisdom of community elders and empowered parents. In child care, Early Head Start, and Head Start programs, young children are learning in two languages, wrestling with cognitively challenging questions and real-world problems, and engaging in rich language and literacy-building activities, rituals, and conversations. And parents are reporting less stress.

A study (Tomopoulos et al, 2008) conducted at a large urban hospital underlined the potential of the parent-empowerment strategies that Touchpoints promotes. Parents who felt more empowered when their babies were 6 months old provided more cognitive stimulation at home, including more frequent reading, when their babies were toddlers. Not surprisingly, their toddlers also showed more advanced cognitive development.

"TEACH MORE. LOVE MORE"

"Teach more. Love more." In Miami-Dade County, Florida, this vision has energized not only families, neighbors, educators, and service providers but also policy makers, philanthropists, and taxpayers. The public engagement campaign began in 1999, when David Lawrence, Jr., publisher of the area's leading newspaper, convened a group of nearly 200 experts to draft a strategic plan for school readiness and teamed up with Mayor Alex Penelas to engage diverse sectors of the community in shaping the draft, prioritizing actions at an Early Childhood Summit, and participating in task forces to advance the priorities that the community selected.

The effort has been wide-ranging, including welcome gifts and visits for newborns, a 24-hour "warm line" for parents and child care professionals who have questions or concerns about a child or need information about community services, a trilingual newsletter that reaches more than 26,000 families, a web site, and a television show. Pediatricians have been trained in the Touchpoints approach, along with early educators and family support professionals. Early care and education programs have improved dramatically as a result of multiple initiatives and alliances with local universities, and the number of professionally accredited programs has soared from just 17 at the outset to more than 335 in 2008. Children with special needs are being identified earlier and offered appropriate services. Parents of all backgrounds are talking, reading, teaching, and learning.

Taxpayers contribute to these initiatives through a dedicated property tax that supports children's services. In 2002, the community voted two to one to initiate this tax and establish a Children's Trust to allocate the resulting revenue. The Teach More/Love More coalition continues to expand its efforts to fulfill its stated mission:

> To ensure that all children in Miami-Dade County have the community's attention, commitment and resources and, hence, the chance to develop intellectually, emotionally, socially and physically so that they are ready and eager to learn by the time they reach first grade. (Teach More/Love More, n.d.)

LAYERS OF THE ONION

The following story is a reflection on the experiences of three communities—Cambridge, Massachusetts; Grand Rapids, Michigan; and

St. Paul, Minnesota—who pioneered separate early language and literacy initiatives, borrowed each other's ideas, and came together to assess and codify what worked in their individual settings and what could be shared with other communities (Agenda for Children, 2008). Lei-Anne Ellis, Literacy Coordinator for the Agenda for Children, told the story:

> Our message resonates with all sorts of parents, and with professionals at all levels. Sometimes, we approach it simply. "Talk with your child. That's how he learns. You don't have to read all the words in a book—or even be able to read any of them. What's important is talking about the book together, making connections to your child's experience." Sometimes, we go into depth: We talk about specific techniques for supporting language at each stage of development and teach all of the question-asking steps of dialogic reading. We discuss the merits of different approaches to introducing children to a second language or tracking children's emergent literacy progress. We showcase techniques for supporting children's progress in their home languages within English-dominant classrooms. We look together at the linguistic and communicative strengths of children from different backgrounds and strategize how best to ensure that our preschools and schools continue to build on them.
>
> But the process is always the same:
>
> - We make people aware of their importance in children's lives—and the importance of talking with children.
>
> - We give permission to do what comes naturally—to have fun together and learn from the child.
>
> - We help people reflect on their own context—what they have grown up with, what seems to work best for a particular child or group of children, the expectations of those around them. Then they can decide what they want to do more of, or less of. They can be more intentional about their parenting or their professional practice.
>
> - We provide supports and opportunities for practicing new techniques and approaches.
>
> - We encourage and support reflection on what's working and what isn't, and what next steps might be. The cycle begins again as people seek new information.
>
> Of course, it doesn't always happen in this neat sequence. It's more like peeling an onion. For most of the parents, home visitors, and teachers we work with, there are a series of "aha moments."

Each one strips away blinders and brings richer understanding, but there is always another layer to explore.

The same is true for us. We keep experimenting, being surprised, and rethinking what we do. We've tried out a number of different methods and approaches—hospital visits to families with newborns, parent workshops, reading parties, parent–child playgroups, regular home visits focused on sharing books and toys, family fun days, library programs, getting our supermarkets to create ABC labels and scavenger hunts that turn shopping into a literacy game, courses and individual coaching for our center-based and family child care teachers, book "prescriptions" at well-child visits, broadcasting our messages on ethnic radio stations, subway posters, and multilingual community television and radio spots— even putting book pages on stakes at our parks so families can follow the trail and read a book together. I think they all add value. When the message comes from everywhere, everybody learns. And the more we peel those onion layers, the more people want to learn.

We had a strong base of community interest to build on, and we worked hard to get some big grants that allowed us to come together and try out some creative solutions. Now, 6 years later, we are seeing results. Our children are flourishing, our families are flourishing, and our community is flourishing. Our policy makers, business leaders, and philanthropists are seeing the value of investing in the early years. We are beginning to get the resources we need to sustain a diverse and healthy village. But we still have work to do (Personal Communication, 2008).

A WEALTH OF WORDS

It takes a lot more than words to ensure that all children thrive. Parents can't do it alone. Neither can policy makers, pediatricians, teachers and caregivers, or other early childhood experts. But every community has assets and initiatives that it can bring together to ensure that its children get a good language start, that its families are supported and support each other, and that its child care programs and schools are ready to build—and build on—the strengths its children bring.

The leadership can come from many places. Pediatricians, politicians, newspaper publishers, librarians, child care providers, philanthropists, business people, and professional advocates have all spearheaded successful initiatives. Change can be guided by a long-term strategic plan that reflects the input and buy-in of many sectors of the community, or it can grow within one institution, program, partnership, or neighborhood and spread from there.

It can begin with a simple idea: Talk to me, baby!—a simple approach: playful conversation—and a basic assumption that all of the children in the community are all of the children of the community and that every child matters. With leadership, collaboration, and outreach, this idea can grow into a communitywide commitment that ensures that every child begins school with a wealth of words.

References

Aardema, V. (1981). *Bringing the rain to Kapiti Plain.* New York: Dial Books for Young Readers.

ACF, Head Start Bureau, *Head Start program fact sheet for fiscal year 2006.*

Ada, A.F. (1988). The Pajaro valley experience: Working with Spanish-speaking parents to develop children's reading and writing skills through children's literature. In T. Skutnabb-Kangas & J. Vummins (Eds.), *Minority education: From shame to struggle* (pp. 223–238). Philadelphia: Multilingual Matters.

Ada, A.F. (2001). *Gathering the sun.* New York: Rayo.

Adams, M.J. (1990). *Beginning to read: Thinking and learning about print.* Cambridge, MA: The MIT Press.

Agenda for Children. (2008). *Let's talk...It makes a difference! program manual: An innovative approach to supporting children's literacy development.* Cambridge, MA: City of Cambridge.

Agenda for Children. (n.d.). *Parent education.* Retrieved June 16, 2008, from http://www.cambridgechildren.org/programs/parent_education.php

Alvarado, C., Burnley, L.V., Derman-Sparks, L., Hoffman, E., Jiménez, L.I., Labyzon, J., et al. (1999). *In our own way: How anti-bias work shapes our lives.* Saint Paul, MN: Redleaf Press.

August, D., Calderón, M., & Carlo, M. (2002). *The transfer of skills from Spanish to English: A study of young learners.* Washington, DC: Center for Applied Linguistics.

Bagnato, S.J. (2002). *Quality early learning—key to school success: A first-phase program evaluation research report for Pittsburgh's Early Childhood Initiative (ECI).* Pittsburgh, PA: Children's Hospital of Pittsburgh, SPECS Evaluation Research Team.

Bardige, B. (2005). *At a loss for words: How America is failing our children and what we can do about it.* Philadelphia: Temple University Press.

Bardige, B.S., & Segal, M.M. (2005). *Poems to learn to read by: Building literacy with love.* Washington, DC: ZERO TO THREE Press.

Barik, H., & Swain, M. (1976). A longitudinal study of bilingual and cognitive development. *International Journal of Psychology, 11,* 251–263.

Bates, E., & Dick, F. (2002). Language, gesture, and the developing brain. *Developmental Psychobiology, 40,* 293–310.

Beatty, A. (2005). *Mathematical and scientific development in early childhood: A workshop summary.* Washington, DC: National Academies Press.

Biemiller, A., & Slonim, N. (2001). Estimating root word vocabulary growth in advantaged and disadvantaged populations: Evidence for a common sequence of vocabulary acquisition. *Journal of Educational Psychology, 93,* 498–520.

Bloom, P. (2000). *How children learn the meaning of words.* Cambridge, MA: The MIT Press.

Bochner, S. (1996). The learning strategies of bilingual vs. monolingual students. *British Journal of Educational Psychology, 66,* 83–93.

Bowman, B. (2007, December). When healthy development is not enough. Luncheon plenary address at the ZERO TO THREE National Training Conference, Washington, DC.

Bramsford, J.D., & Johnson, M.K. (1973). Consideration of some problems of comprehension. In W.G. Chase (Ed.), *Visual information processing.* San Diego: Academic Press.

Brazelton, T.B., & Greenspan, S. (2001). *The irreducible needs of children: What every child must have to grow, learn, and flourish.* New York: Perseus Books Group.

Brazelton, T., & Nugent, J. (1995). *Neonatal Behavioral Assessment Scale* (3rd ed.). Cambridge, MA: MacKeith Press.

Brazelton, T.B., & Sparrow, J.D. (2006). *Touchpoints: Birth to three* (2nd ed.). Cambridge, MA: Da Capo Lifelong Books.

Bricker, D., & Squires, J. (with Mounts, L., Potter, L., Nickel, R., Twombly, E., & Farrell, J.). (1999). *Ages & Stages Questionnaires® (ASQ): A parent-completed, child-monitoring system* (2nd ed.). Baltimore: Paul H. Brookes Publishing Co.

Brown, M.W. (1991). *Goodnight, moon.* New York: HarperFestival.

Brown, R. (1973). *A first language: The early stages.* Cambridge, MA: Harvard University Press.

Brooks, C. and Scott, J. C. (1985). *Tapping potential: English and language arts for the Black learner.* Urbana, IL: National Council of Teachers of English.

Brooks-Gunn, J., & Markman, L.B. (2005). The contribution of parenting to ethnic and racial gaps in school readiness. *Future of Children, 15(1),* 139–168.

Bus, A., Belsky, J., van Ijzendoorn, M.H., & Crnic, K. (1997). Attachment and book-reading patterns: A study of mothers, fathers, and their toddlers. *Early Childhood Research Quarterly, 12,* 81–98.

Bus, A., & van Ijzendoorn, M. (1995). Mothers reading to their 3-year-olds: The role of mother-child attachment security in becoming literate. *Reading Research Quarterly, 30,* 998–1015.

Bus, A., van Ijzendoorn, M., & Pellegrini, A. (1995). Joint book reading makes for success in learning to read: A meta-analysis on intergenerational transmission of literacy. *Review of Educational Research, 65,* 1–21.

Business Partnership for Early Learning. (2007). *BPEL annual report.* Seattle: Author.

California Institute on Human Services, Sonoma State University. (2003). *Language is the key: Follow the car resource guide.* Sonoma, CA: National Head Start Family Literacy Center.

Carle, E. (1994). *The very hungry caterpillar.* New York: Philomel.

Carle, E. (1999). *From head to toe.* New York: Harper Trophy.

Carlsson-Paige, Nancy (2008). *Taking back childhood: Helping your kids thrive in a fast-paced, media-saturated, violence-filled world.* New York: Hudson Street Press.

Center for Law and Social Policy. (2008). *Head Start participants, programs, families, and staff in 2006.* Washington, DC: Author.

Chall, J.S., Jacobs, V.A., & Baldwin, L.E. (1990). *The reading crisis: Why poor children fall behind.* Cambridge, MA: Harvard University Press.

Christakis, D.A., Zimmerman, F.J., DiGiuseppe, D.L., & McCarty, C.A. (2004). Early television exposure and subsequent attentional problems in children. *Pediatrics, 113,* 708–713.

Cisneros, S. (1997). *Hairs/pelitos.* Albuquerque, NM: Dragonfly Books.

Committee on the Prevention of Reading Difficulties in Young Children, National Research Council. (1998). *Starting out right: A guide for promoting children's reading success* (M.S. Burns, P. Griffin, & C.E. Snow, Eds.). Washington, DC: National Academies Press.

Conner, B. (2007). *Unplugged play.* New York: Workman Publishing.

Cowley, J. (1999). *Mrs. Wishy-Washy.* New York: Wright Group/McGraw-Hill.

Cox, P.R., & Cartright, S. (2006). *Frog on a log.* Eveleth, MN: Usborne Books.

Cruz-Contarini, R. (2001). *Las letras hablan.* León, Spain: Everest.

Cummins, J., & Swain, M. (1986). *Bilingualism in education: Aspects of theory, research and practice.* New York: Longman.

DeCasper, A.J. & Spence, M.J. (1986). Prenatal maternal speech influences newborns' perception of speech sounds. *Infant Behavior and Development, 9,* 133–150.

De Rico, U. (1994). *The rainbow goblins.* New York: Thames and Hudson.

Deerr, K., Feinberg, S., Gordon, E., & Schull, D. (2006). Libraries are family places for literacy and learning. In J. Knapp-Philo & S.E. Rosenkoetter (Eds.), *Learning to read the world* (pp. 477–498). Washington, DC: ZERO TO THREE Press.

Dickinson, D., & Smith, M. (1994). Long-term effects of preschool teachers' book readings on low-income children's vocabulary and story comprehension. *Reading Research Quarterly, 29,* 104–122.

Dickinson, D.K., & Sprague, K.E. (2001). The nature and impact of early childhood care environments on the language and early literacy development of children from low-income families. In S.B. Neuman & D.K. Dickinson (Eds.), *Handbook of early literacy research* (pp. 283–280). New York: Guilford Press.

Dickinson, D.K., & Tabors, P.O. (2001). *Beginning literacy with language: Young children learning at home and school.* Baltimore: Paul H. Brookes Publishing Co.

Dickinson, E. (1976). *There is no frigate like a book.* In *The complete poems of Emily Dickinson.* Boston, MA: Back Bay Books (p. 553). (Original work published 1873)

Dunn, L.M. (1981). *Peabody Picture Vocabulary Test-Revised.* Circle Pines, MN: American Guidance Service.

Eastman, P.D. (1960). *Are you my mother?* New York: Random House.

Education Development Center. (2007, December). Diversity in preschool: EDC's professional development program helps both educators and students succeed. *EDC Update.* Retrieved Sept. 9, 2008, from http://main.edc.org /NewsRoom/features/preschool_diversity.asp.

Edwards, C., Gandini, L., & Forman, G. (1998). *The hundred languages of children: The Reggio Emilia approach—Advanced reflections* (2nd ed.). Stamford, CT: Ablex Publishing.

Eggers-Piérola, C. (2005). *Connections and commitments: Reflecting Latino values in early childhood programs.* Portsmouth, NH: Heinemann.

Ehlert, L. (1994). *Eating the alphabet: Fruits & vegetables from A to Z.* New York: Harcourt Big Books.

Eliason, C., & Jenkins, L. (2003). *A practical guide to early childhood curriculum* (7th ed.). Upper Saddle River, NJ: Prentice Hall.

Eliot, L. (1999). *What's going on in there? How the brain and mind develop in the first five years.* New York: Bantam Books.

Emberley, E. (1992). *Go away, big green monster.* New York: Scholastic.

Engel, S. (1997). The emergence of storytelling during the first three years. *ZERO TO THREE Journal, 17,* 1–9.

Fahey, J. (Producer). (2007). *Raising readers* [video]. (Available from Get Ready to Read! at http://www.getreadytoread.org/content/view/396)

Family Communications. (2005). *From Lullabies to Literacy: The importance of relationship* [Multimedia kit with workshop facilitator's guide, video segments, Power Point presentations, and handout masters]. Pittsburgh: Author.

Family Place Libraries. (n.d.). *The core components of a Family Place Library.* Retrieved July 7, 2008, from http://www.familyplacelibraries.org /whatMakes.html

Federation of Child Care Centers of Alabama. (1998). *More is caught than taught: A guide to quality child care.* Montgomery, AL: Author.

Feynman, R. (2001). *The pleasure of finding things out.* London: Penguin Books Ltd.

Fillmore, L.W., & Snow C. (2008). *What Early Childhood Teachers Need to Know about Language and Linguistics* (ERIC Document Reproduction Service No. ED447722, p. 1).

Fivush, R., Haden, C.A., & Reese, E. (2006). Elaborating on elaborations: Role of maternal reminiscing style in cognitive and socioemotional development. *Child Development, 77,* 1568–1588.

Fraiberg, S. (1996). *The magic years: Understanding and handling the problems of early childhood.* New York: Scribners.

Freeman, D. (2007). *Corduroy.* New York: Puffin Storytime.

French, L. (2004). Science as the center of a coherent, integrated early childhood curriculum. *Early Childhood Research Quarterly, 19,* 138–149.

Galinsky, E., Howes, C., & Kontos, S. (1995). *The family child care training study: Highlights of findings.* New York: Families and Work Institute.

Gamel-McCormick, M., & Amsden, D. (2005). *Delaware early care and education baseline quality study.* Newark, DE: Center for Disabilities Studies, University of Delaware.

Gates, H.L. (1989). *The signifying monkey: A theory of African-American literary criticism.* Oxford, UK: Oxford University Press.

Genesee, F., Paradis, J., & Crago, M.B. (2004). *Dual language development and disorders: A handbook on bilingualism and second language learning.* Baltimore: Paul H. Brookes Publishing Co.

Gill, B.P., Dembosky, J.W., & Caulkins, J.P. (2002). *A "noble bet" in early care and education: Lessons from one community's experience.* Pittsburgh: RAND.

Gilligan, C. (1993). *In a different voice: Psychological theory and women's development.* Cambridge, MA: Harvard University Press.

González, N., Moll, L.C., & Amanti, C. (2005). *Funds of knowledge: Theorizing practices in households, communities, and classrooms.* New York: Routledge.

Goodwyn, S.W., Acredolo, L.P., & Brown, C. (2000). Impact of symbolic gesturing on early language development. *Journal of Nonverbal Behavior, 24,* 81–103.

Gopnik, A., Meltzoff, A.M., & Kuhl, P. (1999). *The scientist in the crib.* New York: William Morrow and Company.

Greenspan, S., & Salmon, J. (1996). *The challenging child: Understanding, raising, and enjoying the five "difficult" types of children.* New York: Perseus Books Group.

Hakuta, K., & Diaz, R. (1984). The relationship between degree of bilingualism and cognitive ability: A critical discussion and some new longitudinal data. In K.E. Nelson (Ed.), *Children's language* (Vol. 5, pp. 319–344). Mahwah, NJ: Lawrence Erlbaum Associates.

Hamm, K., Gault, B., & Jones-DeWeever, A. (2005). *In our own backyard: Local and state strategies to improve the quality of family child care.* Washington, DC: Institute for Women's Policy Research.

Hammil, D.D., & McNutt, G. (1980). Language abilities and reading: A review of the literature on their relationship. *Elementary School Journal, 80,* 269–277.

Hammond, B., Hoover, M. & McPhail, I. (Eds.) (2005), *Teaching African American learners to read*. Newark, DE: International Reading Association.

Harley, B., & Lapkin, S. (1984). *The effects of early bilingual schooling on first language development*. Toronto: O.I.S.E.

Harpaz-Rotem, I., & Hirst, W. (2005). The earliest memory in individuals raised in either traditional and reformed kibbutz or outside the kibbutz. *Memory, 13*, 51–62.

Hart, B., & Risley, T.R. (1995). *Meaningful differences in the everyday experience of young American children*. Baltimore: Paul H. Brookes Publishing Co.

Hart, B., & Risley, T.R. (1999). *The social world of children learning to talk*. Baltimore: Paul H. Brookes Publishing Co.

Hayes, S., & Ormerod, J. (1994). *Eat up, Gemma*. New York: Harper Trophy.

Heath, S.B. (1983). *Ways with words: Language, life and work in communities and classrooms*. Cambridge, UK: Cambridge University Press.

Heckman, J.J. (2005). Lessons from the technology of skill formation. (NBER Working Paper No. W11142.) Cambridge, MA: NBER.

Hoban, R. (1964). *Bread and jam for Francis*. New York: Harper.

Hoff, E. (2006). Language experience and language milestones during early childhood. In K. McCartney & D. Phillips (Eds.), *Blackwell handbook of early childhood development* (pp. 233–251). Malden, MA: Blackwell Publishing.

Howes, C., Galinsky, E., Shinn, M., Sibley, A., Abbott-Shim, M., & McCarthy, J. (1998). *The Florida child care quality improvement study: 1996 report*. New York: Families and Work Institute.

Jan, T. (2008, April 2). With babies, words for wisdom: City urges parents to nourish young minds with talk. *The Boston Globe*, pp. A1 and A7. Retrieved July, 7, 2008, from http://www.boston.com/news/local/massachusetts/articles/2008/04/02/with_babies_words_for_wisdom

Jencks, C., & Phillips, M. (1998). *The Black–White test score gap*. Washington, DC: Brookings Institution Press.

Jervay-Pendergrass, D. (2000). Conversational prenarratives: The emergence of talk about past events. In J. Kreeft Peyton, P. Griffin, W. Wolfram, and R. Fasold (Eds.), *Language in action: New studies of language in society: Essays in honor of Roger W. Shuy* (pp. 550–576). Cresskill, NJ: Hampton Press, Inc.

Jervay-Pendergrass, D., & Brown, C. (1999/2000). Something happened! Sharing life stories from birth to three. *The Zero to Three Journal, 20*(3): 25–31.

Kagan, J. (1999). Born to be shy. In R. Conlan (Ed.), *States of mind: New discoveries about how our brains make us who we are* (pp. 29–52). New York: Wiley.

Kalmanson, B. (2006). What babies teach us: The transdisciplinary practice of infant mental health and early intervention. Special address at the ZERO TO THREE National Training Institute, Albuquerque, NM.

Karweit, N., & Wasik, B. (1996). The effects of story reading programs on literacy and language development of disadvantaged pre-schoolers. *Journal of Education for Students Placed At-Risk, 4*, 319–348.

Katz, J.R. & Snow, C.E. (2000). Language development in early childhood. In D. Cryer & T. Harms (Eds.), *Infants and toddlers in out-of-home care*. Baltimore: Paul H. Brookes Publishing Co.

Keats, E.J. (1962). *The snowy day*. New York: Viking Press.

Kellogg, S. (1992). *Much bigger than Martin*. New York: Puffin Books.

Kim, K.H.S., Belkin, N.R., Lee, K.H., & Hirsch, J. (1997). Distinct cortical areas associated with native and second languages. *Nature, 388*, 171–174.

Layzer, J., & Goodson, B. (2006). *National study of child care for low-income families: Care in the home: A description of family child care and the experiences of the families and children who use it, Wave 1 report: Executive summary.* Washington, DC: Administration for Children, Youth, and Families.

Leichtman, M.D., Pillemer, D.B., Wang, Q., Koreishib, A., & Han, J.J. (2000). When Baby Maisy came to school: Mothers' interview styles and preschoolers' event memories. *Cognitive Development, 15,* 99–114.

Lombardi, J. (2003). *Time to care: Redesigning child care to promote education, support families, and build communities.* Philadelphia: Temple University Press.

Lord, J.V., & Burroway, J. (1987). *The giant jam sandwich.* Boston: Houghton Mifflin.

MacDonald, S., Uesiliana, K., & Hayne, H. (2000). Cross-cultural and gender differences in childhood amnesia. *Memory, 8,* 365–376.

Marshall, N.L., Creps, C.L., Burstein, N.R., Glantz, F.B., Robeson, W.W., & Barnett, S. (2004). *The cost and quality of full day, year-round early care and education in Massachusetts: Infant/toddler: Executive summary.* Wellesley, MA: Wellesley Centers for Women and Abt Associates.

Martin, B., & Carle, E. (2007). *Brown bear, brown bear, what do you see?* New York: Henry Holt & Co.

Marzollo, J., & Pinkney, J. (1997). *Pretend you're a cat.* New York: Puffin Books.

Mayer, M. (1998). *Just for you.* New York: Random House.

McClosky, R. (1948). *Blueberries for Sal.* New York: Viking Juvenile.

McMurray, B. (2007). Defusing the childhood vocabulary explosion. *Science, 317*(5838), 631.

Meier, T. (2008). *Black communications and learning to read: Building on children's linguistic and cultural strengths.* Mahwah, NJ: Lawrence Erlbaum Associates.

Moats, L. (2001). Overcoming the language gap: Invest generously in teacher education. *American Educator, 25,* 8–9.

Modigliani, K., & Moore, E. (2005). *Many right ways designing your home child care environment* [DVD and manual]. Columbia, MD: Enterprise Community Partners.

Montie, J.E., Xiang, Z., & Schweinhart, L. (2007). *The role of preschool experience in children's development: Longitudinal findings from 10 countries.* Ypsilanti, MI: High/Scope Press.

Mosel, A., & Lent, B. (1968). *Tikki Tikki Tembo.* New York: Henry Holt and Company.

Mullen, M.K. (1994). Earliest recollections of childhood: A demographic analysis. *Cognition, 521,* 55–79.

Mullen, M.K., & Yi, S. (1995). The cultural context of talk about the past: Implications for the development of autobiographical memory. *Cognitive Development, 10,* 407–419.

National Association for the Education of Young Children, & International Reading Association. (1998). *Learning to read and write: Developmentally appropriate practices for young children. A joint position statement of the International Reading Association and the National Association for the Education of Young Children.* Washington, DC: Author.

National Latino Children's Institute. (n.d.) *Words for the future—Creando el futuro.* Retrieved July 7, 2008, from http://www.nlci.org/kits/Words%20intro.htm

National Research Council. (1998). *Preventing reading difficulties in young children. Committee on the Prevention of Reading Difficulties in Young Children.*

(C.E. Snow, M.S. Burns, & P. Griffin, Eds.). Washington, DC: National Academies Press.

National Research Council, & Institute of Medicine. (2000). *From neurons to neighborhoods: The science of early childhood development.* Washington, DC: National Academies Press.

National Research Council, Committee on Early Childhood Pedagogy. (2000). In B.T. Bowman & M.S. Donovan (Eds.), *Eager to learn: Educating our preschoolers.* Washington, DC: National Academies Press.

National Scientific Council on the Developing Child. (2007). The science of early childhood development: Closing the gap between what we know and what we do. Cambridge, MA: Center on the Developing Child, Harvard University.

Nelson, K. (1973). Structure and strategy in learning to talk. *Monographs of the Society for Research in Child Development, 38*(1–2) (Serial 149):136.

Nelson, K. (ed.) (1989). *Narratives from the crib.* Cambridge, MA: Harvard University Press.

Neuman, S., Copple, C., & Bredekamp, S. (2000). *Learning to read and write: Developmentally appropriate practices for young children.* Washington, DC: National Association for the Education of Young Children.

NICHD Early Child Care Research Network. (Eds.). (2005). *Child care and development: Results from the NICHD study of early child care and youth development.* New York: Guilford Press.

Norton, D.G. (1993). Diversity, early socialization and temporal development: The dual perspective revisited. *Social Work, 38,* 82–90.

Norton, D. (1994). My mommy didn't kill my daddy. In J. Osofsky & E. Fenichel (Eds.), *Caring for infants and toddlers in violent environments: Hurt, healing, and hope.* Washington, DC: ZERO TO THREE Press.

Norton, D. (1996). Early linguistic interaction and school achievement: An ethnographical, ecological perspective. *Zero to Three, 16,* 8–14.

Nugent, J.K., Keefer, C., Minear, S., Johnson, L., & Blanchard, Y. (2007). *Understanding newborn behavior & early relationships: The Newborn Behavioral Observations (NBO) System handbook.* Baltimore, Paul H. Brookes Publishing Co.

Paley, V.G. (1991). *The boy who would be a helicopter.* Cambridge, MA: Harvard University Press.

Paley, V.G. (1993). *You can't say you can't play.* Cambridge, MA: Harvard University Press.

Pancsofar, N., & Vernon-Feagans, L. (2006). Mother and father language input to young children: Contributions to later language development. *Journal of Applied Developmental Psychology, 27*(6), 571–587.

Parish, P. (1992). *Amelia Bedelia.* New York: Harper Trophy.

Piaget, J. (1952). *The origin of intelligence in the child.* International Universities Press.

Pillemer, D. (2000). *Momentous events, vivid memories.* Cambridge, MA: Harvard University Press.

Pinkner, S. (1994). *The language instinct: How the mind creates language.* New York: William Morrow and Company.

Piper, W. (1978). *The little engine that could.* New York: Grosset & Dunlap.

Powell, D. (2005). *Lessons learned: The Bush Foundation Infant/Toddler Program turns 10.* St. Paul, MN: The Bush Foundation.

Primary Phonics Storybooks. (2001). *Mac and Tab book 1.* Cambridge, MA: Educators Publishing Service.

Pruden, S.M., Hirsh-Pasek, K., Golinkoff, R.M., & Hennon, E.A. (2006). The birth of words: Ten-month-olds learn words through perceptual salience. *Child Development, 77,* 266–280.

Raffi. (1988). *Shake my sillies out.* New York: Crown Books.

Raikes, H.H., Raikes, H.A., Pan, B.A., Luze, G., Tamis-LeMonda, C.S., Rodriguez, E.T., et al. (2006). Mother–child book reading in low-income families: Correlates and outcomes during the first three years of life. *Child Development, 77,* 924–953.

Reach Out and Read. (n.d.). *Our mission.* Retrieved June, 16, 2008, from http://www.reachoutandread.org

Rideout, V., Vanderwater, E., & Martella, E. (2003). *Zero to six: Electronic media in the lives of infants, toddlers, and preschoolers.* Menlo Park, CA: Henry J. Kaiser Family Foundation.

Ringgold, F. (1996). *Tar beach.* Albuquerque, NM: Dragonfly Books.

Risley, T., & Hart, B. (2006). Promoting early language development. In N.F. Watt, C. Ayoub, R.H. Bradley, J.E. Puma, & W.A. LeBoeuf (Eds.), *The crisis in youth mental health: Critical issues and effective programs* (Vol. 4, pp. 83–88). Westport, CT: Praeger.

Rolnick, A., & Grunewald, R. (2003). Early childhood development: Economic development with a high public return. Minneapolis, MN: *The Region,* 17 no. 4 Supplement (December, 2003), 6–12.

Rosenkoetter, S., & Knapp-Philo, J. (2006). *Learning to read the world: Language and literacy in the first three years.* Washington, DC: ZERO TO THREE Press.

Ryder, J., & Cherry, L. (1992). *Chipmunk song.* New York: Puffin Books.

Ryder, J., & Rothman, M. (1993). *Sea elf.* New York: HarperCollins.

Ryder, J., & Rothman, M. (1994). *Lizard in the sun.* New York: Harper Trophy.

Scanlon, D., & Vellutino, F.R. (1996). Prerequisite skills, early instruction, and success in first-grade reading: Selected results from a longitudinal study. *Mental Retardation and Developmental Research Reviews, 2,* 54–63.

Scarborough, H.S. (1998). Prediction of reading disability from familial and individual differences. *Journal of Educational Psychology, 81,* 101–108.

Schnetzler, P., & Harris, J. (2000). *Ten little dinosaurs.* Kansas City, MO: Accord.

Segal, M., & Adcock, D. (1983). *Making friends.* Upper Saddle River, NJ: Prentice Hall.

Segal, M., & Adcock, D. (1985). *Your child at play Two to three years.* New York: Newmarket Press.

Segal, M., & Bardige, B. (2000). *Your child at play: Five to eight years.* New York: Newmarket Press.

Seuss, Dr. (1960). *Green eggs and ham.* New York: Random House.

Seuss, Dr. (1989). *And to think that I saw it on Mulberry Street.* New York: Random House.

Seuss, Dr. (1960). *Dr. Seuss's ABC: An amazing alphabet book!* New York: Random House.

Shannon, D. (1998). *No, David.* New York: Blue Sky Press.

Sharmat, M., & Aruego, J. (1989). *Gregory the terrible eater.* New York: Scholastic.

Shaw, N., & Apple, M. (2005). *Sheep in a jeep.* New York: Scholastic.

Snow, C. (1991). The theoretical basis for relationships between language and literacy in development. *Journal of Research in Childhood Education, 6,* 510.

Snow, C.E., Porche, M.V., Tabors, P.O., & Harris, S.R. (2007). *Is literacy enough? Pathways to academic success for adolescents.* Baltimore: Paul H. Brookes Publishing Co.

Snow, C., Tabors, P., Nicholson, P., & Kurland, B. (1995). SHELL: Oral language and early literacy skills in kindergarten and first-grade children. *Journal of Research in Childhood Education, 10*, 37–48

Sonenberg, N. (2005). *Family place libraries: From one Long Island library to the nation.* Americans for Libraries Council.

Sparling, J. (2007). *Getting dressed conversation book.* Hillsborough, NC: MindNurture.

Stanovitch, K.E. (1986). Matthew effects in reading: Some consequences of individual differences in the acquisition of literacy. *Reading Research Quarterly, 21*, 360–407.

Tardif, T., Gelman, S.A., & Xu, F. (1999). Putting the "noun bias" in context: A comparison of English and Mandarin. *Child Development, 70*, 620–635.

Teach More/Love More. (n.d.). *Our mission.* Retrieved July 7, 2008, from http://www.teachmorelovemore.org/AboutUs.asp

Thrive in Five. (2008). *Boston's school readiness roadmap.* Boston: Author.

Tomopoulos, S., Mendelsohn, A.L., Dreyer, B.P., Brazelton, T.B., Berkule, S.B., Fierman, A.H., et al. (2008). *Parent empowerment associated with enhanced parent–Child interactions and cognitive development in young children.* Poster submission at Pediatric Academic Societies & Asian Society for Pediatric Research Joint Meeting.

van Kuyk, J.J. (2003). *Pyramid: The method for young children.* Arnhem, The Netherlands: Cito.

Vernon-Feagans, L., Hurley, M.M., Yont, K.M., Wamboldt, P.M., & Kolak, A. (2007). Quality of childcare and otitis media: Relationship to children's language during naturalistic interactions at 18, 24, and 36 months. *Journal of Applied Developmental Psychology, 28*, 115–133.

Ward, H., & Anderson, W. (2006). *The tin forest.* New York: Dutton Juvenile.

Weinstein, M. (2005). *The surprising power of family meals: How eating together makes us smarter, stronger, healthier, and happier.* Hanover, NH: Steerforth Press.

Weissbourd, R. (1997). *The vulnerable child: What really hurts America's children and what we can do about it.* Cambridge, MA: Perseus Books Group.

Wells, G. (1985). *The meaning makers.* Portsmouth, NH: Heinemann.

Wetherby, A.M., & Prizant, B.M. (1993). *CSBS DP™ Infant-Toddler Checklist and Easy-Score Software.* Baltimore: Paul H. Brookes Publishing Co.

Whitebook, M., & Cost, Quality & Outcomes Study Team. (1995). *Cost, quality, and child outcomes in child care centers: Public report.* Denver: University of Colorado, Economics Department.

Whitehurst, G.J., Arnold, D.H., Epstein, J.N., Amgell, A.L., Smith, M., & Fischel, J.E. (1994). A picture book reading intervention in daycare and home for children from low income families. *Developmental Psychology, 30*, 679–689.

Whitehurst, G., & Lonigan, C. (1998). Child development and emergent literacy. *Child Development, 68*, 848–872.

Winerman, L. (2005). The culture of memory. *Monitor on Psychology, 36*(8), 56.

Wolf, M. (2007). *Proust and the squid: the story and science of the reading brain.* New York: HarperCollins.

Wolpert, E. (2005). *Start seeing diversity: The basic guide to an anti-bias classroom.* Saint Paul, MN: Redleaf Press.

Wood, A., & Wood, D. (2005). *King Bidgood's in the bathtub.* New York: Harcourt Children's Books.

Xue, Y., Leventhal, T., Brooks-Gunn, J., & Earls, F.J. (2005). Neighborhood residence and mental health problems of 5- to 11-year-olds. *Archives of General Psychiatry, 62*, 554–562.

Yopp, H.K. (1992). Developing phonemic awareness in young children. *Reading Teacher, 45*(9), 696–703.

Zelver, P., & Lessac, F. (2005). *The wonderful towers of watts.* Honesdale, PA: Boyds Mills Press.

ZERO TO THREE. (1992). *Heart Start: The emotional foundations of school readiness.* Washington, DC: Author.

ZERO TO THREE. (2008). *Caring for infants and toddlers in groups: Developmentally appropriate practice.* Washington, DC: Author.

ZERO TO THREE Policy Center (2007). State and community policy roundup: Progress on infant-toddler issues across the United States, July 2007. Washington, DC: Author.

ZERO TO THREE Policy Center (2008). State and community policy roundup: Progress on infant-toddler issues across the United States, January–July, 2008. Washington, DC: Author.

Zimmerman, F., & Christakis, D. (2007). Associations between media viewing and language development in children under age 2 years. *Pediatrics, 151,* 364–368.

Resources for Parents and Providers

ACTIVITY BOOKS, DVDS, RESOURCE KITS, AND MANUALS

Agenda for Children. (2008). *Let's talk . . . It makes a difference! program manual: An innovative approach to supporting children's literacy development.* Cambridge, MA: City of Cambridge.

Cronin, S., & Masso, C.S. (2003). *Soy bilingue: Language, culture, & young latino children.* Seattle: Center for Linguistic and Cultural Democracy.

Knapp-Philo, J. (2007). *Celebrating language & literacy with infants, toddlers, and twos* [DVD]. Bethesda, MD: Teaching Strategies.

Lally, J.R., Mangione, P.L., & Young-Holt, C.L. (Eds.). (1990). *Infant/toddler caregiving: A guide to language development and communication.* Sacramento: California State Department of Education.

Lerner, C., Dombro, A., & Levine, K. (2000). *The magic of everyday moments: How the brain, body and mind grows from birth to 3* [Series of booklets for parents, in English and Spanish]. Washington, DC: ZERO TO THREE Press.

Manolson, A. (1992). *It takes two to talk: A parent's guide to helping children communicate* [Guidebook and DVD]. Toronto: Hanen Centre.

National Latino Children's Institute. (2007). *Words for the future—Creando el futuro.* [Multimedia kit with manual, activity cards, poster, story handouts, and CD-ROM]. San Antonio, TX: Author.

Parent/Professional Advocacy League, M-POWER, Inc., & The Massachusetts Department of Mental Health. (2006). *Promoting social and emotional health through early literacy* [Manual with tip sheets and resources for parents and providers]. Boston: Massachusetts Department of Education Family Literacy Consortium.

Sparling, J. (2007). *Learning games* [Series of booklets with language games for children from birth to 5 years, in English and Spanish]. Hillsborough, NC: MindNurture.

Sparling, J. (2007). *Learning games manual for family childcare.* Hillsborough, NC: MindNurture. (Also available in Spanish.)

Sussman, F. (1999). *More than words: Helping parents promote communication and social skills in children with autism spectrum disorder* [Guidebook and DVD]. Toronto: Hanen Centre.

Sussman, F. (2006). *TalkAbility people skills for verbal children on the autism spectrum: A guide for parents* [Guidebook and DVD]. Toronto: Hanen Centre.

Washington Research Institute, & California Institute on Human Services, Sonoma State University. (2003). *Language is the key* [Resource Guide and DVD]. Sonoma, CA: National Head Start Family Literacy Center.

Weitzman, E., & Greenber, J. (2002). *Learning language and loving it: A guide to promoting children's social, language and literacy development* [Guidebook and DVD]. Toronto: Hanen Centre.

WestEd (2006). *A world full of language: Supporting preschool English language-learners* [DVD and guidebook]. Sacramento, CA: California Department of Education.

WEB SITES

Born Learning (http://www.bornlearning.org)

Born Learning, an innovative public engagement campaign that helps parents, caregivers, and communities create quality early learning opportunities for young children, is designed as a tool for long-lasting community change. Among the resources on its web site is the "Your Child @" series, a set of information and tip sheets for parents, covering all areas of development with an emphasis on supporting language, social-emotional connections, and learning.

Circle of Inclusion (http://www.circleofinclusion.org)

The Circle of Inclusion web site is for early childhood service providers and families of young children. This site offers demonstrations of, and information about, the effective practices of inclusive educational programs for children from birth through age 8. Information is available in English, Spanish, Korean, Chinese, and Japanese.

Colorín Colorado (http://www.colorincolorado.org)

The Colorín Colorado web site offers stories, activities, ideas, and strategies to help English language learners master English reading. It also contains a wealth of background information for parents and teachers. Although the site covers children in grades pre-K through 12, many of the resources are helpful for preschool- and kindergarten-age children. This bilingual site can be viewed in English or Spanish.

Get Ready to Read (http://www.grtr.org)

An initiative of the National Center for Learning Disabilities, *Get Ready to Read!* is a national program to build the early literacy skills of preschool children. The site contains a host of resources for children, parents, and early education professionals, including games and activities, screening tools, and checklists for classrooms and family child care homes.

PBS Kids (http://www.pbskids.org)

In addition to games and learning activities for children, this site contains information for parents and teachers on the curriculum and research behind such shows as *Sesame Street*, *Between the Lions*, *Reading Rainbow*, and *SUPER WHY!*

Reading Rockets (http://www.readingrockets.org)

Reading Rockets is a national multimedia project offering information and resources on how young children learn to read, why so many struggle, and how caring adults can help. Its web site contains a wealth of resources to help "launch" young readers, including techniques for teaching reading, strategies to help kids who struggle, articles and other resources for families and teachers, recommended children's books, and interviews with children's authors.

Teach More/Love More
(http://www.teachmorelovemore.org)

In addition to information about school readiness activities and resources in Miami-Dade County, Florida, this web site contains a wealth of information for parents and caregivers on child health and development, supporting language and literacy, and everyday fun activities. This trilingual site can be viewed in English, Spanish, or Haitian Kreyol.

ZERO TO THREE (http://www.zerotothree.org)

ZERO TO THREE is a national organization dedicated to supporting the healthy development and well-being of infants, toddlers, and their families by informing, educating, and supporting adults who influence their lives. This site has multiple free resources for parents and professionals, in addition to those available for purchase, on topics such as play, language and literacy, and social-emotional development.

Talk to Me, Baby!

Study Guide

This study guide is designed to serve as an aid to self-study, as well as a tool for book groups, workshop and course instructors and participants, and parent educators interested in sharing, discussing, and implementing the messages of *Talk to Me, Baby! How You Can Support Young Children's Language Development*. It is designed to foster engaged and reflective conversation among adults as they learn about how young children develop language, reflect on the many ways in which adults can support robust language learning, observe and seek to understand children's behavior, enjoy "conversations" with babies and young children, experiment with language-building strategies that may be unfamiliar, and join with others to build language-rich settings and language-supportive communities.

For each chapter of the book, the guide includes

- **Key Concepts and Vocabulary**

- **Check Yourself** questions that guide review of key information

- **Personal Reflections** that draw on the learner's experience, expertise, and cultural/linguistic background

- **Learning from Each Other** questions designed to spark discussion among participants and tap the expertise of families and colleagues whose backgrounds or perspectives may be different from theirs

- **Observation and Application Opportunities** in home, child care, clinical, and community settings

Depending on your purpose and setting, you might

- Review Key Concepts and Vocabulary before and after reading a chapter

- Find answers to the Check Yourself questions in the chapter

- Take turns answering Check Yourself questions in a study group

- Use Check Yourself questions to organize a PowerPoint presentation

- Record Personal Reflections in a journal

- Share some of your Personal Reflections with others

- Use some Personal Reflection questions to help workshop participants build on prior knowledge and experiences

- Use some Learning from Each Other questions to facilitate discussion

- Reach out to colleagues and friends and talk about a Learning from Each Other question

- Use a Learning from Each Other question to help you learn from a parent's knowledge of his own child

- Assign Observation and Application Opportunities as individual or group projects

- Incorporate some Observation and Application Opportunities into your lesson planning

- Use the handouts at the end of this study guide to record strategies you would like to experiment with or do more of and to share those strategies with colleagues and families

Chapter 1: The Power of Play Talk

Key Concepts and Vocabulary

- **Play talk:** Playful or informative relationship-building talk meant to engage the listener. Includes conversation, running commentary, storytelling, wordplay, chit-chat, explanation, open-ended questioning, and thinking aloud.

- **Business talk:** "No nonsense" talk that directs children's behavior, including demands, commands, directions, and prohibitions. "Stop that right now." "Put on your jacket."

- **Affirmation:** An expression of encouragement, praise, or approval in response to a child's effort, discovery, communication, or achievement. "You can do it!" "Great job!" "High five!" "That's a good idea."

- **Decontextualized language:** Language that goes beyond the "here and now" context that speaker and listener are sharing to include the past, future, far away, hypothetical (what if...), imaginary, or abstract. Characteristic of books and storytelling.

- **Positive guidance:** Age-appropriate support and discipline that helps a child prepare for new or challenging situations, understand what is expected and what is "off limits," avert or cope with frustration, exercise self-control, handle conflicts in positive ways, and learn from mistakes.

- **Virtuous circle:** An upward spiral in which success begets success. For example, rich language input and frequent conversation opportunities build children's vocabularies and their confidence and fluency as speakers. As their spoken language becomes more facile and sophisticated, they elicit more complex language from their conversation partners, which further fuels their language learning.

> **More talk makes a difference**
> **because more talk is richer talk.**

Check Yourself

- Why is it important to talk with babies and young children?

- What makes "play talk" different from "business talk?"

- Hart and Risley found that "meaningful differences" in the quantity and quality of adults' talk with children had a major impact on the children's later vocabularies and school achievement. Explain why each of the following is important for a child's development:

—Amount of "non–business talk" or "play talk": conversation, running commentary, storytelling, wordplay, chit-chat, explanation, and thinking aloud

—Responsiveness to a child's overtures, interests, and attempts to communicate

—Encouraging words, including recognition of accomplishments (affirmations)

—Positive guidance (discipline) techniques, including offering choices, suggestions, and explanations

—Asking the child questions, especially open-ended ones

—Talk that is rich in information and description

—Use of varied vocabulary and uncommon words

- How does reading aloud with young children make a difference to their language development?

- What intellectual, social, and emotional advantages do preschoolers gain when they can "use their words" well? How do these advantages compound over time, creating a "virtuous circle"?

Personal Reflections

- Looking back to your own childhood, what can you remember about learning to talk, either from direct experience or from family stories? Who cared for you? Who played with you? What language(s) did they speak? Can you remember any favorite lullabies, nursery rhymes, games, or rituals? Were you encouraged to speak with adults, or taught that "children should be seen and not heard?" How did the important adults in your life react to your early attempts to talk?

- What do you most enjoy doing with babies and young children?

- How does your talk with young children differ when you are playing with them from when you are trying to get them to do something (or stop doing something)?

- What do you hope to learn from this book?

Learning from Each Other

- What playful techniques have you found to be effective in guiding children's behavior? How do you let children know when you "mean business"?

- How do you help parents and teachers make more time for play talk?

- What challenges do parents face today that may be different from those faced in earlier generations? How might you help today's parents cope with challenges such as media saturation, a shortage of affordable, high-quality child care, and a fast-paced, 24/7 economy?

- Do you work with families who face additional stresses, such as poverty, linguistic or social isolation, family or community violence, or depression? How might these challenges affect the amount of play talking they do with their children? In what situations and settings are they most able to enjoy play talk?

Observation and Application Opportunities

- Partner with a parent or provider to make a joint journal or scrapbook that traces a child's language development. Note words, questions, play themes, favorite books and activities, important people and experiences, and milestones such as babbling, first words, talking in sentences, and learning to read. Be sure to represent all of the languages that the child is learning and the different settings where she spends time.

- Try keeping a "language journal" that traces your interactions with a child or group of children. Record dated observations of your "play talk" activities. Note the children's comments, questions, play interests, and linguistic accomplishments. Also keep track of the strategies you use to support their language and literacy development.

Chapter 2: Baby Babbles

Key Concepts and Vocabulary

- **Newborn Behavioral Assessment Scale:** An examination of a newborn's behavior that helps parents to get to know their baby, appreciate her capabilities, and learn how to approach and interact with her in ways that will support her development. The scale looks at how each baby responds to different kinds of stimuli, maintains equilibrium in the face of challenges like noise or bright light, regulates his body temperature, breathing, movements, and alertness, and marshals energy for social interaction and learning.

- **Attunement:** Building a mutually satisfying responsive relationship; getting "in sync" or "on the same wavelength." Through frequent, positive interaction, babies and adults become attuned to each other.

- **Cortisol:** A hormone secreted in response to stress. High levels of cortisol damage a baby's developing brain circuitry and interfere with learning.

- **Babbling:** Experimenting or playing with speech sounds. Before they can say meaningful words, babies babble strings of sounds that can sound like words or even, eventually, like whole sentences.

- **Parentese:** An engaging, high-pitched, often sing-song and repetitive style used by adults around the world when talking with babies.

- **Infant curriculum:** Infants have their own "curriculum." As they explore their world and interact with people, they are busy finding out what they can do with their bodies and with various objects and materials, how things move and fit in space, how to use objects —and people—as tools, how to make interesting things happen over and over again, and how to remember and retrieve things and people that are out of sight. They are especially interested in learning to communicate!

**Everything that fascinates a baby creates
an opportunity for adult connection and play talk.**

Check Yourself

- What effects do insufficient stimulation and lack of opportunities to engage with people have on a baby's brain development and learning? What are the effects of overstimulation and of chronic or severe stress?

- Why is it important to talk to a baby who is too young to understand? What are some of the ways that very young babies respond when adults talk to them?

- How does babbling change over time? How does hearing more than one language affect a baby's babbling?

- What features of "parentese" help children learn language?

- How do baby songs, knee-bouncing rhymes, Peek a boo and chase games, and show-off routines help babies build language and turn-taking communication skills? What other benefits do these games have for babies?

- When should you begin to read to babies, tell them stories, or narrate their activities with a play-by-play account? What do babies gain from these activities as newborns? At 6 months? At one year?

- In choosing books for babies, what characteristics should you look for?

Personal Reflections

- What differences have you noticed among babies you have known in:

—How they liked to be approached?

—Levels and types of stimulation that engaged their interest without becoming overwhelming?

—What they found soothing when they were upset?

—How they told you when they wanted more and when they had had enough?

- What are your favorite ways to make babies smile or laugh? How do you keep them from getting overexcited, or know when they've had enough?

Learning from Each Other

- What are your favorite games to play with infants of different ages?

- What baby games are traditional in your culture(s)? What do the babies gain from these games?

- How do cultures and individual families differ in their approach to taking babies out in public? What are some ways to help babies feel comfortable with new people and to "include" them in the conversations and activities of a mixed-age group?

Observation and Application Opportunities

- Observe a baby as he plays with a new toy or explores his environment. What is he trying to accomplish or discover? How do adults encourage his exploration and celebrate his successes? How can you make the task more challenging and still hold his interest?

- What new games, activities, or strategies would you like to try (or vary) with the babies in your life or share with their teachers and caregivers?

- What are some fun ways you could **increase** the amount of engaging, responsive, reassuring, and encouraging play talking that you and those you work with do with babies?

Chapter 3: First Words, First Stories

Key Concepts and Vocabulary

- **Symbolic gesture:** A gesture that is used like a word to represent an object or idea. Most children use gestures with communicative and symbolic intent just before or along with their first words.

- **Follow the CAR:** A reminder to parents and caregivers to **follow** a child's lead, to **c**omment on what he is doing, **a**sk a question, or **r**espond to his communication by adding a bit more, and to give him time to formulate a response.

- **Elaborated reminiscing (with a toddler):** Telling simple stories about her past experiences, including interesting details and descriptions, and encouraging her to remember and to help tell the story.

- **Word spurt:** A jump in vocabulary and a noticeable increase in the pace of learning new words that occurs for most children between 15 and 24 months, usually after they have learned to say about 50 words. Word learning rates accelerate at some point for all children, but they accelerate more rapidly when children have had richer language experience.

**Children's early experiences with language
build a reservoir of fuel that powers a language lift-off.**

Check Yourself

- How do young toddlers use gestures to communicate? Give some examples.

- List several reasons why some children may be slower to use words than others.

- Would you worry if a child spoke no recognizable words at 15 months? At 24 months? What other signs would you look for that language and communication are "on track"?

- How can an adult use words to help a toddler who is just beginning to speak to express her feelings and desires, cope with strong emotions, prepare for changes and challenges, stay safe, and avoid meltdowns?

- Does learning two languages as a toddler harm or slow down language development? What does a toddler gain when her parents speak to her in their native (or preferred) language? What are the advantages of bilingualism?

- How can a child who does not yet put words together tell a story? What do toddlers gain when their parents and caregivers involve them in reminiscing about past experiences?

- In choosing books for toddlers, what characteristics should you look for? What are some language-building ways to involve toddlers in "reading" books?

- What are some key characteristics of high-quality child care for toddlers? How do these characteristics contribute to robust language development?

Personal Reflections

- What are some of the favorite activities of toddlers you have known? What concepts are they learning as they go about their day? How can attentive adults enhance their learning of concepts and associated language?

- What strategies have you found effective for connecting with a wary toddler and encouraging him to "talk" with you?

- What positive discipline techniques have you found to be most effective with toddlers? How does each of these techniques build language as well as self-control and emotional resilience?

Learning from Each Other

- What discipline techniques have you observed being used by parents or caregivers whose backgrounds are different from yours? What might children learn from these techniques?

- How might responding in words to a toddler's gestures, pairing gestures with your words, or even teaching "baby signs" facilitate a child's verbal language? Would you recommend these strategies to parents? Why or why not?

- How would you help parents whose 1-year-olds are not yet speaking words to understand that when they begin to talk is far less important than the richness of their communicative experience and word-learning opportunities? What strategies might you recommend for "priming the language pump" and building a strong base for rich vocabulary development?

- How would you build upon parents' and caregivers' cultural and linguistic backgrounds and their relationship with a particular toddler to help them support the child's language? What would you want to know before making specific recommendations? How might you find out?

- How would you help a bilingual or multilingual family decide what language(s) to use with their children? What recommendations would you make for toddler caregivers who are not fluent in a family's preferred language?

- How would you answer a parent's questions about what and how much "educational" television his toddler should be watching? What substitute activities might you suggest that would keep a toddler safely engaged while adults were preparing meals or doing other chores?

Observation and Application Opportunities

- Watch two toddlers playing together or side by side. What is each child trying to accomplish? Do you see any evidence that they are imitating each other or using gestures or words to communicate? Are you able to facilitate their communication, help them "use their words," or otherwise enrich their play and foster their friendship? How does each child respond to your efforts?

- When caring for more than one child, helping a toddler stay "in control" and carrying on one-to-one conversations with each child without neglecting the others can be a real challenge. What strategies have you learned from this chapter that might help with this?

- What are some fun ways you could **increase** the amount of engaging, responsive, encouraging, and concept-building "play talking" that you and those you work with do with toddlers?

Chapter 4: Off Like a Rocket

Key Concepts and Vocabulary

- **Grammatical marker:** A word or word part that indicates a grammatical function or relationship, such as plural (*-s*), possessive (*-'s*), past tense (*-ed*, have been), gender (*–a* or *–o* in Spanish), or negation (*not, ain't*). Different languages and dialects mark grammatical relationships in different ways; elements that are marked in some dialects or languages may not be in others.

- **Telegraphic speech:** "Sentences" that include key words but omit grammatical markers and connectors like *is*. Telegraphic speech is often used by toddlers and second language learners who have mastered some vocabulary and can combine words but are still learning the language's grammatical system.

  - **Simultaneous versus sequential bilingualism:** Children who learn two languages in their first 3 years are considered "simultaneous bilinguals"; they learn and process both languages as a first language. Sequential bilinguals learn a second language later in life, building on their knowledge of their first language.

  - **Inner speech:** Talking silently to oneself or thinking in words. Toddlers often talk to themselves out loud as they remind themselves how to behave, make simple plans, or talk their way through problems. This self-talk gradually becomes inner speech.

  - **Circles of communication:** A concept developed by Dr. Stanley Greenspan to describe how partners in a conversation build on each other's ideas. A conversation flows smoothly when one partner "opens a circle," the other partner responds in a way that "closes" or "completes" it and "opens" another, the first partner responds by closing that circle and opening another, and so forth.

Little children love big words.

So much is new for 1- and 2-year-olds that almost any discussion or explanation or shared fantasy play is likely to introduce new words and concepts.

Check Yourself

- Can young children who are learning two languages at the same time or one after another keep the grammatical rules straight, or does knowing the rules of one language interfere with learning those of another?

- What aspects of language learning are *most* influenced by the richness of the language a young child hears and the frequency of his opportunities for engaged conversation:

—Grammar?

—Vocabulary?

—Speaking at appropriate times and in polite or socially acceptable ways?

—Ability to use language with precision, style, persuasiveness, and humor?

- Should you mostly use short sentences and simple words with toddlers who are just learning to put words together? What benefits do toddlers gain from hearing some longer sentences and some specific, interesting, and hard-to-say words?

- Describe some of the advances that occur in children's pretend play and storytelling as they learn to combine words and sequence ideas. What are some effective techniques for helping a young child tell or act out a story and learn to keep a conversation going?

- In choosing books for 2-year-olds, what characteristics should you look for? What are some language-building ways to involve 2-year-olds in "reading" books that can engage their emerging ability to connect ideas, to pretend, and to tell stories?

- Describe several ways to help 2- and 3-year-olds cope with transitions (from one place or activity to another), frustration, and limits. How do these strategies engage children's emerging sense of humor or ability to follow an explanation and connect ideas? Explain how each "positive guidance" strategy builds a child's competence in acceptable behavior, self-control, and language.

- List at least six features of a child care setting that would make it a language-rich environment for 2- and 3-year-olds.

- Explain why "words are brain food for 2-year-olds." List at least five good ways to teach 2-year-olds new words.

Personal Reflections

- What interesting conversations have you had with a toddler or 2-year-old? What did you learn about the child's interests, perceptions, or thinking? How did you contribute?

- What questions have you heard (or learned of) from 2- and 3-year-olds? What did each reveal about the child's understanding of the world, emotional concerns, or wishes? Besides giving a matter-of-fact reply, what else could you do to build on the child's curiosity or address his underlying concerns?

- What are your favorite books to share with 2- and 3-year-olds? What makes the experience special for you? For the child?

Learning from Each Other

- "When we wonder aloud about whether it will rain, or why the sky is dark, or what we need to bring along on an outing, we invite children to think with us." How might you encourage parents and teachers of toddlers and 2-year-olds to "wonder aloud" and "invite children to think?"

- In your community, how are young children expected to address adults? What "magic words" and polite phrases do they learn? How else do adults teach them to express their needs and desires in socially acceptable ways?

- How are expectations for toddler and preschool behavior alike and different in communities (or cultures) with which you are familiar? How have they changed from when you were growing up?

- What do you consider to be the essential features of a book-sharing experience for 2- and 3-year-olds? How would you encourage a parent or caregiver who could not read aloud comfortably to use books with children of this age?

Observation and Application Opportunities

- Give a 2-year-old a collection of intriguing small objects that could be sorted, counted, arranged in a pattern, or used to play out a story. What does the child say as she plays with the objects? How does she engage you? How does she respond to your attempts to enrich her play with information, questions, and specific, descriptive, fanciful, or mathematical language?

- Create (or describe) a "theme box" that would intrigue a 2-year-old and prompt theme-related pretending. What props would you include? How might you get involved in the play? In the spirit of the game a child is playing, how might you build on his ideas and stretch his vocabulary?

- What are some fun ways you could **increase** the amount of engaging, imaginative, thought-provoking "play talking" that you and those you work with do with 2-and 3-year-olds?

Chapter 5: What Will They Think of Next?

Key Concepts and Vocabulary

- **Magic years:** A term coined by Dr. Selma Fraiberg to describe the first 5 years of life. The term captures not only the magical thinking (fanciful, not bound by reality or adult logic) that is characteristic of preschool children but also the magical inventiveness that so delights their parents and teachers.

- **Hundred languages of children:** All of the ways that preschoolers represent and communicate their observations, feelings, ideas, and stories—with words, drawing, clay, dance, map making, song, block building, drama, and a host of other media.

- **Mature pretend play:** Dramatic or constructive (building, setting up miniature worlds) play in which children co-construct a story or scenario. The play involves planning, gathering of props, negotiation of roles and storylines, and dialog or narration.

- **Funds of knowledge:** The collective wisdom, expertise, and know-how of families and communities, related to their jobs, hobbies, traditions, recent and historic experiences, lifestyles, and everyday skills.

> **Reading aloud frequently from a diverse collection of books that invite conversation may be the single most important thing that adults can do to build preschoolers' language.**

> **It is the talk that surrounds the storybook reading that gives it power, and different kinds of books foster different kinds of talk.**

Check Yourself

- Besides talking in complete and (mostly) grammatical sentences, what are the major linguistic accomplishments of 3- and 4-year-olds?

- Why is it important to use a language in which you are comfortably fluent and educated when talking with a 3- or 4-year-old? List several ways that you can support her home language or dialect if it is different from yours.

- "For most children, the achievement of basic proficiency in their first language (and often a second language or dialect as well) coincides with a flowering of creativity." What characteristics of creative people are preschoolers likely to exhibit?

- What are some of the benefits of mature pretend play for preschool children?

- Describe at least six ways that adults can enhance preschoolers' pretend play. Which ones are most likely to introduce new words or concepts? Which are most likely to enhance friendships and help children develop social skills? Which are most likely to foster flexible thinking and creativity?

- In choosing books for preschoolers, what characteristics should you look for?

- List at least five different kinds of books that should be in a diverse collection of books that invite conversation between preschoolers and adults. What are some language-building ways to involve children in "reading" and learning from each type of book?

- How can teachers tap "funds of knowledge" in their community to enrich their curricula, create a more culturally familiar environment for children, and welcome families into their classrooms?

- How do cultural and family patterns of talking about the past affect what children remember and how they recount it?

Personal Reflections

- What pretend play games or scenarios are favorites among children you know or work with? How might adults enhance these games with welcome but unexpected props, settings, costumes, questions, books, or role-playing?

- What are some of the things that the preschoolers you know or work with seem most "eager to learn"?

- Choose a book that you enjoyed as a child or enjoy sharing with children. What might you do to help children "go deeper" in their understanding of the words and concepts that are key to the story? What real-world experiences, questions, information, and activities might you add to further build on their interest?

- Have you ever caught yourself "working too hard" (by doing something for children yourself rather than soliciting their ideas or letting them help)? How were you able to involve a child or a group in your task or challenge? What did each of you gain?

Learning from Each Other

- What alternatives might you suggest to parents or teachers who are not comfortable engaging in pretend play with young children or who don't think that this is an appropriate role for adults?

- "A program that encourages children to experiment, to think and talk about new ideas, to approach situations with an open mind, and to engage in a range of self-chosen activities will support the child's development. On the other hand, programs that approach early childhood education in an overly didactic way, teaching concepts and skills mainly through adult talk and rote child response, stifle children's creative thought processes—and restrict their language development."

  —What evidence backs up this statement?

  —How would you explain it to parents searching for a "high-quality" preschool program? What would you suggest they look for?

- What funds of knowledge does your family and community have that you can share with young children? How can you help the families you work with to share their funds of knowledge more intentionally? How can you bring these themes and concepts into a child care environment?

- What daily, weekly, and special occasion rituals are important to the families you work with? How do these rituals build language? How might their language-building power be enhanced? What new rituals can you create together?

- What strategies have you found most effective for helping children to include a less popular peer or a child with a disability, language difference, or other social challenge?

- What strategies have you found most effective for helping a child who tends to be excluded approach a peer or group and actively engage in play with other children?

Observation and Application Opportunities

- Collect some preschool questions from parents, teachers, or your own observations. Record them as accurately as possible. What does each question reveal about the child's logic, knowledge, wishes, observations, worries, and/or intellectual interests? What commonalities and differences do you see in the questions? How might you address and build on one or more of the questions in an educational experience?

- What are some fun ways in which you could **increase** the amount of information-rich, imaginative, thought-provoking "play talking" that you and those you work with do with 3- and 4-year-olds?

Chapter 6: From Language to Literacy

Key Concepts and Vocabulary

- **Emergent reader:** A child who is learning a lot about how books, print, and stories work but cannot yet read unfamiliar text without help.

- **Concepts of print:** Understanding of how print works in a particular language and its corresponding writing system. For example, readers of English learn that words are written with letters and separated by spaces, that print is read from left to right and top to bottom, and that sentences begin with capital letters and end with punctuation marks.

- **Phonemic awareness:** Awareness of the sounds (phonemes) that make up words. Includes the ability to segment words into their separate sounds and blend sounds together into words.

- **Alphabetic principle:** The idea that (in an alphabetically written language) the letters represent the phonemes that are combined into words.

- **Inside-*out* and outside-*in* strategies:** Use of information that is "inside" a written word (including letters, letter combinations, and syllables, along with knowledge of letter–sound correspondence and skills such as segmenting and blending) to figure out what the word "says." Use of context clues from "outside" the word (including storyline, pictures, vocabulary and word knowledge, and "what makes sense in the sentence" along with general knowledge) to figure out what the word "says" and what it means. Beginning readers work from the inside out and from the outside in.

> Children who know lots of words and concepts have
> rich background knowledge. They also know a lot about
> words. They understand—intuitively—how
> parts of words fit together, and can make new words
> and nonsense words by playing around with word
> parts. This provides a strong foundation for reading.

> The key to literacy is language development,
> fostered in caring relationships through frequent,
> vocabulary-stretching conversations
> that build on young children's natural curiosity.

Check Yourself

- How is written or literary language different from everyday spoken language? Why would conversations involving "decontextualized language" (talk about past, future, far away, and imaginary events and abstract ideas) prepare children for reading?

- Explain why a strong language foundation, including a robust vocabulary and lots of experience with word play and stories, is essential for literacy.

- What "concepts of print" is a 4-year-old who has been read to a lot and has had many experiences with books and other forms of reading and writing likely to know?

- Why does knowing the names of many of the letters help a child learn to read a language such as English?

- Describe some of the "outside-*in*" and "inside-*out*" clues and strategies that beginning readers use to decode text and understand its meaning.

- What features of texts support beginning readers? How else can adults provide scaffolds or supports as they share books with beginning readers?

- What other features of books appeal to 4-, 5-, and 6-year-olds, whether they are hearing a story read aloud, reading parts with adult help, or reading the book independently?

- List at least 10 things that you might see in a "writing-rich environment" for preschoolers or kindergartners.

Personal Reflections

- Describe some of the intellectual and linguistic accomplishments of 4-, 5-, and 6-year-olds that make them interesting conversationalists, probing questioners, and compelling storytellers. Give examples from your own experience.

- When did you first learn to read? How did you feel about the learning process? What did important people in your life do (or not do) to promote your love of language, storytelling, and reading?

- What games and strategies have you found to be both fun and effective for engaging preschoolers or kindergartners in word play and building their phonemic awareness?

- Explain the statement: "For most children, the best strategy for teaching beginning reading is not 'either' phonics 'or' whole language, but rather an integrated or 'whole-part-whole' approach." Describe an effective reading lesson or book-sharing experience that incorporates both kinds of strategies.

Learning from Each Other

- What listening games or strategies have you found to be particularly helpful to second-language learners, children whose dialects differ markedly from standard written forms, or children who have difficulties with auditory processing?

- The *Science Start!* program (described in Chapter 5) serves as a central "evidence-based" component of several federally funded Early Reading First projects. What features of the program seem especially conducive to promoting literacy? Do you know of (or use) another program or approach that might have similar impact, although literacy is not its central goal? What do you see as its strengths? How might you enhance its literacy impact?

- How would you explain to a parent that writing with "invented spelling" can help a child learn to read? What teaching techniques might you suggest to a parent who is concerned that his child is "learning it wrong" when he writes, "I luv bks"?

- Why would a parent continue to read aloud to a child who has learned to read independently? How can parents who do not enjoy reading aloud or do not read fluently support children who are learning to read? What other strategies would you recommend to parents you work with to promote their children's love of reading?

Observation and Application Opportunities

- Read a nonfiction book with older preschoolers or kindergartners, or share information about an area in which you are an expert. What questions do the children have? What do these questions reveal about their thinking and their intellectual interests? How might you engage them in reading and writing as you help them find answers?

- Interview a 4-, 5-, or 6-year-old about a topic on which she is an expert. The conversation may relate to her family or culture, her favorite place, toy, or activity, something she made, or something that she learned about from books or other sources. What did you learn about the topic? About the child? Did you learn any new words? How did your taking on the role of learner affect the flow of the conversation and the ways in which you and the child talked and listened?

- Observe in a prekindergarten or kindergarten classroom or a home setting where one or more of the children are between 4 and 6 years old. What materials, activities, and child-created products do you see that

—Model reading and writing as valued grown-up activities?

—Involve children in reading and writing for their own purposes?

—Convey messages that are meaningful to children—helping them organize materials and activities, explore intellectual interests, enrich their play, celebrate their accomplishments, and share what they have learned?

—Stimulate questions, conversations, and enriched vocabulary?

—Help children link spoken and printed words?

—Build phonemic awareness by helping children hear and manipulate the sounds that make up words?

—Deepen children's understanding of multiple meanings of words, of words with related or opposite meanings, and of multiple ways to say similar things?

—Help children learn letter names and associated sounds?

—Support or scaffold children as they learn to read independently?

—Engage children in various forms of storytelling, including drama, art, and bookmaking?

—Support literacy in more than one language?

- What could you add to build on the children's interests and further enrich the language and literacy environment?

Chapter 7: Building Language—Supporting Communities

Key Concepts and Vocabulary

- **Anticipatory guidance:** Conversation designed to help someone know what to expect and prepare for it. Pediatricians and family support providers use anticipatory guidance to make parents aware of the disorganization, backsliding, stress, and "falling apart" that often accompany developmental advances, and to help them support their children through these transitions.

- **Black communications:** An African American communication system with a distinctive vocabulary and rules and patterns for grammar, pronunciation, word usage, and appropriate ways of using language in different situations. Like all language varieties, it is deeply rooted in culture and history.

- **Family Place Library:** A public library that welcomes very young children and their families with a set of onsite and outreach programs that help families connect with a network of community resources and supports.

- **Community School Readiness Wiring:** A process that builds on existing neighborhood leadership in order to integrate key information on how to support children's healthy development and school readiness into parents' daily lives—through the workplace, grocery stores, hair salons, playgrounds, child care programs, and other places that families frequent.

- **Touchpoints:** A practical approach for building strong family–child relationships from before birth through early childhood, based on the work of Dr. T. Berry Brazelton. Providers trained in the Touchpoints approach build relationships and alliances with parents and work together across disciplinary boundaries. They "touch" into the family system at the predictable points where a child's behavior is likely to be confusing or challenging, helping parents carefully watch and understand their child's behavior and strengths.

> **At the critical age for language learning, public investments in children's education are lower than they will be at any time during childhood.**

> **Change can begin with a simple idea: Talk to me, baby!—a simple approach: playful conversation—and a basic assumption that "every child matters." With leadership, collaboration, and outreach, it can grow into a communitywide commitment that assures that every child begins school with a wealth of words.**

Check Yourself

- A series of studies in the 1990s assessed the quality of child care settings and found that fewer than half of American toddlers were likely to get consistently good care. In terms of language development, why should this be of particular concern?

- What challenges do providers face in providing consistently high-quality, language-enriching care to infants, toddlers, and preschoolers? What additional challenges do providers and families face in neighborhoods of concentrated disadvantage? What are some of the factors that can mitigate these challenges?

- According to Terry Meier, what are some of the linguistic strengths children gain from growing up in communities in which African American Vernacular English is spoken and black communications play a central role in community and family life?

- Why is it important for early childhood professionals to

  —Build relationships with parents that highlight their knowledge of their own children and the important roles they play in their development?

  —Help parents understand the developmental process and anticipate upcoming issues, achievements, and learning opportunities?

  —Bring families together for fun activities and foster networks of mutual support?

  —Work together across professional disciplines, agencies, and other "silos"?

  —Spread the word about the importance of early language development and the ways in which adults can promote it?

  —Learn from the community?

  —Build community and state-wide support for high-quality programs for young children and their families, and the public as well as private resources needed to sustain these programs?

- Give examples of community efforts that are achieving one or more of these goals.

Personal Reflections

- What do you see as particular strengths of your own community or culture in terms of language facility and supports for social-emotional and linguistic development? What strengths have you observed in other communities and cultures you have worked with?

- Using the core messages of *Words for the Future/Creando el futuro* as an example, create a list of key messages to share with families in your community. Phrase the messages in ways that you think will resonate with those particular families.

Learning from Each Other

- What are the scientific and economic arguments for public investments in programs that serve young children and their families?

Based on what you have read in this book, what additional arguments would you make to a policy maker or voter who wanted to know why this should be a priority public investment?

- According to language and literacy experts Lucy Wong Fillmore and Catherine Snow,

  > High quality early childhood education programs have great potential for preventing later school failure, particularly if they place a strong emphasis on language development. For this reason, early childhood teachers need thorough knowledge about language and how to help children develop language and literacy skills. (2008, p. 1)

  What do you think early childhood teachers need to know about language development and about how to support language and literacy?

- How can you help families you work with to enrich their conversations with their children and adopt (or strengthen) language-building habits? What further supports might they need from the community to make this a realistic goal?

- What assets and initiatives does your community have that can be brought together to ensure that children get a good language start, that families are supported and support each other, and that child care programs and schools are ready to build—and build on—the strengths children bring?

- What policies and programs in your state help families, caregivers, and teachers to build young children's language? What needs to be strengthened, expanded, or changed? How would you make the case to policy makers and voters?

Observation and Application Opportunities

- Considering your particular context and communication style, what can you intentionally do (or do more of) to enrich your conversations with young children and create more frequent opportunities for them to engage in rich, language-building conversations?

- What can you do to help spread the word about the importance of talking with young children, to help get the message "into the drinking water?"

- How else can you work with others to build supports in your community and ensure that every child begins school with a wealth of words?

Worksheets and Handouts for Practitioners and Parent/Teacher Educators

The Questions We Ask Young Children

Instructions: As adults, we ask young children many kinds of questions. Quizzing has its place—many children love to show off their knowledge by answering factual questions. But open-ended and reflective questions can be more intellectually challenging. They are more likely to elicit interesting responses and to build children's language skills. Add examples of each type of question from your own experience with parents, teachers, and children. Talk with others about some of the interesting responses children have given to your open-ended and reflective questions.

Strategies	Toddler examples (can be answered nonverbally or with few words)	Older toddler/ preschool examples
Quizzing: Asking for known right answers	"Give me the red block, please."	"What color is this block?"
Open-ended Questioning: Asking for opinions, descriptions, predictions, choices, and other unknown information that the child can supply	"What color block would you like?"	"What are you building?"
Reflective Questioning: Asking questions related to a child's activity that provide insight into his thoughts, expand his play, or prompt further exploration	"Where will the people go in your house?"	"I see you are building a tall tower. How will you help it to balance?"

Language-Building Habits

Instructions: Use this form to keep track of all of the ways that you support young children's language development. In the second column, check off things that you already do frequently and effectively, and add some specific examples of words, stories, songs, routines, conversations, questions (yours and the children's), and other strategies. Look through this book for new ideas that you would like to try, and record some of them in the third column. Talk with colleagues, parents, and other caregiving partners about what you can do together to support children's language. Keep the completed form handy as you work on enhancing your "language-building habits."

Language-Building Strategies	We do this a lot! Examples:	Let's do more! Ideas
Talk a lot. Tell babies and toddlers what you are doing and what they are doing. Describe what you see, hear, and feel. Talk about what is right in front of you, and also talk about what has happened, will happen, and might happen. Use words to soothe and reassure, to prepare children for transitions, to celebrate their accomplishments, and to share your delight in their discoveries.		
Sing. Use lullabies to calm children and cheery songs to teach words and concepts or to accompany routine tasks. Make up new words to familiar tunes as you sing about children's experiences. Sing the songs you like as well as the children's favorites.		

(Continued)

Language-Building Strategies	We do this a lot! Examples:	Let's do more! Ideas
Be silly. Share jokes, nonsense words, tongue twisters, silly songs, nursery rhymes, traditional hand rhymes, finger plays and movement games, and other forms of word play. Encourage children to join you in having fun with sounds and words.		
Use caregiving routines for private conversations. When you change a baby's diaper, play Peekaboo and talk about what "the baby in the mirror" is doing. When you help a toddler put on her coat, talk about what she wants to do outside. When you greet a 2-year-old on Monday morning, ask about her weekend activities.		
Follow the child's lead. Stoop down to his level, make eye contact, and tune in to what he may be trying to say with his words, sounds, and gestures. Make a comment, ask a question, or offer a response. Wait patiently for the child to respond, then add a bit more to keep the conversation going.		

Language-Building Strategies	We do this a lot! Examples:	Let's do more! Ideas
Ask open-ended questions whose answers you really want to know. Children's rapidly developing minds are fascinating. Ask children for their opinions and choices. Ask about what they see and hear, what they think, wish, and imagine. Often, their answers will amaze you.		
Wonder with children. Share your questions and speculations and encourage theirs. Use books, experiments, outings, and interviews to find answers and spark new questions. Use your local library and the Internet to explore children's interests in depth.		
Use interesting words. It is a myth that simple language is best for young children. Little children love big words. Many 2-year-olds can name half a dozen dinosaurs, pasta varieties, or vehicles. Specific, descriptive words intrigue them— and build their vocabularies.		

(Continued)

Language-Building Strategies	We do this a lot! Examples:	Let's do more! Ideas
Think out loud. Let children hear how you make a plan, approach a problem, or react to something that happened. Toddlers will imitate your words and soon begin to use their own words to talk themselves through problems and control their own behavior. Their thinking out loud will eventually become inner speech and verbal reasoning.		
Set up "provocations" and "communication challenges." Provide children with interesting things to talk about and interesting problems to solve. Make a "volcano" with vinegar and baking soda; build a raceway for toy cars from cardboard tubes; explore light with flashlights, glasses, and mirrors; take a rain walk. Put some attractive items in sight but out of reach so children will ask for them; provide collections of props and costumes that suggest pretend play themes, then add unexpected items to expand the play.		
Join children in pretend play. Don't just watch—join the fun. Eat the play cookies and help the child bake more. Stay with the child's game, but add a few ideas of your own.		

Language-Building Strategies	We do this a lot! Examples:	Let's do more! Ideas
Help children use their words. Encourage children to use words to ask for what they want. Teach toddlers words like "stop," "careful," "touch gently," and "my turn." Help a preschooler to make a plan or solve a conflict with a friend.		
Strategies used in my home country/culture or by the children's families: • •		
Strategies that support bilingualism: • •		
Strategies for children with special needs: • •		
More ways to build language: • •		

When You Have Concerns

Instructions: Because language is key to so much of later development, it is best to err on the side of caution when concerns arise. It can be difficult to distinguish transient language delays from problems likely to persist, and earlier intervention is likely to be more effective. Use the following chart to monitor the language and communication development of children in your care and note any areas of concern. Make a checkmark in one of the four columns provided for each area of concern. **Consider referring a child for further assessment for items for which you checked "I'm really worried" or if several "minor issues" are evident in more than one setting (e.g., home and child care) and persist over time.** See Chapter 3 for further discussion and recommended instruments.

Area of concern	No concern	Minor issue	Real concern	Not sure
Difficulties with attachment				
Little responsiveness to sounds, language, or interactive play in first 6–12 months				
Limited vocalization or excessive oral–motor sensitivity, weakness, drooling, or feeding problems continuing beyond 6 months				
Little or unvaried babbling by 12 months; no words or expressive jargon by 18 months				
Little use of or understanding of conventional gestures (shaking head, waving) by 15 months				
Little understanding of words or verbal directions by 18 months				
Little symbolic pretend or constructive play by 18 months				
Little use of words or signs at age 18–24 months				

Area of concern	No concern	Minor issue	Real concern	Not sure
Communicating primarily through grunts and actions (e.g., pulling someone by the hand) after 18 months				
Continuing difficulty responding to communications and participating in turn-taking games (e.g., as Peekaboo or Catch) or conversations				
Slow development of speech combined with difficulties in other communication areas				
Very limited vocabulary or little use of word combinations at age 2–3				
Little creative or pretend play, or only stereotypic play at age 2–5				
Difficulty following multistep directions after age 3				
Difficulty carrying on responsive conversations after ages 3–4				
Not talking in full sentences or recounting experiences, in preferred language, by age 3–4				
Difficulty making self understood by peers and adults who speak the same language after age 4				
Excessive tantrumming, aggression, or difficulty using words when upset after age 4				
Continuing lack of interest in books, stories, songs, verbal humor, and storytelling in early childhood or later				

Myth or Fact?

Instructions: Check the statement in each pair that is TRUE. Explain why.

- There is no point in talking to a baby who is too young to understand your words.
- Talking, singing, and playing with babies build their brainpower and emotional security.

- When talking with young children, you should always use very simple words.
- Using interesting words with young children helps build their vocabularies.

- Young children need to practice language, not just hear it.
- A young child can learn a language just from watching television.

- Two year olds are too young for choices; it is best to tell them what to do.
- Toddlers develop richer language when they hear more questions and fewer commands.

- Parents who are English language learners should speak with their young children in their home language.
- The more young children hear and speak another language, the harder it will be for them to learn English.

- It is important to correct a young child's grammar so that she learns to speak properly.
- Young children's "mistakes" often show their understanding of language patterns.

- Young children who speak racial or ethnic dialects are not using good English and should be corrected.
- When speaking with a young child, teachers should respond to what he says – not how he says it.

- Learning a second language or dialect makes children smarter. They will soon learn which to use when.
- It is hard for children to learn more than one language or dialect. It is important that all of the adults in their lives talk the same way.

Answers: 1b, 2b, 3a, 4b, 5a, 6b, 7b, and 8a are true.

Index

Boxes, figures, and tables are indicated by *b*, *f*, and *t*, respectively.